CYPHER SYSTEM

EXPANDED WORLDS

CREDITS

Writer/Designer:	Bruce R. Cordell
Creative Director:	Monte Cook
Managing Editor:	Dennis Detwiller
Proofreader:	Charles A. Conley
Graphic Designer:	Bear Weiter
Cover Artist:	Lie Setiawan

Artists

Jacob Atienza, Marco Caradonna, Milivoj Ceran, chrom, Florian Devos, Dreamstime.com, Jason Engle, Erebus, David Hueso, Baldi Konijn, Guido Kuip, Brandon Leach, Eric Lofgren, Patrick McEvoy, Jeremy McHugh, Brynn Metheney, Grzegorz Pedrycz, Mike Perry, John Petersen, Roberto Pitturru, Scott Purdy, Nick Russell, Joe Slucher, Lee Smith, Matt Stawicki, Cyril Terpent, Cory Trego-Erdner, Tiffany Turrill, Shane Tyree, Chris Waller, Cathy Wilkins, Ben Wootten, Danar Worya, Kieran Yanner

Monte Cook Games Editorial Board

Scott C. Bourgeois, David Wilson Brown, Eric Coates, Gareth Hodges, Mila Irek, Jeremy Land, Laura Wilkinson, Marina Wold, George Ziets

As we agree with the growing consensus that "they" can and should be used as a gender-neutral, singular English language pronoun when one is needed, we have adopted that as the style in our products. If you see this grammatical construction, it is intentional.

MonteCook
Games

TABLE OF CONTENTS

INTRODUCTION

USING EXPANDED WORLDS

Expanded Worlds is a companion to the *Cypher System Rulebook* that presents several robust sub-genres of the broader genres introduced in the original. This means you won't find introductions to the Cypher System, how to create characters, rules of the game, or other concepts here. *Expanded Worlds* assumes you've got all that in the *Cypher System Rulebook*, and that you're ready to turn the page and dive right into some new content. Enjoy!

Throughout this book, you'll see page references to various items accompanied by this symbol. These are page references to the *Cypher System Rulebook*, where you can find additional details about that rule, ability, creature, or concept. Often, it will be necessary to look up the referenced item in the rulebook, especially if the item is a descriptor or focus ability that isn't replicated here. Other times, it might not be necessary to reference the item, but doing so will provide useful information for character creation and gameplay.

Expanded Worlds is a companion tome to the *Cypher System Rulebook*. In this book, you'll find additional descriptors, foci, creatures, and genre chapters for you to create and play in even more Cypher System games.

To that end, I've got a few questions for you. Your answers might inspire some fun encounters in your next RPG game, or maybe even kick off a whole new campaign. Alternatively, you can think of these as book club-style questions. Feel free to answer them in your favorite social media. I'll start.

What's your favorite genre? Is it your favorite RPG genre, too? Fantasy, science fiction, or horror? Maybe it's a subgenre, like childhood adventure, fairy tales, or post-apocalyptic?

My favorite subgenre to read is hard science fiction (or to watch, like SyFy's The Expanse). There's just something more gritty and real about hard science fiction that's lost when PCs are warping through multiple star systems, at least for me.

How were you introduced to post-apocalyptic fiction? Was it a movie about a disease ravaging the population, or a piece of fiction about life in the aftermath of a nuclear war? Or maybe it was a video game where survivors hid in vaults to avoid atomic holocaust before emerging to find a world changed beyond recognition.

For me, it was a story I found in one of the Reader's Digest Condensed Books that littered my house growing up. My grandmother gave them to my mom as gifts. One of the stories was about a world ravaged by fire, and how the protagonist survived by never giving up. Rebuilding a demolished world is the theme that sticks with me. I guess that's hope in the face of despair. Thus, in any post-apocalyptic-themed RPG I run or write, no matter how dark, it also must include some path forward for hope.

Do you like to mash-up genres? You know, like horror and science fiction, or horror and childhood adventure, or horror and... anything.

Me? Yes. *Hell* yes. I love mixing genres to create new scenarios. For years, fantasy and science fiction was my favorite mash-up. Yes, you guessed it, Expedition to the Barrier Peaks is one of my all-time favorite D&D adventures. Are you telling me the dungeon is a crashed alien spaceship? Sign me up!

PART 1
CHARACTERS

CHAPTER 1

CHARACTER DESCRIPTOR

DESCRIPTORS

Descriptors, page 64

Part 2: Fantastical
Genres, page 71

Part 3: Gritty Genres,
page 103

Post-apocalyptic, page 72

Chaotic, page 8

Meddlesome, page 11

Young, page 13

The *Cypher System Rulebook* details fifty descriptors. You can choose from any of the descriptors there, regardless of type, or from one of the new descriptors presented in this chapter.

The *Cypher System Rulebook* selection of descriptors is robust and in most cases, covers all the bases for creating most player characters (PCs). That said, descriptors like Chaotic, Meddlesome and Young, provided in this book, give the players an opportunity to create a character with traits they might not be able to replicate using the *Cypher System Rulebook* alone. Some of the descriptors described here pair well with the new genres described in Part 2: Fantastical Genres and Part 3: Gritty Genres. For instance, the Relentless descriptor was created for the post-apocalyptic genre (though it is useful in many genres). Game masters (GMs) can mine these genre sections for ideas on settings, adventures, characters, and more.

NEW DESCRIPTORS

Adroit
Beneficent
Chaotic
Earnest
Heroic
Insolent
Lawful
Meddlesome
Obsessive
Relentless
Serene
Young

The Cypher System Rulebook details fifty descriptors. You can choose from any of the descriptors there, regardless of your type, or from one of the new descriptors presented in this chapter.

ADROIT

Thanks to your background and perhaps some natural talent, you're adept at lots of things. Although you might have a specialty, you're also quite good at picking up new skills on the fly, regardless of whether they are physical or mental tasks. Need to repair the exterior of a large vessel in less-than-inviting circumstances or a toxic environment? You can probably pull it off because you're just that adroit.

You have the following characteristics:

Competence Pool: You have an additional Pool called Competence that begins with 3 points (and with a maximum value of 3 points). When spending points from any other Pool, you can take 1, some, or all the points from your Competence Pool first. When you make a recovery roll, your Competence Pool is one additional Pool in which you can place recovered points. When your Competence Pool is at 0 points, it does not count against your damage track. Enabler.

Quick Learner: The first time you attempt and fail a roll, you can try again without having to use Effort (if you don't want to). Additional retries require applying Effort as normal. Enabler.

Initial Link to the Starting Adventure: From the following list of options, choose how you became involved in the first adventure.

1. You were asked to join because you're competent.

2. You need money to get out of a bad situation.

3. In a stunning coincidence, a mechanical failure put the PCs in danger until you saved them.

4. Another PC asked you to join them.

BENEFICENT

Helping others is your calling. It's why you're here. Others delight in your outgoing and charitable nature, and you delight in their happiness. You're at your best when you're aiding people, either by explaining how they can best overcome a challenge or by demonstrating how to do so yourself.

Retrying a Task After Failure, page 195

Some people in hard science fiction scenarios are adroit.

Near future, page 118

You have the following characteristics:

Generous: Allies who have spent the last day with you add +1 to their recovery rolls.

Altruistic: If you're standing next to a creature that takes damage, you can intercede and take 1 point of that damage yourself (reducing the damage inflicted on the creature by 1 point). If you have Armor, it does not provide a benefit when you use this ability.

Skill: You're trained in all tasks related to pleasant social interaction, putting other people at ease, and gaining trust.

Helpful: Whenever you help another character, that character gains the benefit as if you were trained even if you are not trained or specialized in the attempted task.

Inability: While you are alone, the difficulty of all Intellect and Speed tasks is increased by one step.

Initial Link to the Starting Adventure: From the following list of options, choose how you became involved in the first adventure.

1. Even though you didn't know most of the other PCs beforehand, you invited yourself along on their quest.

2. You saw the PCs struggling to overcome a problem and selflessly joined them to help.

3. You're nearly certain the PCs will fail without you.

4. The choice was between your tattered life and helping others. You've haven't looked back since.

CHAOTIC

Danger doesn't mean much to you, mainly because you don't think much about repercussions. In fact, you enjoy sowing surprises, just to see what will happen. The more unexpected the result, the happier you are. Sometimes you are particularly manic, and for the sake of your companions, you restrain yourself from taking actions that you know will lead to disaster.

You have the following characteristics:

Tumultuous: +4 to your Speed Pool.

Skill: You are trained in Intellect defense actions.

Chaotic: Once after each ten-hour recovery roll, if you don't like the first result, you can reroll a die roll of your choice. Regardless of the outcome, if you do, the GM presents you with a GM intrusion.

Inability: Your body is a bit worn from occasional excesses. The difficulty of Might defense tasks is increased by one step.

Initial Link to the Starting Adventure: From the following list of options, choose how you became involved in the first adventure.

1. Another PC recruited you while you were on your best behavior, before realizing how chaotic you were.

2. You have reason to believe that being with the other PCs will help you gain control over your erratic behavior.

3. Another PC released you from captivity, and to thank them, you volunteered to help.

4. You have no idea how you joined the PCs. You're just going along with it for now until answers present themselves.

EARNEST

You always speak from the heart, rarely remembering that dissembling isn't always a negative trait but sometimes useful for smoothing over awkward interpersonal situations. That's because you're sincere and feel things deeply. You like to get to the meat of whatever problem prevents you from succeeding, whether that's a person, a physical obstacle, or a puzzle of some kind.

You have the following characteristics:

Purposeful: +2 to your Intellect Pool.

Skill: You're trained in persuasion.

Skill: You have a passion. You are trained in an area of lore or knowledge of your choice.

Skill: You're trained in defense rolls to resist disease and poison.

Skill: You're trained in all tasks involving providing consolation and emotional support to others.

Inability: You could never detect falsehood. The difficulty of any task that involves seeing through lies or trickery is increased by one step.

Additional Equipment: You make deep and abiding friendships. Thanks to your earnest nature, a friend has given you an additional expensive item.

Initial Link to the Starting Adventure: From the following list of options, choose how you became involved in the first adventure.

1. A PC confided in you as to what they were up to, and you joined them.

2. Hard times overwhelmed you, and having no funds, you joined the PCs.

Some characters in historical settings are defined by their earnest natures.

Historical, page 104

Expensive item, page 183

GM Intrusion, page 372

3. It was either join the PCs or be kidnapped into a far worse situation.

4. You suspect that the other PCs won't succeed without you.

HEROIC

You are courageous, daring, and altruistic in equal measures. You're not afraid to face horrors that make others quaver, especially if it means helping someone else who couldn't succeed (or survive) without you. Some say you're made of the stuff of legends and that your exploits will one day become the stories that inspire a new generation.

You have the following characteristics:

Mighty: +2 to your Might Pool.

Heroic Guise: You hold yourself in a way that inspires others. You are trained in all social interactions.

Hero's Complication: Although the GM can use GM intrusions on you normally (awarding XP), they can also introduce a GM intrusion on you without awarding XP (as if you had rolled a 1 on a d20 roll) based on how your heroic nature tends to attract danger. However, if this happens, 50% of the time, your heroic nature works to your advantage. Your weapon breaks, but that allows you to notice something everyone else missed. A trap catches you, but it also catches your enemies. A new foe enters the fray, but your current foe mistakes it for your ally and attacks it instead of you. You and the GM should work together to determine the details.

Skill: Things tend to go your way. You are trained in tasks involving perception and finding hidden things.

Inability: You tend to take others at their word. The difficulty of any task that involves detecting falsehoods is increased by one step.

Initial Link to the Starting Adventure: From the following list of options, choose how you became involved in the first adventure.

1. You were hunting a great foe and hired the other PCs to accompany you.

2. The PCs were looking for someone like you to round out their number.

3. A mentor recommended you to the other PCs.

4. You killed a mighty foe, and the other PCs were aided (or rescued from captivity) by that act.

A fair number of wanderers in mythological and fantasy setting are heroic.

Mythological, page 82

INSOLENT

Why should you have to put up with others' shortcomings? In your opinion, most people are idiots (friends excluded, of course). If you're completely honest, compared to your obvious superiority, most people are misguided, thick-headed, and a waste of space. If someone wants your attention, you usually make them prove themselves. That doesn't win you many new friends. But it's funny to see them fume.

You have the following characteristics:

Flip: +2 to your Intellect Pool.

Goad: If a creature within short range has not yet attacked you, you can use your action to goad it so that it does. It becomes so angry at your impertinence that the difficulty of its first attack is increased by one step.

Skill: You're not afraid of anything, nor do you put up with others' mental games. You are trained in Intellect defense tasks.

Inability: The difficulty of all tasks relating to social interaction is increased by one step.

Additional Equipment: Thanks to your insolent behavior, you have an additional oddity, given to you by someone who, having reached the breaking point over your

impudence, offered it to you if you would just go away.

Initial Link to the Starting Adventure: From the following list of options, choose how you became involved in the first adventure.

1. You browbeat one of the other PCs until they told you their plans.

2. From afar, you observed that something interesting was going on and invited yourself along.

3. Someone took violent exception to your insolence, but the PCs saved you.

4. You told your friend that nothing could impress you because you'd seen it all. They brought you to the PCs to prove you wrong.

LAWFUL

You live by a code. It might be your own set of rules or rules handed down to you by a religious, military, or other organization steeped in dogma to which you once belonged. The important thing is that you're not governed by passions, but by your steadfast confidence that to follow the law is to live in grace.

You have the following characteristics:

Justified: You are an enthusiastic upholder of the law. You are trained in any noncombat task when you are directly upholding the law.

Skill: You are trained in tasks related to knowing, understanding, and interpreting the laws of the land.

Inability: You can't abide law-breaking, especially when you're the culprit, however unjust those laws might be. While engaged in any activity that breaks the law, the difficulty of all Intellect-based tasks is increased by one step.

Initial Link to the Starting Adventure: From the following list of options, choose how you became involved in the first adventure.

1. You heard what the other PCs were up to and knew they could use your expertise.

2. You gathered a group of PCs to accomplish a lawful task.

3. You agreed to provide money for the upkeep of an organization you were previously affiliated with and find yourself in need of new funds, so you joined the PCs.

4. You think the PCs will help you bring law to areas that suffer lawlessness, once you get them on board with your way of thinking.

MEDDLESOME

Some say you're nosy and ask too many questions. It's true, you constantly ask "why?" because the world is a big place full of both wonderful and terrifying things. If you don't investigate when strange things happen, how will you ever know what's going on? You relish knowing the full story, and the only way to get that in difficult situations is to meddle.

You have the following characteristics:

Analytical: +2 to your Intellect Pool.

Skill: You see things other people miss. You are trained in perception and detecting falsehoods.

Skill: Sometimes you find things that you wish you hadn't. You are trained in stealth tasks.

Skill: You get a thrill from knowing the right answer. You're trained in tasks related to calling up a pertinent detail on a topic you once read about in a book, heard discussed in class, or saw on a documentary.

Initial Link to the Starting Adventure: From the following list of options, choose how you became involved in the first adventure.

1. You noticed that strange noises were coming from an abandoned area, so you gathered the other PCs to check it out.

2. One of your mutual friends has gone missing, and you and the other PCs are determined to find them.

3. You believed that the PCs' task might lead to important and maybe even amazing discoveries.

4. Frightened by something, you ran away, but you came back with the other PCs to watch your back.

OBSESSIVE

Few things are as wonderful as getting lost in doing what you love. Time slips past, hour after hour, while you're in the flow. Whether you are obsessed with studying secrets, insects, mutants, or killing bandits, your ability to sink into what most interests you is what allows you to succeed. Everything else somehow seems less important, and this allows you to focus.

You have the following characteristics:

Your Obsession: At the beginning of each day, choose one concept on which you will concentrate. For the rest of that day, you're obsessed with that choice. This doesn't mean you ignore anything not related to

It's not uncommon for characters in childhood adventure scenarios to be called meddling.

Childhood adventure, page 96

11

Many investigators and operatives in crime and espionage scenarios are Serene.

your obsession—it just means you are at your best when performing tasks related to the obsession, and slightly inattentive when performing tasks that are not.

Enthralled: When you attempt a task that is directly related to your current obsession, the difficulty is one step lower. The player and GM can decide whether a particular situation warrants the step reduction.

Preoccupied: When you attempt a task that is not related to your current obsession, the difficulty is one step higher. The player and GM can decide whether a particular situation warrants the step increase.

Initial Link to the Starting Adventure: From the following list of options, choose how you became involved in the first adventure.

1. You wouldn't take no for an answer when you asked the PCs if you could join their mission.

2. You were preoccupied with something else and didn't realize what you'd agreed to until it was too late.

3. You believed that you could learn a lot by joining the other PCs.

4. One of the PCs asked you to come along, believing that your obsessive nature would be invaluable to the mission.

RELENTLESS

Life has thrown a lot of trouble your way. Disasters large and small have tried to stamp you out. But you've emerged from each alive and moving forward. Stronger, too, but also scarred by what you had to do to survive. People less unyielding than you are gone now. That's not going to happen to you because you never give up.

You have the following characteristics:
Survivor: +2 to your Might Pool.
Skills: You are trained in tasks related to healing and finding food and water.

Survivor's Intuition: You can come up with a random fact pertinent to the current situation when you wish. It is always a matter of fact and must be something you could have logically read or seen in the past. You can do this one time, although

the ability renews each time you make a recovery roll.

Inability: You're not a people person. The difficulty of your deception and persuasion tasks is increased by one step.

Inability: You have an aversion to studying. The difficulty of all Intellect-based tasks is increased by one step.

Initial Link to the Starting Adventure: From the following list of options, choose how you became involved in the first adventure.

1. You found the PCs in trouble and decided to help.

2. Uncharacteristically, you were caught in a bind. The PCs helped to free you.

3. It was either do what needed doing or die. Now, here you are along with the PCs.

4. To protect a loved one, you agreed to join the PCs because their quest was related to your own.

SERENE

You are as still as untroubled water and as smooth as glass. Even when difficulties arise, you maintain your cool, your self-control, and your serene demeanor. Part of it comes to you naturally, but serenity also requires discipline and conscious control of your emotions. Rising to the bait offered by an ally, a foe, or a chance-met lout in the street is only something you do if it advances your own agenda, not because you've lost control.

You have the following characteristics:
Self-Possessed: +2 to your Intellect Pool.
Skill: You are trained in Intellect defense tasks.

Keep Your Cool: You are trained in all actions that involve overcoming or ignoring the effects of fear, intimidation, or panic.

Initial Link to the Starting Adventure: From the following list of options, choose how you became involved in the first adventure.

1. By staying calm in a difficult situation, you gained the trust of the PCs.

2. No one else would take up the task, but you weren't afraid to try.

Crime and espionage, page 110

Many survivors of post-apocalyptic scenarios are relentless.

Post-apocalyptic, page 72

If a PC plays a Young character long enough, at some point it's reasonable for the player to update their character descriptor to something that applies in their adult life.

3. You were investigating a series of strange occurrences, which led you to the PCs and your current situation.

4. Sometimes you need to blow off a little steam and helping the PCs seemed like a way to do that.

YOUNG

Small and inexperienced, you're somewhere between nine and thirteen years old. But you don't let that stop you because you're not afraid of anything. Adults say that you're bold only because you're too young to know better, and that one day you'll grow out of it. You don't believe them because come on, what do they know? They're old.

You have the following characteristics.

Resilient: +2 to your Speed Pool.

Curious: +2 to your Intellect Pool.

Vulnerable: Adults look out for you. You are trained in all pleasant social interactions with adults.

Skill: Your curiosity often leads to destruction. You are trained in tasks involving breaking things.

Inability: The difficulty of any Might-based task is increased by one step.

Inability: The difficulty of any task involving knowledge is increased by one step.

Additional Equipment: You have a sling (or a similar light ranged weapon with a short range).

Initial Link to the Starting Adventure: From the following list of options, choose how you became involved in the first adventure.

1. A friend of yours and the other PCs is in trouble (or missing) and needs your help.

2. You got lost, and the PCs helped you.

3. You and the PCs are all the same age.

4. You ran away from home and found the PCs.

CHAPTER 2

CHARACTER FOCUS

The *Cypher System Rulebook* describes what foci are, how to choose them, and how to understand and use the focus as presented. The Character Focus chapter also includes a section on how to customize foci, tweaking a particular focus that isn't quite right for a character concept.

The Foci in Different Genres table from the *Cypher System Rulebook* lists foci sorted by different genres, including fantasy, modern, horror, science fiction, and superheroes. In *Expanded Worlds,* similar tables are provided, though we've sorted the new foci by the genres introduced here. So

instead of finding the Wears Power Armor focus under a Science Fiction header, you'll see it under the post-apocalyptic and hard science fiction genres.

Because we've sorted a focus into a genre doesn't mean that the focus is unavailable in other genres, even if you're not creating or playing in a mash-up game. You might find that the Wears Spurs (which we've listed as a focus suited for the historical genre) works well in a crimes and espionage game. Likewise, the Mutates focus (listed under the post-apocalyptic genre) is probably great for fairy tales and maybe mythological settings.

On the other hand, not all new foci are appropriate for every genre. The genre chapters provide guidance, but this section offers some broad generalizations. The GM can include whatever foci are available in their setting. Foci turn out to be an important distinction in this case, because Mutates, for example, specifies that something super-science (or magical) is happening, just as Eliminates Occult

> *Not all foci are appropriate in every genre. Other foci can be adjusted to fit into a genre that they might not appear to work with at first glance. Of course, the GM can include—and adjust—whatever foci appear most appropriate for the setting.*

Threats implies the existence of something occult to investigate.

CHANGES SHAPE

You can change your shape in subtle and dramatic ways. A fairy ancestor, divine bloodline, experiment with mutating radiation, or some other extreme or mythological intervention granted you your metamorphic ability. You can only take simple forms at first, changing only your face and posture. But eventually, you can become anything: a cloud, a fish, a furnace, or even a colossal creature capable of smashing buildings with your mighty limbs.

Since you can change shape, you probably are fastidious about your appearance, which means you tend to dress well and groom yourself. On the other hand, maybe you rely on your ability to change shape to keep up appearances.

Connection: Choose one of the following.

1. Pick one other PC. Even when you change shape, that character always recognizes you.

2. Pick one other PC. For some reason, that character can trigger you to revert to your normal shape once per day, even if you don't want to.

3. Pick one other PC. When you change shape, that character changes into that shape too, if they're touching you, and only for one round before they revert.

4. Pick one other PC. At great risk to themselves, they pulled your transformed, unconscious body from a bad situation and saved your life.

Minor Effect Suggestion: You can retain your transformed shape for twice as long.

Major Effect Suggestion: All opponents within short range are so startled by your sudden change in shape that they are dazed, during which time the difficulty of all tasks they perform is modified by one step to their detriment.

Tier 1: Mimic. You can transform your face, height, and posture to resemble someone of about your size that you know or have watched for at least a few minutes. For the

**Changes Shape
GM Intrusion:** *Your transformation draws unwelcome attention, leads to a shape different than was specified, or is unstable.*

NEW FOCI IN DIFFERENT GENRES

POST-APOCALYPTIC

Drives Like a Maniac
Governs
Mutates

Plays a Deadly Instrument
Scavenges
Serves in an Elite Military Squad

Walks the Wasteland
Wears Power Armor

CRIME AND ESPIONAGE

Collects Bounties
Drives Like a Maniac
Eliminates Occult Threats†

Finds the Flaw in All Things
Governs
Learns Quickly

Negotiates Matters of Life and Death
Serves in an Elite Military Squad
Works for a Living

FAIRY TALE

Changes Shape
Eliminates Occult Threats
Fell Through a Rabbit Hole

Is Hunted by Moths
Keeps a Magic Ally
Likes to Break Things

Runs Away
Was Foretold
Wonders

CHILDHOOD ADVENTURE

Figures Things Out
Helps their Friends

Likes to Break Things
Plays Too Many Games

Runs Away
Wonders

MYTHOLOGICAL

Changes Shape
Finds the Flaw in Everything
Gazes into the Abyss

Keeps a Magic Ally
Makes Prophecy
Revels in Trickery

Rules the Sea
Touches the Sky
Was Foretold

HARD SCIENCE FICTION

Conducts Rocket Science
Hacks Networks
Loves the Void

Negotiates Matters of Life and Death
Resides in Silicon
Serves in an Elite Military Squad

Transcends Humanity
Wears Power Armor
Works for a Living

HISTORICAL

Descends from Nobility
Explores

Sailed Beneath the Jolly Roger
Is Sworn to the Crown

Is Wanted by the Law
Wears Spurs

†Only if elements of the occult become part of the setting.

next hour, the difficulty of all tasks related to disguise yourself as someone else is decreased by two steps. Action.

Tier 2: Transform (3 Intellect points). You can transform yourself to take on the shape of any natural creature no larger than yourself and no smaller than a large rat for up to one hour. Your equipment becomes part of the transformation, rendering it unusable unless it has a passive effect, such as armor. You retain normal stats and abilities, including the ability to talk. Also, you gain one minor ability associated with the creature you become. For instance, if you transform into a cat, you become specialized in climbing. If you transform into a bird, you can fly up to long distance each round. If you transform into a fish, you can breathe underwater. Action to initiate. Action to end.

Tier 3: Vigor of Proteus (6 Intellect points). You restore points to your Might Pool or Speed Pool in one of two ways: either the chosen Pool regains up to 6 points, or that Pool is restored to a total value of 12. You make this decision when you initiate this

A character who becomes colossal can accomplish a variety of additional tasks based on their new size, such as make melee attacks against low flying aircraft, move a long distance each round, and climb large structures.

ability. Points are restored at a rate of 1 point each round. This ability can never raise a Pool higher than its maximum. Action.

Tier 4: Bestial Shape (4+ Intellect points). You change into a monstrous beast, such as a wolf, bear, or other predatory creature up to three times your normal size. In your new form, you add 8 points to your Might Pool, gain +2 to your Might Edge, and gain +2 to your Speed Edge. Reverting to your normal form is a difficulty 2 task. While in beast form, you are prone to forgetting that you were once not a beast (this memory loss is triggered by a GM intrusion), during which you may wander off or take some other action more in keeping with your new form. The only way to end the amnesia is to revert to your normal form. Either way, after you revert, you suffer a –1 penalty to all rolls for one hour. Action to change. Action to revert or take some other shape.

Tier 5: Embrace the Multitude (5 Intellect points). You can use this power in one of two ways: you can become a single insect, or become of swarm of biting, stinging insects.

Insect. You become a single insect you're familiar with for up to one hour. While transformed, you retain your Speed Pool, Intellect Pool, and special abilities (work with your GM if an ability provided by your descriptor or type requires additional modification). Your Might Pool is reduced to 1 point. You have no equipment—you are your equipment. Intellect tasks that do not require physical manipulation are not penalized. Because of your size, foes often ignore you, and you're hard to hit, so the difficulty of your stealth tasks and defense rolls is decreased by three steps. Otherwise, you interact with the world as the creature you've transformed into might. Action to change. Action to revert or take some other shape.

Swarm. You discorporate into a swarm of tiny, flying insects for one minute. While discorporate, you can't affect or be affected

by normal matter or energy. Only mental attacks can affect you, but likewise, you can't attack, touch, or otherwise affect anything directly. Like a swarm of flying insects, you can move up to a long distance each round, or as your action, swarm about a single creature and modify all tasks it attempts by one step to its detriment. Action to change. Action to revert or take some other shape.

Tier 6: Extreme Shape (9+ Intellect points). You can use this power in one of two ways: you can become an inert object or transform into a creature of colossal size.

Object. You become an inert object (such as a hammer, pool of water, or rock) or a simple piece of equipment (such as a microphone or radio) that you are familiar with for up to one minute. As an object, you can't move or take actions, though you retain a hazy sense of your environment (the difficulty of all perception tasks is increased by two steps). You gain +5 Armor against physical attacks. If you attempt to take on the semblance of a particularly complex piece of equipment—such as a supercomputer or some magical artifact—the GM will assign a difficulty to the task equal to the object's level. Action to change. Action to revert or take some other shape.

Colossal Shape. You change shape into a monstrous creature up to 60 feet (18 m) tall for one minute. When you do, you become practiced in using whatever natural weapons—teeth, claws, tail, and so on—your new shape possesses. Also, you add a total of 15 temporary points to your Might Pool, +3 to Might Edge, and you deal 4 additional points of damage with melee attacks. For each level of Effort you apply to increase your mass further, it increases by 10 feet (3 m), and you add 1 additional point to your Might Pool.

Taking a colossal shape is taxing. While colossal, the difficulty of your Speed defense rolls is increased by two steps. After you revert to normal size (or take some other shape), you are exhausted and descend one step on the damage track. Finally, each additional time you become colossal before your next ten-hour recovery roll, you must apply an additional level of Effort. Thus, the second time you use Extreme Shape to become colossal, you must apply one level of Effort; the third time you use become colossal, two levels of Effort; and so on.

Action to change. Action to revert or take some other shape.

COLLECTS BOUNTIES

Nothing beats the adrenaline rush when you finally apprehend someone you've tracked across three counties—except maybe collecting the reward for bringing them in. When someone charged with a crime is released on bail bond money and then skips town, you're the best shot the system has for locating the perpetrator and making the world a safer place by putting the bad guy behind bars.

You wear heavy boots, a leather jacket, and an obvious holster for your weapon (whatever it is). Concealed weapons are not your style; you want everyone to know you mean business.

Connection: Choose one of the following.

1. Pick one other PC. They accidentally provided information to a competing bounty hunter that lost you the reward on a particularly lucrative bond.

2. Pick one other PC. You happened to see a few documents while tracking down something unrelated, which leads you to believe they're not exactly who they claim to be. You've since grown comfortable with them, but remain vigilant in case they turn out to be dangerous.

3. Pick one other PC. They rescued you from a vehicle accident, pulling you out of the wreckage at great risk to themselves.

4. Pick one other PC. They know a secret story about your past that doesn't reflect especially well on your character. But back then, you were young and stupid. Not like today. Right?

Additional Equipment: Heavy leather trench coat (light armor).

Minor Effect Suggestion: The difficulty of your next attack against your target is decreased by one step.

Major Effect Suggestion: Make an immediate extra attack on your target.

Tier 1: Tracker and Hunter. When tracking, looking for, or hiding from living people, the difficulty of the task is decreased by one step. Enabler.

Trained and Licensed. You had to demonstrate a basic level of competence to get your license. That license grants you the legal ability to arrest those who signed a bail bond contract and skipped their court date. You are trained in all tasks related to knowledge of bail, bonds, and your rights to enforce a bail bond contract.

Tier 2: Expert Combatant. Choose one type of attack in which you are not already trained: light bashing, light bladed, light ranged, medium bashing, medium bladed, medium ranged, heavy bashing, heavy bladed, or heavy ranged. You are trained in attacks using that type of weapon. Enabler.

Know Where It Hurts. You inflict 2 additional points of damage when fighting people. Enabler.

Tier 3: Roll With the Punches. Sometimes a "skip" gets rough, and you've got to evade an attack. You are trained in Speed defense tasks. Enabler.

Tier 4: Thinking It Through. Skips with bails set at astronomical levels are the most lucrative bounties. They are also the hardest to track. Thankfully, street smarts are your secret weapon. You add 4 points to your Intellect Pool. Enabler.

Tier 5: Master Combatant. You deal 2 additional points of damage with one weapon attack in which you are specialized. Enabler.

Tier 6: Knock out Blow (5+ Might points). These days, bounties are rarely dead or alive. To get your commission, you need to bring your target in alive. If you strike a living human target of level 3 or less with a melee weapon you're trained or specialized in, the target is rendered unconscious (and can take no actions) for one minute. Instead of applying Effort to decrease the difficulty, you can apply Effort to increase the maximum level of the target. Thus, to knock out a level 6 target (3 levels above the normal limit), you must apply 3 levels of Effort.

A "skip" is bounty hunter slang for someone who accepts a bail bond loan and then skips his court date.

When someone signs a bail bond contract, they waive their constitutional rights and agree that they can be arrested by the bail bond agent.

Collects Bounties GM Intrusions: *A weapon misfires, your documents are not in order, the target was misidentified, or police mistake you for a criminal.*

COMMANDS MONSTERS

Part of you shudders to the beat of the savage heart. Monsters that would happily feast on the intestines of still-living prey bow in your presence. They recognize something of you in them. That essence—which could stem from your heritage, a magical curse, an artifact you carry, or divine right—gives you the ability to command horrors both mundane and supernatural. When you reach your full potential, you might one day be crowned as the sovereign of all monsters. What defines a monster, precisely? Does my ability work on tigers, dogs, or just on manticores and vampires? The easiest definition is this: *a monster is anything that would attack and kill a human to feed on it.* For example, your power might not work on domesticated dogs, but it would work on a pack of wild dogs, and it certainly would apply to vampires!

Connection: Choose one of the following.

1. Pick one other PC. A monster you control will take commands both from that character and from you. But if it ever receives conflicting commands, it turns on you both.

2. Pick one other PC. You captured a monster for that character, but it promptly tried to kill them. They still have scars from the incident.

3. Pick one other PC. You are pretty sure you can command that PC as a monster if you apply enough Effort (though you don't think you can capture the PC). You haven't tried, and you're not sure you should; it might unlock some previously bestial part hidden in them.

4. Pick one other PC. You saved them from a monster attack, and they owe you their life.

Additional Equipment: A leash.

Minor Effect Suggestion: The monster's slash causes the foe to bleed, increasing the difficulty of all tasks the foe takes next round by one step.

Major Effect Suggestion: A monster you control takes an immediate extra action of your choice.

Tier 1: Control Monster (2+ Intellect points). You can verbally control a creature within short range for one minute, commanding it to do simple tasks on your behalf. It must be a level 2 or lower creature, whose primary motivation is hungers for flesh.

Alternatively, you can force up to three such creatures within range to take no actions for as long as you focus all your attention on them. Instead of applying Effort to decrease the difficulty, you can apply Effort to increase the maximum level of the affected creature. Thus, to affect a level 4 creature (two levels above the normal limit), you must apply two levels of Effort. Action to initiate.

Bestiary. You are trained in the lore of monstrous creatures—recognizing them, knowing their weaknesses, and knowing their habits and behaviors. Enabler.

Tier 2: Capture Monster. If you've successfully used Control Monster on a target of up to level 3, you can attempt to capture it. Doing so is a difficulty 3 Intellect task. A "captured" creature becomes tame

in your presence and will accompany you and follow your instructions. At tier 2, you can only have one captured creature at a time. However, the difficulty for using your Control Monster on the creature you have captured is decreased by one step.

You'll make rolls for your captured monster when it takes actions. In combat, you can use your action to direct the creature's attack, providing an asset if you're next to it, or vice versa. Enabler.

Tier 3: Monster Mentor. You know how to get more out of the monsters under your command. When helping your monster in combat, you can use your action to direct the creature's attack (or other ability) and reduce the difficulty of the monster's actions by a total of two steps. (This replaces the asset described under Capture Monster.) Enabler.

Tier 4: Evolve Monster. When using Capture Monster, you can attempt to capture a creature of up to level 4. Doing so is a difficulty 4 Intellect task. With your GM's permission, you could instead increase the level of a lower level creature you've previously captured to level 4. Enabler.

Tier 5: Menagerie. You can have two captured monsters accompany you at any one time instead of just one. Enabler.

Improved Bestiary. You are specialized in the lore of monstrous creatures. If you are already specialized, you instead gain +1 to any roll related to using this skill. Enabler.

Tier 6: Evolution Master. When using Capture Monster, you can attempt to capture a creature of up to level 5. Doing so is a difficulty 5 Intellect task. With your GM's permission, you could instead increase the level of a lower level creature you've previously captured to level 5. Enabler.

CONDUCTS ROCKET SCIENCE

You are specialized in a form of aerospace engineering called astronautics. You build ships designed to fly through the empty void of space where vacuum, radiation, temperature differentials, and extremes of gravitational and centripetal forces work constantly to tear apart what you build. This means your mind is sharp, your hands are clever, and your motivation is to break the

bonds of gravity and travel to other worlds of the solar system (or perhaps beyond).

Though some of your colleagues fit the stereotypical mold of mussed hair and stained lab coats, that's not your style. As a rocket scientist, you have a certain reputation to uphold, and that extends to how you dress.

Connection: Choose one of the following.

1. Pick one other PC. That character was involved in an accident that could've seen their craft's orbit decay and burn up, but you solved the problem and saved them.

2. Pick one other PC. They seem strangely interested in your rocket designs. You suspect they have a secret agenda. It's up to them whether they really do or not.

3. Pick one other PC. Based on a few comments you've overheard, you suspect that this character doesn't hold math in the highest regard.

4. Pick one other PC. When this character is standing next to you, something about them throws off your calculations. Instead of a GM Intrusion being triggered on a roll of 1, they're triggered on a roll of 1 or 2. Like all GM intrusions however, they do not always lead to a bad outcome.

Additional Equipment: Field science kit, marker for writing calculations.

Minor Effect Suggestion: You don't have to spend an action observing to make your next trajectory calculation.

Major Effect Suggestion: Intuition flares, and you can ask the GM one question about what you're looking at, and the GM will provide a general and true answer.

Tier 1: Calculate Trajectory (2 Intellect points). You observe or study a problem, puzzle, or object for at least one round. The next time you interact with it (possibly in the following round), the difficulty of a related task such as solving the problem or puzzle, or understanding more about an object is reduced by one step. Action.

Scientist: You are trained in astronautical engineering plus one other area of scientific knowledge of your choice in which you are not already trained. Enabler.

Tier 2: Modify Device (4 Intellect points). You jury-rig a piece of mechanical or electrical equipment to make it function above its rated spec for a very limited time. To do so, you must use spare parts equal to an expensive item, have a field science kit or a permanent lab, and succeed at an Intellect-based task equal to the level of the item you are modifying. When complete, using the device modifies all tasks performed in conjunction with the device by one step in the user's favor, until it inevitably breaks. For example, you could improve the spacecraft thrusters to increase a spacecraft's speed, modify the decryption module to more quickly decrypt a message, improve the sensitivity of a scientific instrument package, and so on. Each use of the modified device requires a depletion roll of 1–2 on a d6. Action to initiate, one hour to complete.

Tier 3: Genius. The more you use your brain, the better it gets. You add 3 points to your Intellect Pool. Enabler.

Continuous Learning. You are trained in another area of scientific knowledge of your choice in which you are not already trained. Enabler.

Tier 4: Extensive Training. You are specialized in one area of knowledge of your choice. Enabler.

Theory of Mind. You are trained in Intellect defense tasks. Enabler.

Tier 5: Orbital Mechanic (1 Intellect point). When you use Effort to decrease the difficulty of solving a problem or puzzle, you decrease the difficulty by two steps for the first level of Effort you apply. (This ability works in conjunction with Calculated Trajectory on applicable problems.) For example, if you used Calculate Trajectory in the previous round on the problem to decrease the difficulty one step, then use Orbital Mechanic this round in conjunction with a level of Effort to decrease the difficulty, the total difficulty of the problem or puzzle is decreased by three steps. Enabler.

Tier 6: One Giant Leap (6 Intellect points). Your research leads to a breakthrough, and you imbue an object with a truly amazing property, though you can only use the item once. To do so, you must buy spare parts equivalent to an expensive item, have a field science kit or a permanent lab, and succeed at a difficulty 4 Intellect-based roll to create a random cypher of up to level 2.

The GM decides the nature of the cypher. When attempting to create a specific cypher or a cypher of up to level 4, the difficulty is increased by two steps. Creating a cypher does not allow you to surpass your normal cypher limit. Action to initiate, one hour to complete.

DESCENDS FROM NOBILITY

You descend from privilege, wealth, and power. Your family once owned land (perhaps they still do), wielded political control, and accumulated vast wealth. You've stepped away from that somewhat, though you still carry a noble title, whether you want to or not. People recognize your name, and sometimes they recognize you as being descended from nobility.

Different cultures have different noble titles. One example: hereditary Western European titles of nobility include duke/duchess, marquis/marchioness, earl/countess, viscount/viscountess, and baron/baroness. Work with your GM to determine your title.

Since you were raised a certain way, you probably dress smartly and carry yourself in such a way that inspires, endears, or intimidates. You have a voice suited to drawing attention (unless you disguise it).

Connection: Choose one of the following.

1. Pick one other PC. That character was once in service to your parent's household, but you have since grown to think of them as a peer.

2. Pick one other PC. You're pretty sure that they are descended from a rival house, even if they don't know it.

3. Pick one other PC. You used your nobility—your influence, your wealth, or the promise of a favor—to intercede on that character's behalf.

4. Pick one other PC. You were once very close with that character in the distant past.

Additional Equipment: A set of expensive clothing suitable for nobility.

Noble Advantage: If you wish, you can swap an ability gained from your type for the following.

Retinue. Your name entitles you to a retinue that accompanies you wherever you go unless you purposefully disband it. The retinue is composed of five level 1 servants. You can ask them to deliver things for you, run messages, pick up objects of interest or items on a list—pretty much whatever

Descends From Nobility GM Intrusions: *Debts incurred by a family find the last living heir. A long-lost sibling seeks to disinherit rivals. A shake-up in the lineage puts a spotlight on surviving nobles.*

you want, within reason. They can also run interference if you're trying to avoid someone, help hide you from the attention of others, help you muscle through a crowd, and so on. If a situation becomes physically violent, they provide an asset to your Speed defense rolls and, if you command it, try to hold a foe's attention while you escape. Enabler.

Minor Effect Suggestion: The next time you attempt to command, captivate, or otherwise influence the same foe, the difficulty of the task is decreased by one step.

Major Effect Suggestion: The foe is influenced, captivated, or otherwise affected by your ability for twice as long as normal.

Tier 1: Privileged Nobility. You are adept at claiming the rewards that being of the nobility can generate. When recognized, you can be seated at any eating establishment, be let into any court or other structure where laws are decided or nobility rules, be invited to any gala, and get a seat at a private function of any sort. When dealing with someone who can't or won't immediately give in to your desire, you gain an asset on all tasks related to persuasion if that person recognizes you (or is convinced that you're a noble even if they don't recognize you). Enabler.

Tier 2: Trained Interlocutor. You were tutored by the finest teachers in the arts of rhetoric. Through wit, charm, humor, and grace (or sometimes rudeness, threatening posture, and obscenity) you are trained in all interactions. Enabler.

Tier 3: Command (3 Intellect points). Through sheer force of will, you can issue a simple imperative command to a single living creature, who then attempts to carry out your command as its next action. The creature must be within short range and able to understand you. The command can't inflict direct harm on the creature or its allies, so "Commit suicide" won't work, but "Flee" might. In addition, the command can require the creature to take only one action, so "Unlock the door" might work, but "Unlock the door and run through it" won't. Action.

Improved Retinue. If you have a retinue, they are level 2. Enabler.

Tier 4: Trained Duelist. The finest teachers in the arts of weaponry tutored you in the use of one type of weapon. When wielding that kind of weapon, you inflict 1 additional point of damage and are trained in Speed defense tasks. Enabler.

Tier 5: Claiming Your Title (3 Intellect points). Acting only as someone who is a noble and used to privilege can, you verbally harangue a foe who can hear you so forcefully that it is unable to take any action, including making attacks, for one round. Whether you succeed or fail, the difficulty of the next action the target takes after your attempt is modified by one step to its detriment. Action.

Tier 6: Mind of A Future Ruler (6 Intellect points). When you develop a plan that involves your followers, you can ask the GM one very general question about what is likely to happen if you carry out the plan, and you will get a simple, brief answer. Action.

DRIVES LIKE A MANIAC
Your skill behind the wheel is legendary. When the engine is racing, and the wind is in your hair, you feel alive. Where you go, others fear to follow, for the wastes are cruel to those whose vehicles break down. Whether balancing on two wheels (or even one), jumping another vehicle, or driving head-on toward an oncoming enemy car, you don't think about the risks. You live to drive, and your fondest wish is to die behind the wheel. But before it comes to that, you'll run anyone that crosses your path off the road.

Driving is a job for the elite and the dangerous, so you wear dangerous-looking clothing and body ornamentation, including a long leather coat, driving gloves, tattoos, piercings, and possibly even an arresting hairdo.

Connection: Choose one of the following.

1. Pick one other PC. You promised that character a trip anywhere they wanted to go in your vehicle. They haven't yet taken you up on your offer.

2. Pick one other PC. You drove a getaway vehicle for them after they committed an offense against a powerful organization. Trouble hasn't found you because of it. Yet.

3. Pick one other PC. That character tells you they were hired to kill you, but they didn't, because they like the way you drive.

4. Pick one or more other PCs. You accidentally crashed your vehicle when those characters were your passengers. Everyone was hurt to some extent.

Equipment: A motorcycle or car and one full tank of fuel.

Minor Effect Suggestion: You can drive an additional 50 feet (15 m) this round.

Major Effect Suggestion: You can take an immediate extra action related to driving a vehicle.

Tier 1: Driver. You are trained in all tasks related to driving a car, truck, or motorcycle, including mechanical repair tasks. Enabler.

Driving on the Edge. You can make an attack with a light or medium ranged weapon and attempt a driving task as a single action. Enabler.

Tier 2: Car Surfer. You can stand or move about on a moving vehicle (such as on the hood, roof, in the open door well, etc.) with a reasonable expectation of not falling off. Unless the vehicle veers sharply, stops suddenly, or otherwise engages in extreme maneuvers, standing or moving about on a moving vehicle is a routine task for you. If the vehicle engages in extreme maneuvers like those described, the difficulty of any task to remain on the vehicle's surface is decreased by one step. Enabler.

Stare Them Down. One doesn't play games of chicken with other maniac drivers without gaining mental strength. You're trained in Intellect defense tasks. Enabler.

Tier 3: Expert Driver. You are specialized in all tasks related to driving a car, truck, or motorcycle, including mechanical repair tasks. Enabler.

Tier 4: Sharp-Eyed. Because you must always keep an eye out when you're on the road, you are trained in all tasks related to perception and navigation. Enabler.

Road Reflexes. You add 3 points to your Speed Pool. Enabler.

Tier 5: Something in the Road. When you use a vehicle as a weapon (described under Run 'Em Down) you inflict 5 additional points of damage. Enabler.

Tier 6: Trick Driver. While driving a car, truck, or motorcycle, your Might Edge, Speed Edge, and Intellect Edge increase by 1. When you make a recovery roll while driving, you recover 5 additional points. When you attempt a driving task or an extreme trick—such as jumping a ravine or other vehicle, spinning in the air, landing safely on another vehicle, and so on—the difficulty of the task is reduced by one step. Enabler.

ELIMINATES OCCULT THREATS

Maybe you didn't want to learn magic. Perhaps it was either learn about the occult or die. Or maybe you had friends or family who were killed by a mysterious occult presence, which was what spurred on your early interest. In which case, you made it your single goal to pierce the heart of that mystery, and you discovered it was supernatural. Whether you've gotten to the bottom of the original series of occult events that set you on your path, you've become something of an occult detective and have the capacity to help others with their brushes with the supernatural.

Connection: Choose one of the following.

1. Pick one other PC. Through a quirk of fate, your magic cannot harm or affect that character.

2. Pick one other PC. You recently discovered that if they stand near you when you use your Track the Supernatural ability, your range expands by an order of magnitude. They must remain within immediate range of you to retain the effect.

3. Pick one other PC. They had a devastating experience with magic in the past and must decide how to react to your constant study (and use) of magic.

Run 'Em Down. *Training in driving makes the character practiced in using a vehicle as a weapon. If the vehicle is used to run over a victim or ram an enemy vehicle, treat a motorcycle as a medium weapon and treat a car or truck as a heavy weapon.*

Eliminates Occult Threats GM Intrusions: *Complicated spells can be forgotten. Using unfamiliar magic can sometimes draw attention from Unseelie or demonic realms. Clients sometimes have hidden agendas.*

Though by no means required, adepts and similar characters are usually most likely to choose Eliminates Occult Threats as a focus.

"So. Magic. What's it all about, then? I wonder what you were after when you got into the game. It's usually something. Something specific that you think is worth taking risks for. Money. Sex. Revenge. Power. Enlightenment."

~Constantine

4. Pick one other PC. For some reason, they are particularly vulnerable to your magic. Occasionally when you use Pocket Eclipse or Enchant Creature, and they are within short range of you, they are affected as well (blinded by darkness or enchanted).

Additional Equipment: Occult paraphernalia, such as a tarot deck or similar, incense sticks, some vials filled with various substances (including dust, blood, and mercury), and an amulet of supposed ancient vintage.

Spellcasting Special Abilities: If you have special abilities that seem supernatural, you perform them as minor spells you invoke, which involve an arcane gesture or two, a few mystical words, and possibly a pinch of dust or other material. This alteration changes nothing except how you trigger the effects.

Also, you can choose to learn the minor spell Pocket Eclipse instead of one of the abilities granted by your type.

Pocket Eclipse (2 Intellect points). For the next ten minutes, light drains from an area within long range that is no bigger than an immediate distance in diameter. Light cannot enter the area of eclipse, and creatures that normally can see in the dark cannot see in the area. If you cast Eclipse on an object, the effect moves with the object and could be temporarily suppressed if the object is enclosed in wrapping or a container. Action to initiate.

Minor Effect Suggestion: Your foe is surprised by or has a bad reaction to your magic for one round, during which time the difficulty of all its tasks is modified by one step to its detriment.

Major Effect Suggestion: An important item on the target's person is destroyed.

Tier 1: Occult Knowledge. You have studied ancient tomes, scrolls, and from stone tablets unearthed in distant parts of the world. You are trained in all tasks related to knowledge of the occult, supernatural, and magic. Enabler.

Track the Supernatural (2+ Intellect points). You have learned various arcane tricks and occult divinatory spells, enough to allow you to track down a range of occult activity within a mile. You normally can't track entities themselves but instead the places where magic or other supernatural effects were used. When you use this ability,

you must burn an ancient parchment and observe the smoke, draw a magic circle and meditate inside, or take some other occult action that occupies you for about a minute. Then you can track occult effects of up to level 2 (and gain a vague sense of what has happened even before you get there, which might allow you to discriminate between multiple hits) to its location. Instead of applying Effort to decrease the difficulty, you can use it to increase the level of the effect you can detect; each level of Effort applied increases the level by one. A minute to initiate; your tracking sense lasts for about an hour.

Tier 2: Resist Occult Influence. You are naturally resistant to supernatural influence that seeks to seize control of your will. You have an asset to all defense tasks against magic, occult, and supernatural attacks and effects. Enabler.

Investigator. To shine as an occult detective, you must engage both mind and body in your deductions. You can spend points from your Might Pool, Speed Pool, or Intellect Pool to apply levels of Effort to any Intellect-based task. Enabler.

Tier 3: Enchant Creature (2+ Intellect points). You know a spell for affecting the minds of other creatures. A level 2 target within immediate range does as you suggest on its next action (but will not follow suggestions to harm itself or its allies). Instead of applying Effort to decrease the difficulty, you can apply Effort to increase the maximum level of the target. Thus, to suggest a course of action to a level 5 target (three levels above the normal limit), you must apply three levels of Effort. Action.

Tier 4: Draw Conclusion (3 Intellect points). After careful observation and investigation (questioning one or more NPCs on a topic, searching an area or a file, and so on) lasting a few minutes, you can learn a pertinent fact. This ability is a difficulty 3 Intellect task. Each additional time you use this ability, the task difficulty increases by one step. The difficulty returns to difficulty 3 after you rest for ten hours. Action.

Tier 5: Pass Through Barrier (5 Intellect points). You know a spell for getting around most obstacles. You or a willing target you touch, along with all carried equipment, is transformed into a colorless mist for up to one minute. Someone transformed to mist can flow in any direction, including upward, an immediate distance each round (even against a strong wind), penetrate any area that isn't hermetically sealed and enjoy immunity to mundane physical attacks. Someone transformed to mist cannot speak, interact with objects or carried equipment, or use special abilities. If you begin falling a short or longer distance, you can invoke this ability quickly enough to avoid striking the bottom (shorter falls do not provide enough time). Action to initiate.

Tier 6: Summon Demonic Entity (8+ Intellect points). You know a spell for summoning a malefic entity into your presence. Work with your GM to determine the creature's nature and relationship with you (if any); otherwise, you summon a chain demon. The creature appears within immediate range, plucked from the realm of its origin. If you applied a level of Effort as part of the summoning, the demon is amenable to your instructions; otherwise, it acts according to its nature. The demon persists for up to one minute before returning to its nether realm, though at the GM's option, it may stay longer. Action.

EXPLORES

The Royal Geographical Society of London was founded in 1830 to advance geographical knowledge and science, and as a place for explorers to come together and share their discoveries. The Geographical Society fosters such famous explorers as Livingstone, Stanley, Scott, Shackleton, Hunt, Hillary, and a host of others. Maybe even you. But even if you're not a member (or a member of some similar explorer's club), the same yearning to see far horizons and discover new places fires your imagination.

You probably wear sensible, all-weather garments and carry sturdy gear that won't get ruined in the rain or heat. A hat to keep off the sun, and extra water for when the trail peters out in the middle of nowhere.

Connection: Choose one of the following.

1. Pick one other PC. This character has been your adventuring partner in previous expeditions, and the two of you work so well together that you both gain +1 to any

roll when you collaborate on the same task, fight the same foe, and so on.

2. Pick one other PC. That character nearly drowned while following you on one of your expeditions. It's up to them whether they trust you to lead an expedition again.

3. Pick one other PC. You think they suspect that you were involved with tomb robbers or other criminals. Whether you were or not is up to you.

4. Pick one other PC. You suspect this character possesses secret knowledge of a hidden tomb, lost city, or treasure. Whether they really do or not remains up to them to decide.

Additional Equipment: You carry an explorer's pack with rope, enough rations for two days, a bedroll, and other tools needed for outdoor survival. If you wish, you also carry proof of membership in an explorer's club.

Explorer's Club: If you wish, you can swap an ability gained from your type for the following.

Membership Benefits: You not only belong to a well-regarded and well-funded club of explorers, but you have also purchased a founding membership. This provides several benefits, including a base of operations for extended periods, somewhere to conduct research on a variety of geographical and historical topics, contacts among other explorers, and access to a variety of leads about sites of interest that no one else has yet explored. Sometimes the explorer's club will mount expeditions, or fund your explorations if you make your case well enough. Also, you can always claim one item from collections (where ancient jewelry, documents, and relics are kept), in return for an artifact of equal value. Finally, you gain an asset in all tasks related to navigation and finding your way. Enabler.

Minor Effect Suggestion: You can take an extra action. You may use this action only to perform a movement-related activity, or a knowledge-based activity, such as trying to climb a treacherous cliff or attempting to decipher strange cave markings.

Major Effect Suggestion: The difficulty of any Speed defense action you take before the end of the next round is reduced by one step.

Tier 1: Trained Explorer. You are trained in searching, listening, climbing, balancing, and jumping tasks. Enabler.

Chain Demon, page 133

Explores GM Intrusions: *Strange diseases are common in uncivilized regions. Food runs out on long expeditions. Porters become scared or demoralized and flee.*

PCs who don't take the Explores focus can still join the Royal Geographical Society and gain the Membership Benefits ability instead of taking a skill.

Tier 2: Resilient. In your explorations of uncivilized regions, you've been exposed to all sorts of terrible things and have developed a general resistance. You gain +1 to Armor and are trained in Might defense tasks. Enabler.

Tier 3: Apprentice Explorer. You gain a level 2 NPC apprentice explorer who is completely devoted to you. You and the GM must work out the details of the fellow explorer who demurs to you.

You'll probably make rolls for your apprentice when they take actions. In combat, they usually don't make separate attacks, but helps you with yours. On your action, if the

NPC is next to you, they serve as an asset for one attack you make on your turn.

If your fellow explorer dies, you gain a new one after at least two weeks and proper recruitment. Enabler.

Tier 4: Explorer's Intuition (4 Intellect points). Your competence in the skills of exploration gives you an uncanny intuition when it comes to finding things. While in the wilderness, you can extend your senses up to a mile in any direction and ask the GM a very simple, general question about that area, such as "Where is the native camp?" or "Is my friend Dr. Livingstone still alive?" If the answer you seek is not in the area, you receive no information. Action.

Tier 5: Survive Nature's Wrath (3 Speed points). When low rations, disease, and bad morale threaten to wreck an expedition, you always double down and try harder. You can reroll any of your Might, Speed, or Intellect defense rolls and take the better of the two results. Enabler.

Tier 6: Survival In Extremity (4 Intellect points). If you have the time and the freedom to scrounge for everyday materials in your environment, you can fashion a temporary asset that will aid you once to accomplish a specific task. For example, if you need to climb a wall, you could create a climbing device; if you need to break out of a cell, you can fashion a lockpick; if you need to create a small distraction, you could put together something to make a loud noise; and so on. The asset lasts for a maximum of one minute, or until used. Alternatively, you find or create a significant shortcut, secret entrance, or emergency escape route where it looked like none existed. You and the GM should work out the details. Action.

FELL THROUGH A RABBIT HOLE
You weren't always this way, but something happened to you when you fell through a "rabbit hole" (either metaphorically, or literally) into a surreal realm of magic, faeries, nonsense entities, or something so otherworldly that you can't quite explain it. You've returned, but the connection remains, and you're no longer the same. Not only do you think about things differently—possibly even in ways that

confuse your friends—but you also can do things that defy reality. At least reality on *this* side of the rabbit hole.

Connection: Choose one of the following.

1. Pick one other PC. It was while following that character you first learned of the surreal realm to which you are now connected.

2. Pick two other PCs. You know about an important connection between them that they don't know.

3. Pick one other PC. You accidentally draw that character to the attention of a dangerous creature that lives within the surreal realm to which you are connected.

4. Pick one other PC. Whenever this character is near, your abilities seem to take twice as long to activate.

Additional Equipment: You have a ring of keys, which sometimes work on locks when you least expect it.

Minor Effect Suggestion: A small animal—a cat, a raccoon, or a rabbit—trips up your foe, and your foe falls.

Major Effect Suggestion: A stranger appears and helps you for a few rounds.

Tier 1: Legerdemain (1 Speed point). You can perform small but seemingly impossible tricks. For example, you can make a small object in your hands disappear and move into a desired spot within reach (like your pocket). You can make someone believe that they have something in their possession that they do not have or vice versa. You can switch similar objects right in front of someone's eyes. Action.

Fell Through a Rabbit Hole GM Intrusions: *Sometimes silly strangers are dangerously insane. Nonsense influence from a surreal realm can cut both ways, creating impediments and calling attention. Sometimes the surreal realm calls those who've previously visited back, whether they want to return or not.*

NONSENSE TABLE

1	**Escape (2 Intellect points).** You gain a notion on how to escape, wriggle free from bindings, or squeeze through a tight spot, gaining an asset to any escape task. Alternatively, you can gain an asset to any defense task to throw off an ongoing negative effect like poison or a curse. Action.
2	**Pierce to the Heart (1 Intellect point).** You are inspired by trickery. If you succeed on a Speed-based task against one creature within immediate range, the difficulty of your next attack against that creature before the end of the next round is reduced by one step. Action.
3	**Unexpected Trapdoor (3 Intellect points).** A surface is not as solid as it first appeared, and you find a trap door. You can use the door to access the basement, the attic, or go through a wall up to 10 feet (3 m) thick if you succeed on an Intellect task equal to the level of the impediment. Alternatively, a foe within short range drops through said trapdoor to whatever lies beneath (which might just be a ten-foot deep pit). The trapdoor persists for about a minute. Action to initiate.
4	**What's This In My Pocket? (3 intellect points).** You're sure it wasn't there before, but it is now. You pull a cypher from your pocket. The GM determines what kind. If you are already at your cypher limit, one cypher you already have goes missing. Action.
5	**Premonition (2 Intellect points).** You learn one random fact about a creature or location that is pertinent to a topic you designate. Alternatively, you can choose to learn a creature's level; however, if you do so, you cannot learn anything else about it later with this same ability. Action.
6	**Fetch (3 Intellect points).** You cause an object to disappear and reappear in your hands or somewhere else nearby. Choose one object that can fit inside a 5-foot (2 m) cube and that you can see within long range. The object vanishes and appears in your hands or an open space anywhere you choose within immediate range. Action.
7	**You're Not So Hurt As All That (3 Intellect points).** When you touch an impaired or debilitated character, you can move them up one step on the damage track (a debilitated PC becomes impaired, and an impaired PC becomes hale). Alternatively, if you use this ability on a PC during a rest, you grant them a +2 bonus to their recovery roll. Action.
8	**What Kind of Beast is That? (3 Intellect points).** A creature from the surreal realm to which you have a connection appears of up to level 3. The creature aids you for up to one minute before leaving. Action to initiate.
9	**Because I Said So (3 Intellect points).** You're inspired by a crazy impulse. For one minute, you gain an asset to tasks related to deceiving, persuading, and intimidating. Action to initiate.
10	**Begin at the Beginning (2 Intellect points).** For one hour, you can see in complete darkness within short range as if it were dim light. Also, you gain an asset to all tasks related to finding your way and tracking other creatures. Action to initiate.

Tier 2: Nonsense. Something that just happened doesn't sit right with you, and you put your foot down. You call on your connection to a surreal realm and hope things change for the better. At the very least, they'll change. Gain an effect from the Nonsense Table by rolling randomly. If you roll an effect and do not wish to pay the stat point cost, nothing happens. Alternatively, you can pay the cost and apply a level of Effort to choose a result within 2 results of your rolled result. Enabler.

Tier 3: Red Queen Running (2 Speed points). Sometimes fleeing is the only way to keep your head. After your action on your turn, you can move up to a short distance or get behind or beneath cover within immediate range. Enabler.

Tier 4: Curious and Quick. You gain 6 new points to divide among your Intellect and Speed stat Pools however you wish. Enabler.

Tier 5: Nonsense Deluge. You've become more practiced when you call on your connection to the surreal realm to which you are connected. When you refer to the Nonsense Table, you can select the result you want rather than rolling randomly on the table. Enabler.

Tier 6: Surreal Protection. Your long-term connection to a surreal realm, whether you welcome that connection or not, has changed you in many ways. It also protects you. An invisible, implausible influence provides you with +2 Armor. Also, if struck by a melee attack, the protective influence creates a backlash that inflicts 4 points of nightmare damage to the attacker. Enabler.

FIGURES THINGS OUT

You're a natural when it comes to applying your brain to a problem and coming up with a workable solution. The world is a chaotic place, filled with unpredictable people and crazy situations that adults think of as normal. You're young, the future is wide open, and everything seems equally interesting. Which is what helps you come at things in a novel way, which sometimes gets to the root of issues that others say can't be figured out.

You probably carry a day pack where you collect interesting stuff, a journal where you

Insight, page 216

Figures Things Out GM Intrusion: *An Insight gained is an unwelcome piece of news. An NPC is as good or better than the character at figuring out what the next step is.*

Scan, page 32

Premonition, page 27

keep notes about unexpected situations, and all your doodles and reminders.

Connection: Choose one of the following.

1. Pick one other PC. If it weren't for you, they never would've made it through a difficult situation.

2. Pick one other PC. You figured out that they have a secret that they haven't told anyone yet. You don't know what that secret is, but you can tell it weighs on them.

3. Pick one other PC. Based on a couple of comments you've overheard, you suspect that this character thinks brawn and force, not reason, are the solutions to most problems.

4. Pick one other PC. When this character stands next to you, you have a hard time concentrating. You're not sure why.

Additional Equipment: A journal and "space pen" that writes underwater.

Minor Effect Suggestion: You don't have to spend an action observing to use With Fresh Eyes or attempt Filling in the Details.

Major Effect Suggestion: Intuition flares, and you gain an asset on your task.

Tier 1: With Fresh Eyes. You observe or study a creature, object, or location for at least one round. The next time you interact with it (possibly in the following round), the difficulty of a related task (such as persuading the creature, attacking it, or defending from its attack) is reduced by one step. Action.

Tier 2: Gain Insight. Once after each long rest, you can ask the GM if there is an Insight related to your current situation. The Insight might help you with a plan, your method of research, gathering information, scouting, or in the pursuit of some other goal. An Insight is a single bit of special knowledge from the GM that you can count on with certainty. Normally, gaining an Insight costs 3 Intellect points. When you use this ability, it costs you nothing. Action.

Tier 3: Filling in the Details (2+ Intellect points). If you've used With Fresh Eyes on a creature, object, or location within the last few days, you can learn one random fact about the subject that is pertinent to a topic you designate. If you also have the Scan or Premonition special ability, one use of either ability grants you two facts about the subject. Also, you can use Filling in the Details on the same subject multiple times (even if you've learned a creature's level), but each time you do, you must apply one additional level of Effort than on your previous use. Action.

Tier 4: Insight Gained. Sometimes the GM alerts players that there is an Insight to be gained in a particular situation. Normally, a character must spend 2 XP to follow up on the GM's comment. However, once after each long rest, you can follow up on the GM's comment without spending XP. Action.

Tier 5: Genius. The more you use your brain, the better it gets. You add 5 points to your Intellect Pool. Enabler.

True Knowledge. You've figured enough things out that you've become trained in any one task that you're not already trained in, including combat tasks. Enabler.

Tier 6: Know When To Evade. You've become so good at figuring things out that you subconsciously avoid danger even when your conscious mind isn't yet aware of the threat. You're specialized in all defense tasks.

FINDS THE FLAW IN ALL THINGS

You can see the weak points in objects, in people, and even in the way people think, plan, and dream. Those flaws are always apparent, even when you don't want to see them. If you don't hold your tongue, you risk leaving a trail of angry and embittered people in your wake. Your burden of knowledge makes it difficult to stay in relationships long, so you cherish those who you call friends, even their flaws (though you try not to call those out too often). Some believe that your ability is the power of fate and that one day, you will find the flaw in reality itself, and transcend.

Connection: Choose one of the following.

1. Pick one other PC. Through a quirk of fate, you cannot sense that character's flaws.

2. Pick one other PC. You recently discovered that if they stand near you when you attempt to use your abilities to sense the flaw in others, your abilities sometimes don't work. Other times, they seem to work better than ever. You're not sure what's going on.

3. Pick one other PC. When you first met, you told them exactly how much of a failure they were as a person, laying bare all their worst fears and doubts. You've since apologized, but they must decide how to react to you.

4. Pick one other PC. This character has a treasured item that was once yours, but that you lost in a game of chance.

Flaw Abilities: If you wish, you can swap an ability gained from your type for the following.

Find the Flaw: If an opponent has a straightforward weakness (takes extra damage from fire, can't see out of their left eye, and so on), the GM will tell you what it is. If you also have the Sharp-Eyed descriptor and its associated Find the Flaw ability, you have an asset on the first action you take against a target when you exploit the straightforward weakness identified by Find the Flaw. Enabler.

Minor Effect Suggestion: The display of your ability leaves a creature confused and even a little frightened. The difficulty of defense actions to resist the creature's attacks decreases by one step for one minute.

Major Effect Suggestion: An important item on the target's person is destroyed.

Tier 1: Perfect Submission (1+ Intellect point). You know exactly where to grab, prod, or apply pressure to a creature to keep its undivided attention. For as long as you take no physical actions or movements except to hold the submission, the other creature can take no physical actions, even over multiple rounds. If the creature is attacked, the effect ends. You can affect creatures up to twice as large as you. To affect creatures three, four, or more times larger than you, you must apply increasing levels of Effort. For instance, to affect a creature three times larger than you, you must apply two levels of Effort. Action.

Tier 2: Reckoning. If you attack an opponent who you have observed in combat (against another creature or yourself) for at least one round, the difficulty of your next attack is reduced by one step. On a successful hit with this attack, you inflict 2 additional points of damage. Enabler.

Tier 3: Fly in the Ointment. The difficulty of all tasks related to detecting falsehoods and

Sharp-eyed, page 83

Find the Flaw, page 83

Finds the Flaw in All Things GM Intrusions: *Sometimes the flaw in oneself is recognized. It's difficult not to blurt out flaws noticed in an ally. Pointing out a foible or failing can easily create a long-term enemy.*

disguises, and recognizing fallacies, flawed arguments, and bad plans is reduced by two steps. Enabler.

Tier 4: Flaw of Worldly Works (5 Intellect points). You see where objects are most likely to break. The difficulty of any task that would normally depend on brute force (but which you accomplish with an apparently light touch) is decreased by three steps. Examples include opening a barred door or a locked container with a deft touch instead of smashing it, shifting a heavy object without lifting it, opening a hole in a solid barrier by finding a keystone, and so on. Enabler.

Tier 5: Flaw of Mortal Flesh (6+ Intellect points). You recognize where flesh fails. With a swift and sudden attack, you strike a foe in a vital spot. If the target is level 3 or lower, it is killed outright. For each two levels of Effort you apply, you can increase the maximum level of the target by 1. Action.

Tier 6: Flaw in Everything (3 Intellect points). You see flaws in everyone and everything, so much that you usually veil your flaw-finding eye. However, sometimes you raise that veil, if for just a moment. Usually, you see the flaw in others, but sometimes you see the flaw in yourself. When you use this ability, the task you're attempting is modified by two steps in your favor. However, the difficulty of all defense tasks you attempt until your next turn is modified by one step to your detriment. Enabler.

GOVERNS

Governs GM Intrusions: *Someone begins spreading rumors that the governor is weak, unfit to lead, or corrupt. A vote of no-confidence is called. Supplies for the community are stolen.*

Someone's got to lead these people, but everyone who's tried has screwed up, abdicated, or worst of all, led people down a path that you're certain is dangerous. So now it's your time, even if you come from a position of not wanting to take on the role. But people seem drawn to you. They tend to listen when you talk. You might as well put that ability to good use. If you don't step up, you're convinced the situation will continue to degrade. You might have to resort to a few underhanded tricks; if so, maybe it's not the first time you've had to lie to protect others. Most people can't handle the truth.

You are probably a somewhat striking person, whether because you're taller than normal, are attractive, or affect an attire and composure that puts people at their ease when they're around you.

Connection: Choose one of the following.
1. Pick one other PC. This character begins the game having known you in a leadership role in the past.
2. Pick one other PC. They know a secret of yours, and you desperately hope that they don't tell anyone.
3. Pick one other PC. They believe that your intervention saved a community they were part of or have heard of, and they are grateful. They're mistaken, but you haven't disabused them of their belief.
4. Pick one other PC. You secretly believe that they distrust your motives. Whether they do is up to that character to decide.

Additional Equipment: One medium ranged weapon.

Minor Effect Suggestion: The next time you attempt to influence the same target, the difficulty of the task is decreased by one step.

Major Effect Suggestion: The foe is influenced by your ability for twice as long as normal.

Tier 1: Natural Charisma. You are trained in all social interactions, whether they involve charm, learning a person's secrets, or intimidating others. Enabler.

Good Advice (1 Intellect point). You have a clear mind for determining the best way to proceed. When you give another character a suggestion involving their next action, the character is trained in that action for one round. Action.

Tier 2: Lead from the Front. No one is going to allow themselves to be governed by someone not willing to lay it on the line themselves. Thus, you constantly test yourself, which toughens you. You gain 3 new points to divide among your stat Pools however you wish. Enabler.

Hard Choices. Sometimes, you believe that you've got to lie to those who trust you for their own good. You are specialized in deception tasks. Enabler.

Tier 3: Punish The Guilty. To govern means to punish those who disobey the rules or who otherwise betray the trust of the people, as represented by you. You deal 1 additional point of damage with every attack you make. Enabler.

Tier 4: Captivate or Inspire. You can use this ability in one of two ways. Either your words keep the attention of all NPCs that hear them for as long as you speak, or your words inspire all NPCs (of your choosing) that hear them to function as if they were one level higher for the next hour. Action.

Tier 5: Confidence. Governors inspire confidence, and confidence comes from real ability. You gain 6 new points to divide among your stat Pools however you wish. Enabler.

Tier 6: Deep Reserves. When others are exhausted, you can push through. Once each day, you can transfer up to 5 points among your Pools in any combination, at a rate of 1 point per round. For example, you could transfer 3 points of Might to Speed and 2 points of Intellect to Speed, which would take a total of five rounds. Action.

HACKS THE NETWORK

AI and the countless networks integrated into every part of life are as ubiquitous as air, and to most people, about as noticeable. Not you. From the moment you first realized that networks ran on an underlying "Ur" tongue, a code of mathematics and logical symbols, you were hooked. It wasn't your goal to learn everything you could about hacking computers so much as there was nothing else for you. As a thrown stone follows its trajectory, you learned to hack the network.

What you wear doesn't matter, because you live in the code (as long as you have access to a computer, hand terminal, or some other connection). You might have a few extra pockets for high-energy snacks and spare storage medium, as well.

Connection: Choose one of the following.

1. Pick one other PC. You believe that this character shows potential for being an excellent network hacker, but you don't know if they would be interested in the rigorous training and practice required.

2. Pick one other PC. This character once accidentally wrecked your computer.

3. Pick one other PC. You promised this character you would ease their debts by hacking the places where they owe money and adjusting their balance downward.

4. Pick one other PC. Something about that character interrupts your flow. If they're next to you while you are attempting a coding-related task, the task's difficulty is one step higher.

Additional Equipment: You have an expensive portable computer of your choice.

Minor Effect Suggestion: The network security measures or linked cameras are blinded for one round.

Major Effect Suggestion: The network and all nearby connected machines power down for several rounds, up to one minute.

Tier 1: Perfect Hack (3 Intellect points). You persuade a networked machine, computer, connected server, or similar information-relaying appliance to do your bidding. You can discover an encrypted password, break through security on a website, briefly turn off a machine such as a surveillance camera, or disable a robot with a moment's worth of fiddling. Action.

Computer Programming. You are trained in using (and exploiting) computer software, you know one or more computer languages well enough to write basic programs, and you are fluent in various network protocols. Enabler.

Tier 2: Network Tap (4 Intellect points). You can ask the GM one question and get a very short answer. Action.

Tier 3: Expert Hacker. The more you practice hacking, the more proficient you become. You gain 3 additional points to your Intellect Pool and +1 to your Intellect Edge. Enabler.

Hacks the Network GM Intrusions: *It's nearly impossible to write perfect code on the first try. Hackers who make a name for themselves can become targets of other hackers. Hacking requires a working computer, hand terminal, or similar device.*

"A simple program, a worm that can make data unreadable, malware that took Darlene maybe two hours to code. Is that really all it takes to kill the world?"
~Mr. Robot

Tier 4: Erased. You infiltrated the networks so completely that networked cameras can't identify you. If your face comes up on automated recording devices, vulnerabilities you've previously exploited keep you from being recognized. Even when station security physically recognizes you, upon checking their records and hand terminals, they're told that you're not who you seem to be, but rather someone unimportant, which you can use as an asset in any related persuasion or deception interaction. Enabler.

Tier 5: Control Machine (5 Intellect points). You can control the functions of any machine, no matter how far from you it is, that you've previously exploited using Perfect Hack, as long as it is networked to your current location. This effect lasts for ten minutes. Action.

Tier 6: Power Nap. In addition to your normal recovery rolls each day, you can take as many ten minute recovery rolls as you have the time for, so long as you add the points recovered to your Intellect Pool. Action.

HELPS THEIR FRIENDS

Helps Their Friends GM Intrusions: *People who portray themselves as friends or patrons sometimes have ulterior motives. The law takes an undue interest in recent activities. Even when everything goes right, repercussions can follow, especially if powerful people were thwarted.*

You just naturally help your friends in the little things and the big. They're your friends. Maybe you never had friends before and are grateful to be part of something bigger than yourself. Or maybe you had friends but lost them, and this is your chance to redeem yourself. It's not an obligation that makes you so selfless. Maybe it's not even a choice. When you see that they need a helping hand, you offer it without thinking; that's what friends do.

If you choose this foci in a childhood adventure scenario, you probably wear sneakers, jeans, a button-up shirt, a jacket, and carry some kind of backpack to keep your stuff.

Connection: Choose one of the following.

1. Pick one other PC. The first time you saw a friend in trouble, you got scared and ran. You don't know if your friend saw you

or not. You suspect not, and you haven't told your friend what you did.

2. Pick one other PC. You helped your friend break into a place where food was sold and make off with a few bags of sweets. Now you feel guilty about it, and a bit angry at your friend even though it was your choice to help.

3. Pick one other PC. They've always been there for you and helped you when you couldn't help yourself.

4. Pick one other PC. You tried to help a mutual friend but failed. Now that mutual friend is gone (dead, lost, moved away, or made new friends) and you feel like it's your fault. You're not sure if your friend blames you, or not.

Additional Equipment: Picture of you and your friends.

Also, if you wish, you can swap an ability gained from your type for the following.

Advice From A Friend (1 Intellect point). You know your friend's strengths and weaknesses, and know how to motivate them to succeed. When you give an ally a suggestion involving their next action, the character is trained in that action for one round. Action.

Minor Effect Suggestion: You coach a friend, and reduce the difficulty of their next action by one step.

Major Effect Suggestion: You provide aid to a friend, and grant them a free, no-action recovery roll.

Tier 1: Friendly Help. If your friend tries a task and fails, they can try again without spending Effort if you help. You provide this advantage to your friend even if you are not trained in the task that your friend is retrying. Enabler.

Courageous. You are trained in Intellect defense tasks and initiative tasks. Enabler.

Tier 2: Weather The Vicissitudes. Helping your friends means being able to stand up to everything the world throws at you. You have a +1 bonus to Armor. Also, you resist heat, cold, and similar extremes and have

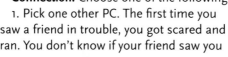

"A friend is someone that you'd do anything for. You lend them your cool stuff, like comic books and trading cards. And they never break a promise."

~Stranger Things

an additional +1 bonus to Armor against ambient damage or other damage that would normally ignore Armor.

Tier 3: Buddy System (3 Intellect points). Choose one character standing next to you. That character becomes your buddy for ten minutes. You are trained in all tasks involving finding, healing, interacting with, and protecting your buddy. Also, while you stand next to your buddy, both of you have an asset on Speed defense tasks. You can have only one buddy at a time. Action to initiate.

Tier 4: In Harm's Way (3 Intellect points). When you put your friends before yourself as your action, you decrease the difficulty of all defense tasks by one step for all characters you choose that are adjacent to you. This lasts until the end of your next turn. If one of your friends would be damaged, you can choose to share up to half the number of points they would otherwise take, but only if you're not already impaired or debilitated. Enabler.

Resilient. You grow more resilient, which grants you 3 new points to divide among your stat Pools however you wish. Enabler.

Tier 5: Instant Motivation (4 Intellect points). Thanks to your cheer of inspiration and heartfelt motivation, one creature you choose within short range is granted an additional, immediate action, which they can take out of turn. Action.

Tier 6: Deep Consideration (6 Intellect points). When you develop a plan that involves you and your friends working together to accomplish a goal, you can ask the GM one very general question about what is likely to happen if you carry out the plan, and you will get a simple, brief answer. In addition, all of you gain an asset to one roll related to enacting the plan you developed together, so long as you put the plan into action within a few days of the plan's creation. Action.

IS HUNTED BY MOTHS

You took too much interest in faerie ways and in your studies, you stole the language of the moths, learning it for yourself. You gained power over moths, but in the process gained the ire of a greater power, entities dark, mysterious, and vengeful. You

call them cryptic moths. Now they hunt you. Or at least, that's the story you tell, and maybe it's true. Or maybe you're a fugitive from some Unseelie court and have taken on the shape and personality of something else to hide what you are and what you've done. But you're still hunted by your kind. You probably wear clothing designed to draw as little attention to yourself as possible.

Connection: Choose one of the following.
1. Pick one other PC. You have a strong emotional connection to this character, and when in their presence, you can choose to radiate light from your palms.
2. Pick one other PC. They are allergic to moths, and occasionally your presence leaves them feeling congested and itchy-eyed, increasing the difficulty of their defense actions by one step while standing next to you.
3. Pick one other PC. This character once ran into you while running away from . . . something. You stopped them just by being in the wrong place at the wrong time, but they seem to hold it against you.
4. Pick one other PC. Every so often, you're sure you see moths following them.

Additional Equipment: You have a moth-shaped tattoo or birthmark on your neck or the back of your wrist, a gift your enemies managed to brand you with once before you escaped.

Moth Language Abilities: If you have special abilities that seem supernatural, you perform them as minor charms you invoke that are accomplished either directly by a swarm of moths, or the effect is accompanied by the appearance of fluttering moths or moth wings. Also, you can choose to gain the Cloak of Moths ability instead of one of the abilities granted by your type.

Cloak of Moths (2 Intellect points). You call a swarm of fluttering insects from nearby and, speaking in the language of moths, ask them to protect you. The swarm wraps itself around you in a halo of fluttering moth wings, granting you an asset to Speed defense tasks for up to ten minutes. Action to initiate.

Minor Effect Suggestion: Moths flutter around the foe's face, increasing the difficulty of attacks the foe attempts on its next turn by one step.

Major Effect Suggestion: Your foe accidentally ingests a moth, and coughing and choking, loses its next turn.

Is Hunted By Moths GM Intrusions: *Sometimes when a swarm of moths is called, a cryptic moth responds instead, and it isn't friendly.*

Tier 1: Moth Zapper (1 Intellect point).
You're hunted, but you can defend yourself. When you will it, your hands crackle with electricity, and the next time you touch a creature, you inflict 3 points of damage. Alternatively, if you wield a weapon, for ten minutes it crackles with electricity and inflicts 1 additional point of damage per attack. Action for touch; enabler for weapon.

Cryptic moth, page 132

Lantern Shine (1 Intellect point). Your eyes shine lantern-bright for ten minutes, allowing you and anyone near you to see in the dark to a short distance. This effect has been known to attract moths, both natural and unnatural. Action to initiate.

Tier 2: See the Unseen. You can perceive creatures and objects that are normally invisible, out of phase, or only partially in this universe. When looking for things more conventionally hidden, the difficulty of the task is also reduced by one step. Enabler.

Tier 3: Fury of Moths (3 Intellect points). You call a swarm of fluttering insects from nearby and, speaking in the language of moths, ask them to protect you. The swarm wraps itself around you in a halo of fluttering moth wings for up to ten minutes.

The moths automatically inflict 2 points of damage to anyone who tries to touch you or strike you with a melee attack and you gain +1 Armor. Action to initiate.

Tier 4: Cryptic Servitude. Though they hate you all the more for it, you've captured and bound one of your hunters so that now it serves you. Invisible until you call upon it, your cryptic moth captive follows your instructions. You and the GM must work out the details of your cryptic moth. You'll probably make rolls for your moth when it takes actions. Your moth in combat usually doesn't make separate attacks but helps with yours. On your action, if the moth is next to you, it serves as an asset for one attack you make on your turn. If the moth is killed, you call and capture another within a week. Enabler.

Tier 5: On Wings of the Night (7 Intellect points). You call a massive swarm of fluttering insects from nearby and, speaking in the language of moths, ask of them to carry you and up to six of your allies through the air to a distant location. The swarm can travel at a rate of 1,000 feet (305 m) per round for up to eight hours. At this speed, most dangerous encounters are ignored. If the moths are attacked or otherwise harmed while ferrying you and your allies, they drop you and disperse. Action to initiate.

Tier 6: Veil of Wings (8 Intellect points).
You call a massive swarm of fluttering insects from nearby and, speaking in the language of moths, ask them to blind up to three foes within long range of you. The swarms flutter around the eyes and head of the targets like a halo, either completely blinding the targets on a successful Intellect act, or effectively distracting the target even on a failed attack so that the target acts as if one level lower. Targets are blinded (or distracted) for up to one minute.

IS SWORN TO THE CROWN
You are part of a well-trained mercenary group that fights with a royal mandate or with the backing of some other government, group, or breakaway confederacy (or you used to do so). Mercenaries fight for pay, not necessarily for a cause, but that doesn't mean that the contract your mercenary company signs isn't vitally important to you. A mercenary group that routinely fails to fight under the flag that paid it to do so soon finds itself without future patrons who will trust the company, and worse, a vengeful former patron to steer clear of. You probably wear the colors or even the uniform of your mercenary group, or the uniform of the political entity to which you're currently pledged.

Connection: Choose one of the following.

1. Pick one other PC. That character is interested in your mercenary company. You would like to induct them, but you're not necessarily authorized to do so (that's up to you), and they might not be interested in actually joining (that's up to them).

2. Pick one other PC. If that PC is within immediate range when you're in a fight, sometimes they help and sometimes they accidentally hinder (50% chance either way, determined per fight). When they help, you gain +1 to all attack rolls. When they hinder, you suffer a –1 penalty to attack rolls.

3. Pick one other PC. They once saved your life, and now you're on the lookout for a way to repay the favor.

4. Pick one other PC. This person recently mocked your commitment to your military company. How you deal with this (if at all) is up to you.

Additional Equipment: Uniform of your mercenary order and a firearm.

Minor Effect Suggestion: The target becomes demoralized so that it is dazed for one round, during which time the difficulty of all tasks it performs is modified by one step to its detriment.

Major Effect Suggestion: Make an immediate additional attack with a firearm as part of your turn.

Tier 1: Military Training. You have received instruction on the use of firearms (or some other style of weapon appropriate to the setting). You inflict 1 additional point of damage with firearms. Enabler.

Seal of Service. You have papers, a seal, or other proof that identifies you as a member of an auxiliary military order fighting on behalf of a particular state. You can use this identification as an asset to interactions if the particular state or the mercenary group to which you belong is relevant to the interaction. For instance, if you are interrogating a captive, you might suggest that your connection to the military or state could provide leniency if answers were forthcoming. Even if the identification is out of date, you might still get some use out of it if an NPC you're interacting with doesn't realize it. Enabler.

Tier 2: Skirmish Team. You designate two additional characters to be part of your skirmish team. You can change this freely every round, but you can only have up to two people plus yourself in your skirmish team at one time. As long as one or both of your skirmish team comrades are within immediate range of you, two of the three of you gain an asset to Speed defense tasks because you have each other's backs. You can freely change who gains the Speed defense asset each round. Enabler.

Tier 3: Improved Military Training. You can choose from one of two benefits: either you are trained in using firearms, or you have the Spray ability (which costs 2 Speed

Historically famous mercenary groups "sworn to the crown" include the Hessians, the Swiss Guard, and the White Company.

points). If a weapon can fire rapid shots without reloading (usually called a rapid-fire weapon), you can spray multiple shots around your target to increase the chance of hitting. This move uses 1d6 + 1 rounds of ammo (or all the ammo in the weapon, if it has less than the number rolled). The difficulty of the attack roll is decreased by one step. If the attack is successful, it deals 1 less point of damage than normal. Enabler (being trained in using guns) or action (Spray).

Tier 4: Commanding Presence. As you work your way up in your military order, you develop a command presence. You can use this ability in one of two ways. Either your words keep the attention of all NPCs that hear them for as long as you speak, or your words inspire all NPCs (of your choosing) that hear them to function as if they were one level higher for the next hour. Action.

Tier 5: Improved Skirmish Team. Everyone in your skirmish team gains one additional advantage: You each inflict 2 additional points of damage with firearms because you're all working together. Enabler.

Tier 6: Fusillade. Every time you succeed at an attack roll with a firearm, you can make an immediate attack against that same foe. Your attack can use a different firearm than the one that initiated the fusillade if the first weapon doesn't have the ability to fire multiple times without reloading as long as the next weapon is close at hand. In any case, the difficulty of each successive fusillade attack is one step higher than the previous attack. Enabler.

Is Wanted By The Law GM Intrusions: Most people do not take well to discovering a wanted outlaw in their midst.

IS WANTED BY THE LAW

"WANTED, DEAD OR ALIVE" posters have appeared featuring your face. You've either done something—or people mistakenly *think* that you've done something—that has made you a target of the law. Sheriffs, rangers, and even bounty hunters are looking for you, which means you need to keep a low profile. Whether or not you did rob some establishment back east, or if you actually would kill a man just for looking at you is up to you. Maybe it's all true, but maybe it's all a mistake that snowballed out of control. Either way, you might be looking to set the record straight or for redemption. Of course, some people will embrace what the world thinks of them and become it.

You're probably called an outlaw or desperado. In addition to your normal clothing, you probably wear a hat that you can pull low, and maybe a kerchief that you can pull up to cover your face when necessary.

Connection: Choose one of the following.

1. Pick one other PC. You feel the overwhelming need to impress this character, although you're not sure why.

2. Pick one other PC. That character knows your real identity, profession, and background. To all others, the truth about you is a closely guarded secret.

3. Pick one other PC. You feel very protective of this character and don't want to see them harmed.

4. Pick one other PC. One night after perhaps too much celebrating, you loudly claimed responsibility for a robbery that you

didn't commit. This character was the only one who heard. Whether they believe you or not is up to them.

Minor Effect Suggestion: You restore 2 points to your Might Pool.

Major Effect Suggestion: The difficulty of your next action is decreased by two steps.

Tier 1: Desperado Reflexes. You gain 3 additional points to your Speed Pool. Enabler.

Quick Draw. You are trained in initiative. Enabler.

Tier 2: Surprise Attack. If you attack from a hidden vantage, with surprise, or before an opponent has acted, the difficulty of your attack is reduced by one step. On a successful hit with this surprise attack, you inflict 2 additional points of damage. Enabler.

Tier 3: Outlaw Reputation (3 Intellect points). People know of your notorious exploits, which have been told and retold so many times that they bear little resemblance to reality. But people fear your name when they recognize you (or you declare yourself). They become so afraid that the difficulty of all attacks affected targets within earshot make against you is increased by one step until one or more of them successfully inflicts damage on you or one of your allies, at which time their fear abates. Enabler.

Tier 4: Quick Draw (2 Speed points). You know how to kill quickly. When you hit with a melee or ranged attack, you deal 4 additional points of damage. You can't make this attack in two consecutive rounds. Action.

Tier 5: Band of Desperados. Your reputation draws a band of six level 2 desperado NPC followers who are completely devoted to you. You and the GM must work out the details of these followers. If a follower dies, you gain a new one after at least two weeks and proper recruitment. Enabler.

Tier 6: Legendary Outlaw. You've survived more than one scrape that should've seen you dead. Maybe your legendary outlaw status helps keep you alive. When you would normally die, you instead fall unconscious for one round and then awaken. You immediately gain 1d6 + 6

points to restore your stat Pools and are treated as if impaired until you rest for ten hours. If you die again before you take your ten-hour recovery roll, you are truly dead. Enabler.

KEEPS A MAGIC ALLY

You discovered, were given, or otherwise obtained an allied magic creature bound to an object (perhaps a minor djinn in a lamp, but work with your GM if either of you would prefer a different kind of creature and object). It requires a fair bit of your attention and energy to keep the minor djinn happy and satisfied, but it's usually worth it. The djinn grants you aid and companionship, and eventually it may grant minor wishes.

You wear comfortable, flashy, and somewhat striking clothing, possibly provided by your magic ally, who is at pains to tell you how fabulous you look, even if others suggest something to the contrary.

Connection: Choose one of the following.

1. Pick one other PC. They gave you the lamp as a present. Only afterward did it become apparent that a magic ally lived inside.

2. Pick one other PC. You promised that character that one day you'd ask the magic ally to grant you a wish to bring back their dead sibling, parent, or friend. However, you're not sure that your ally can accomplish that wish or what the result will be. You've read "The Monkey's Paw."

3. Pick one other PC. You wonder if they are human or are a fairy tale creature pretending to be human.

4. Pick one other PC. That character is half convinced that your magic ally is a servant of evil, perhaps a demon in disguise, and is watching you for signs of demonic influence.

Additional Equipment: A lamp or similar object.

Minor Effect Suggestion: The difficulty of the next task attempted by your magic ally is decreased by one step.

Major Effect Suggestion: Your magic ally can take an immediate extra action of its choice (possibly making an attack on its own).

Tier 1: Bound Magic Creature. You possess a magic ally bound to a physical object (perhaps a minor djinn bound to a lamp, a lesser demon bound to a coin, or a spirit

> **Keeps a Magic Ally GM Intrusions:** *The creature unexpectedly disappears into its bound object. The bound object cracks. The creature disagrees and doesn't do as asked. The creature says it's leaving unless a task is performed for it.*

> **Bound magical creature:** *level 3*

bound to a mirror). The magic ally doesn't yet have the full power that one of its kind could possess when mature. Normally, the ally remains quiescent in its bound object. When you spend an action to manifest it, it appears next to you as a level 3 creature that can converse with you. The creature has its own personality determined by the GM and is a level higher than its base level for one area of knowledge (such as local history). The magic ally may have a long-term goal of its own if the GM determines.

Each time the magic ally becomes physically manifest, it remains so for up to one hour. During that period, it accompanies you and follows your instructions. The magic ally must remain an immediate distance from you; if it moves farther away, it is yanked back into its object at the end of your following turn and cannot return until after your next ten-hour recovery roll. It doesn't attack creatures, but it can spend its action to serve as an asset for any one attack you make on your turn. Otherwise, it can take actions on its own (though you'll likely roll for it).

Bound magical creature: level 4

If the creature is reduced to 0 health, it dissipates. It reforms in its object in 1d6 + 2 days.

If you lose the bound object, you retain a sense of the direction in which it lies. Action to manifest magic creature.

Tier 2: Object Bond (3 Intellect points).
When you manifest your magic ally, it can move up to 300 feet (91 m) from you before being returned to its bound object. Also, it can remain manifest for an extended period, lasting until the end of your next ten-hour recovery roll. Finally, if you give permission, the magic ally can emerge from and enter the bound object on its own initiative. Enabler.

Hidden Closet. The magic ally can store items for you within its bound object, including extra sets of clothing, tools, food, and so on. The interior of the object is, in effect, a 10-foot (3 m) square pocket dimension that normally only the magic ally can access. Enabler.

Tier 3: Minor Wish.
At your request, the magic ally can spend its action casting a minor spell on you. Afterward, it must retreat to its bound object to rest for one hour. The effects it can produce include the following. Action to initiate.

Golden Ward. You gain +1 to Armor for one hour from a translucent sheen of golden light.

Touch of Grace. With the magic ally's touch, you add 3 points to any stat Pool. If you are not damaged, you add the points to your chosen Pool's maximum. They remain until you expend them, you lose them to damage, or an hour passes.

Golden Anger. A golden light touches your eyes. For the next several minutes, if you attack a target, you inflict 2 additional points of damage.

Light of Truth. Whenever you attempt to discern falsehood during the next hour, the difficulty of the task is decreased by two steps.

Tier 4: Improved Object Bond (5 Intellect points).
When you manifest your magic ally, it's a level 4 creature. Also, the creature gains a pulse attack that renders all artifacts, machines, cyphers, and lesser magic devices within short range inoperable for one minute. After the creature uses this ability, it must retreat to its object to rest for three hours. Enabler.

Tier 5: Moderate Wish.
At your request, the magic ally can spend its action casting a moderate spell on you. Afterward, it must retreat to its bound object to rest for at least one hour. The effects it can produce include the following. Action to initiate.

Golden Armor. You gain +3 to Armor for one hour from a translucent sheen of golden light.

MAKING A WISH
If a character asks the magic ally for a real wish instead of a minor or moderate spell, the creature may grant it, especially if the PC is tier 3 or higher. If so, the magic ally is then free of its compulsion to serve the character and should work with the GM to adopt a new focus. Even if the wish is granted, the character may not get exactly what they want, especially if a wish is poorly worded or has multiple interpretations. The level of the effect granted is no greater than level 7, as determined by the GM, who can modify the effect of the wish accordingly. (The larger the wish, the more likely the GM will limit its effect.)

Improved Touch of Grace. With the magic ally's touch, you add 6 points to any stat Pool. If you are not damaged, you add the points to your chosen Pool's maximum. They remain until you expend them, you lose them to damage or an hour passes.

Golden Fury. A golden light blazes in your eyes. For the next three minutes, if you attack a target, you inflict 5 additional points of damage.

Invisible. With a touch, the magic ally bends light that falls on you, so you seem to disappear. You are invisible to other creatures for ten minutes. While invisible, you are specialized in stealth and Speed defense tasks. This effect ends if you do something to reveal your presence or position—attacking, using an ability, moving a large object, and so on. If this occurs, you can regain the remaining invisibility effect by taking an action to focus on hiding your position. Action to initiate.

Tier 6: Object Bond Mastery (7 Intellect points).
When you manifest your magic ally, it's a level 7 creature. It can remain manifest for only three minutes, after which it must return to its object and rest for three days before you can manifest it again.

The magic ally can make its own magic touch attacks (when it does, you roll for it). If it uses its pulse attack from Improved Object Bond (tier 4), instead of deactivating items, it can take control of one item within short range for one minute, if applicable.

Finally, the magic ally can transform into smoke and flame as its action, giving it +10 to Armor but rendering it incapable of attacking foes. In this form, it can fly a long distance each round, and the first time each day it returns to flesh (as an action), it regains 25 points of health. Enabler.

LEARNS QUICKLY
You might not have your dream job, but you do all right. Perhaps events beyond your control set you down a path that led to where you are today, making the best of a mediocre or even a bad situation. Or maybe you're young, and your break just hasn't come along yet. Either way, you work hard to get ahead, deal with bad situations as they arise, and learn quickly whether you're working retail, in a warehouse, or out on the street after a horrific event left you homeless.

You don't stand out in a crowd because you've learned that doing so can draw unwanted attention. That's why you usually wear nondescript clothing, cover up any ink you have, and wear glasses whether you need eye correction or not.

Connection: Choose from the following.
1. Pick one other PC. That character helped you get your current job.
2. Pick one other PC. Through no fault of their own, that character got you fired from your last job by pointing out a problem with something you were connected to only indirectly.
3. Pick one other PC. That character is your cousin.
4. Pick one other PC. You're pretty sure that character hates you, though you don't know why.

Additional Equipment: Two tickets to see a show at a local movie theater.

Minor Effect Suggestion: The difficulty of your next task, attack, or defense (if made within one minute) is decreased by one step.

Major Effect Suggestion: Treat the result of your next task, attack, or defense (if made within one minute) as if you rolled a natural 18.

Tier 1: Still Waters Run Deep. You have a greater-than-average capacity to think things through. You add 3 points to your Intellect Pool. Enabler.

There's Your Problem. You are trained in tasks related to figuring out how to solve problems with multiple solutions (like the best way to pack a truck, calm an enraged customer, give a cat a shot of insulin, or find a route through the city for maximum speed). Enabler.

Tier 2: Quick Study. You learn from repetitive actions. You gain a +1 bonus to rolls for similar tasks after the first time (such as operating the same device or making attacks against the same foe). Once you move on to a new task, the familiarity with the old task fades—unless you start doing it again.

Tier 3: Put It Behind You. Mentally dwelling on bad outcomes rarely serves to improve matters. Moving on to whatever's next is the best way to cope. You gain +1 to your Intellect Edge. Enabler.

Learns Quickly GM Intrusions: *The character is fired. An NPC recipient of criticism turns violent. The character absent-mindedly loses their keys, a card, or another small but required item.*

Hard to Distract. You are trained in Intellect defense tasks. Enabler.

Tier 4: Pay It Forward (3 Intellect points). You can pass on what you've learned. When you give another character a suggestion involving their next action that is not an attack, the difficulty of their action is decreased by one step for one minute. Action.

Tier 5: Quick on the Uptake. You add 3 points to your Intellect Pool.

Learned A Few Things. You are trained in two areas of knowledge of your choice, or specialized in one area of knowledge of your choice.

Tier 6: Two Things at Once (6 Intellect points). The ultimate test: you divide your attention and take two separate actions this round. Enabler.

LIKES TO BREAK THINGS

You enjoyed smashing whatever you could get your hands on when you were a child. You still do (maybe because you're still a child). You're burly, so destroying stuff comes easy. The sound things make when they shatter is magical.

You've shattered so many things that you're developing a knack for seeing the weak point not only in objects, but also in people, and in some cases, in the way people think, plan, and dream. It's up to you whether you want to exploit that talent or continue mostly with breaking objects, which don't cry and make you feel guilty afterward.

Connection: Choose one of the following.

1. Pick one other PC. You promised that character to break the first thing they named to you, whatever it was. They haven't yet taken you up on your offer.

2. Pick one other PC. They wrongfully accused you of smashing something they treasured. Later they apologized, and you've mostly forgotten the incident. Mostly.

3. Pick one other PC. You broke a keepsake that character kept, and hid the evidence. That character has no idea you did it, and just thinks they lost the object. You haven't told them the truth, and now worry too much time has passed to come clean.

4. Pick one or more other PCs. You accidentally destroyed a bridge that you and

they were using at the time. Everyone was hurt, and one other former comrade was killed in the incident.

Additional Equipment: You carry a hammer.

Minor Effect Suggestions: The difficulty of the next task to break something is reduced by one step.

Major Effect Suggestions: The object held by the NPC shatters.

Tier 1: Feat of Strength (1 Might point). The difficulty of any task that depends on brute force is decreased by one step. Examples include smashing down a barred door, tearing open a locked container, lifting or moving a heavy object, or striking someone with a melee weapon. Enabler.

Tier 2: Powerful. Your Might Pool increases by 5 points. Enabler.

Tier 3: Conceptual Breakthrough. Perhaps it's a revelation, but sometimes breaking things is more about using your mind than using your brawn. Your Intellect Pool increases by 3 points, and you gain 1 to your Intellect Edge.

Tier 4: Smarter Not Harder (5 Intellect points). You see where objects are most likely to break. The difficulty of any task that would normally depend on brute force (that you accomplish with an apparently light touch) is decreased by three steps. Examples include opening a barred door or a locked container with a deft touch instead of smashing it or tearing it open, shifting a heavy object without lifting it, opening a hole in a solid barrier by finding a keystone or nexus, and so on. Enabler.

Tier 5: Breaking Bones (6+ Might or Intellect points). You recognize where flesh fails. With a swift and sudden attack, you strike a foe in a vital spot. If the target is level 3 or lower, it is killed outright. For every two levels of Effort you apply, you can increase the maximum level of the target by 1. Action.

Tier 6: Breaking Everything. Your attacks against objects inflict 8 additional points of damage when you use a melee weapon that you wield in two hands. If attacking a creature using a melee weapon wielded in one hand, you inflict 4 additional points of damage. Enabler.

Likes to Break Things GM Intrusions: *Something valuable breaks along with the intended target. An item owned by an ally is broken. The character says something without thinking that risks mentally breaking an NPC ally.*

LOVES THE VOID

The vicissitudes of vacuum? The fear of falling forever? The terror of endless space? Those are afflictions of people stuck at the bottom of a gravity well. You've broken free of the ties that kept you grounded, both physically but especially mentally. Rather than fear the endless blackness of the void, you love it. When it's just you, your suit, and the panorama of stars wheeling out forever and always, you are at peace.

When you're not wearing your spacesuit, you probably wear a jumpsuit or other dress suitable for moving about in a weightless environment.

Connection: Choose one of the following.

1. Pick one other PC. You suspect this character has a paralyzing fear of open spaces, so you keep on eye them, so they don't freeze up at the wrong moment.

2. Pick one other PC. Whenever this character is next to you, you swear that instruments on your spacesuit glitch and give you problems.

3. Pick one other PC. You are indebted to this character for an act of kindness in the past.

4. Pick one other PC. The patterns on a piece of equipment or clothing this character usually wears reminds you of an obscure constellation. Does it mean something?

Additional Equipment: You have a basic spacesuit that can keep you alive in space for up to three hours at a time before requiring a recharge. Replace this option with a better suit if you select the Space Enthusiast ability.

Space Enthusiast: If you wish, you can swap an ability gained from your type for the following.

Have Spacesuit, Will Travel. Somehow or another, you became the legal owner of a fully functional and advanced spacesuit. The spacesuit provides +1 Armor and more importantly, allows you to survive in the vacuum of space using suit reserves for up to twelve hours at a time with enough reaction mass to get around in zero gravity on jets of ionized gas for that same period. After each use, the suit must be recharged, either with already-charged cartridges for air and reaction mass or by allowing the suit to sit idle in an area with breathable atmosphere for at least two hours, during which time it will recharge both air and reaction mass using integrated solid state mechanisms. The suit's power supply is via a radioisotope thermoelectric generator, which means it'll function for a few decades before needing to be changed out.

Minor Effect Suggestion: You restore 2 points to your Speed Pool.

Major Effect Suggestion: You can take a second action this round.

Tier 1: Vacuum Skilled. You are trained in two of the following skills: vacuum welding, algae farming, ecosystem design, circuit design, spacecraft maintenance and repair, or some similar skill related to traveling and colonizing planets, moons, and stations located in the solar system. Enabler.

Microgravity Adept. You ignore all the ill effects of low gravity and no gravity on movement; you are trained in low gravity maneuvers and zero gravity maneuvers. (You might still be subject to negative biological effects of long-term exposure if any). Enabler.

Tier 2: Space Monkey. By taking advantage of microgravity conditions, you gain +1 to your Speed Edge while in zero gravity or low gravity conditions. Enabler.

Fit. To stay fit in low gravity, you must exercise constantly. You gain 3 new points to add to your Might and/or Speed Pools. Enabler.

Tier 3: Space Fighting. By taking advantage of microgravity conditions, you can use inertia and mass to your advantage if engaged in melee. If you spend a round setting up a melee (or a thrown or launched object) attack while in zero gravity or low gravity conditions, the attack inflicts +6 points of damage. Enabler.

Tier 4: Silent As Space. By taking advantage of microgravity conditions, you gain an asset to stealth and initiative tasks while in zero gravity or low gravity conditions. Enabler.

Push Off and Throw (3 Speed points). You can make precise, point-to-point jumps in microgravity, which means you can move up to a long distance and make a melee attack or attempt to grab a foe of your size or smaller. If you attempt to grab your foe and are successful, you move your foe up to a short distance from its original position. Alternatively, while you come to a standstill (or move off in an immediate distance per round in any direction you choose) you

Loves The Void GM Intrusions: *Spacesuits develop glitches. Air refill cartridges sometimes misreport capacity. Micrometeorites are common in space.*

Effects of Gravity, page 121

can launch your foe in a chosen direction through space at a rate of a short distance per round. Action.

Tier 5: Microgravity Avoidance. By taking advantage of microgravity conditions, you gain an asset to Speed defense tasks while in zero gravity or low gravity conditions. Enabler.

Tier 6: Weightless Shot. You have a sixth sense when it comes to lining up trajectories and moving in low and zero gravity environments, which also translates to making ranged attacks. When you hit a target with a ranged attack in microgravity conditions, you can choose to reduce the damage by 2 points but hit the target in a precise spot. Some of the possible effects include (but are not limited to) the following:

- You punch a hole in the target's suit, so it begins to leak air into the vacuum slowly, or all at once (your choice).
- You hit the target's maneuvering pack's reaction mass, which means the target can no longer change their trajectory, or they go spinning off in a random direction (your choice).
- You can shoot a spacecraft, and degrade one ship system by one step (systems include engines, weapons, and atmosphere).

Enabler.

MAKES PROPHECY

You are a prophet, or maybe something even more profound. You can discern the strands of fate that underlie and hold reality together. This vision gives you knowledge of things that are normally hidden. More than that, you can twist fate and alter destiny as you desire, and eventually even speak true prophecy that comes to fruition. Knowing what destiny holds in store for others gives you power over them. To be a prophet—or a demigod of fate—is to be a force of creation and change.

You probably wear dark colors and maybe even a hood, because you don't give much thought to outward appearance. The true beauty and color of life are revealed to you in the weft and warp of fate's tapestry that stretches all around you.

Connection: Choose one of the following.
1. Pick one other PC. Through a quirk of fate, you can't see that character's destiny.

To your eyes, it seems as if that no strands connect them to the tapestry of existence. You worry that means they'll soon be dead.

2. Pick one other PC. You recently discovered that if they stand near you when you use your Premonition ability, you learn something about them, too. It's up to you whether you've told this character about what you can do.

3. Pick one other PC. You once boasted that your ability to make prophecy meant that you could never lose in games of chance. That character asked you to take them to a place where bets could be laid down for money. It's up to you whether you want to go through with your boast or if you've had second thoughts.

4. Pick one other PC. That character has a missing sibling or loved one, and asked you to help find them using your power to trace the lines of fate. So far, you've had no luck.

Minor Effect Suggestion: You learn a deeply buried secret the target was trying to hide.

Major Effect Suggestion: Foes within short range are dazed for one round upon seeing you manipulate fate. During this time, the difficulty of all tasks they perform is modified by one step to their detriment.

Tier 1: Premonition (2 Intellect points). You learn one random fact about a creature or location that is pertinent to a topic you designate. Alternatively, you can choose to learn a creature's level; however, if you do so, you cannot learn anything else about it later with this ability. Action.

Never Surprised. You are trained in initiative and perception tasks. Enabler.

Tier 2: More Than Luck. You can sense violent events moments before they occur, giving you to better chance to avoid them. You are trained in Speed defense tasks. Enabler.

Tier 3: Weave Their Fate (3 Intellect points). You see the lines of destiny stretching out from a creature within short range of you. Seeing that gives you an asset on any interaction you have with that target for the next minute, whether that interaction is social or martial. Action to initiate.

Tier 4: Finder (4+ Intellect points). You can see behind the world and the shadows that

Makes Prophecy GM Intrusions: *The strands of fate resist meddling, and the difficulty of the task is one step higher. The strands of fate snap back after being meddled with and damage the character's mind. A foe appears who can also see and manipulate fate.*

Special rolls, page 10

all creatures and significant objects cast. If you have interacted with a creature or object in the past, you can attempt to learn where it is right now. Alternatively, you can apply a level of Effort and cause an object you have personally handled in the past to be transported into your hands so long as the object can fit inside a 5-foot (2 m) cube. If successful, the object vanishes from wherever it was and appears in your hands or in an open space anywhere you choose within immediate range. Action.

Tier 5: Tapestry of Fate (6+ Intellect points). If you've previously used Weave Their Fate on a target, you can attempt to control the target's actions if it is within short range and can hear and understand you. If you succeed, you control the target's actions for two rounds by verbal command. Instead of applying Effort to decrease the difficulty, you can apply Effort to increase the duration of control; each level applied extends the duration of Tapestry of Fate by one round. When the effect ends, the target recalls being under your control unless you prevent that by succeeding on an Intellect attack whose difficulty is equal to the target's level. If you succeed, the target still remembers but thinks they took the actions themselves, even if they don't know why. Action to initiate.

Tier 6: Speak Prophecy (7+ Intellect points). Seeing the many strands of fate, you can reach out and change the design. Usually, you do so by affecting the fate of another creature or object within long range, by introducing a major special effect upon it either immediately or sometime within the next few days, in accordance with your prophecy. The major special effect is akin to what occurs when you roll a natural 20 on an attack. If you want to try for a larger effect, and if the GM allows it, you can attempt to alter a destiny with a more far-reaching effect, which is more like the kind of GM intrusion initiated by the GM on their players. In this case, you must also apply a level of Effort. Even then, the effect may not work out exactly as you hope. Action.

MUTATES

Savage forces strong enough to destroy a world left you transformed. Either through latent mutations passed down from ancestors that survived the apocalypse, or because something about you reacts when you're exposed to radiation or some other mutagenic source, you are prone to mutation. You might begin your days looking relatively normal, or as a freak of nature that clearly reveals your mutant heritage. Either way, your body continues to change and adapt as you grow older and add to your store of experience. The longer you live, the more you mutate.

You might have a purely cosmetic mutation, such as oddly colored skin, striped hair, horns, a tail, glowing eyes, red teeth, feathers for hair, or something else that's purely cosmetic, which you could choose to hide if you wished, or proudly display.

Connection: Choose one of the following.

1. Pick one other PC. They found you in a mutant cocoon and pulled you out after weeks, months, or years of sleep. You are either grateful or angry at being released from your hibernation.

Mutates GM Intrusions:
A mutant-hunter tracks the character down.
A temporary harmful mutation arises.
Radiation dependency develops, like a drug addiction.

2. Pick one other PC. You were once convinced that they wanted to kill you because of your mutant abilities, but you have since grown to think that what you believed wasn't true, or at least no longer is so.

3. Pick one other PC. Whenever you go near them, your skin begins to glow as brightly as a candle.

4. Pick one other PC. Your mutant ability grants you a limited telepathic bond with them; you always know the direction (though not the distance) to that character if they become separated from you.

Minor Effect Suggestion: You can immediately regain 2 points to any Pool.

Major Effect Suggestion: You can instantly take another action.

Tier 1: Stronger Body And Mind. Your body mutates, granting you 6 new points to divide among your stat Pools however you wish. Enabler.

Distinctive Mutation. Your Beneficial mutation comes with a distinctive mutation, which involves a dramatic physical change to your character's appearance. Your distinctive mutation might be an extra mouth, a snakelike arm, tendrils instead of fingers or eyes, scales or a carapace, or some other distinctive mutation suggested by your GM. Work with the GM to determine the details. Enabler.

Tier 2: Defensive Response. Being a mutant singles you out as visibly different, which is enough to elicit dangerous attention in many you meet. You become trained in Speed defense tasks. If you're already trained in Speed, choose Might or Intellect defense to become trained in. Enabler.

Tier 3: Beneficial Mutation. Your body mutates, granting you one of the abilities noted below, or an ability determined by the GM. If choosing from the list below, you can roll randomly or choose one.

Comfortable In Your Skin. In addition to gaining a Beneficial Mutation, you gain 3 new points to divide among your stat Pools however you wish. Enabler.

Tier 3: Powerful Mutation. Your body mutates, granting you one of the abilities noted below, or an ability determined by the GM. If choosing from the list below, you can roll randomly or choose one.

Tier 4: Mutant Weapon. Your mutation produces a gland that can store and discharge radiation, allowing you to fire a blast of energy that inflicts 5 points of damage with a range of 200 feet (61 m). There is no cost for you to use this ability. Action.

Tier 5: Adapted to the Apocalypse. Your mutant physiology renders you immune to environments that would kill normal people. You never get overheated or too cold, never need to worry about dangerous radiation, diseases, or gases, and can always breathe in any environment (even the vacuum of space). Enabler.

If the GM has access to more complete lists of mutations from other publications, they might decide to ask a character to use those as supplements, or instead of, the mutation lists provided here.

BENEFICIAL MUTATION TABLE

1	*Thick hide:* You gain +1 to Armor.
2	*Increased lung capacity:* You can hold your breath for one hour.
3	*Slippery skin:* You secrete a slippery oil, giving you an asset in any task involving slipping from another's grip, slipping from bonds, squeezing through a small opening, and so on.
4	*Telekinetic shield:* You reflexively use telekinesis to ward away attacks, giving you an asset in Speed defense tasks.
5	*Poison and disease immunity:* You are immune to all poisons and disease.
6	*Tough:* You have +1 Might edge.
7	*Fire resistance:* You have +3 to Armor against damage from fire.
8	*Acid resistance:* You have +5 to Armor against damage from acid.
9	*No scent:* You cannot be tracked or located by scent, and you never have offensive odors.
10	*Scent:* You can sense creatures, objects, and terrain by scent as well as a normal human can by sight. You can detect scents with that degree of accuracy only in short range, but you can sense strong odors from much farther away (far better than a normal human can). Like a hound, you can track creatures by scent.

Tier 6: Master of Mutation. Your body mutates further, granting you 4 new points to divide among your stat Pools however you wish. Also, you can change out your Powerful Mutation and Beneficial Mutation once after each ten-hour rest, and substitute one ability for a different ability from the same list. Enabler.

NEGOTIATES MATTERS OF LIFE AND DEATH

You are called upon to deliver messages between heads of state, broker agreements between rival factions, and find a way to bring a swift end to conflict. You're a diplomat, and though you usually attend events as the representative of another power, now and then your skills are the difference between a truce and ongoing bloodshed and war.

You care a lot about your appearance, because how you look is one more tool you can bring to bear when you negotiate. In addition to a good haircut, you wear expensive though understated clothing and stylish shoes. You also carry an impressive briefcase.

Connection: Choose one of the following.

1. Pick one other PC. Your work on that character's behalf secured them a visa, allowing them to escape from a bad situation.

2. Pick one other PC. That character provided vital information you needed to secure a peace deal between two warring states.

3. Pick one other PC. You're pretty sure that your failure to bring two antagonistic factions to an accord is indirectly responsible for the deaths of that character's parents. So far, you've kept quiet on that topic.

4. Pick one other PC. They asked you to get a friend of theirs out of a bad situation abroad. You agreed, but you're still working on the details.

Additional Equipment: Impressive briefcase.

Minor Effect Suggestion: Your entreaty gains an additional small concession, such as the release of a single prisoner.

Major Effect Suggestion: Foes within earshot are dazed for one round after hearing your entreaty. During this time, the difficulty of all tasks they perform is modified by one step to their detriment.

Tier 1: World Traveler. You are trained in finding your way around new places,

Negotiates Matters of Life and Death GM Intrusions: *Briefcases full of important documents are tempting targets for theft. Assassins from a foreign embassy sometimes target diplomats. A social faux pas gets the meeting off on the wrong foot. A stomach ailment leads to accidental regurgitation on a foreign dignitary.*

POWERFUL MUTATION TABLE

1	*No breath:* You do not need to breathe. Enabler.
2	*Chameleon skin:* Your skin changes colors as you wish. This is an asset in tasks involving hiding. Enabler.
3	*Savage bite:* Your mouth widens surprisingly, and hidden, pointed teeth emerge when you wish it. You can make a bite attack that inflicts 3 points of damage. Enabler.
4	*Face dancing:* You can alter your features enough that you possess an asset in all tasks involving disguise.
5	*Stinger in finger:* You can make an attack with your hand that inflicts 1 point of damage. If you make a second successful attack roll, your stinger also injects a poison that inflicts 4 points of Speed damage. Action.
6	*Spit needles:* You can make an attack with immediate range. You spit a needle that inflicts 1 point of damage. If you make a second successful attack roll, the needle also injects a poison that inflicts 4 points of Speed damage. Action.
7	*Spit webs:* You can make up to 10 feet (3 m) of a strong, ropelike material each day at the rate of about 1 foot (0.3 m) per minute. The webbing is level 3. You can also spit globs of webbing in immediate range, and if they hit, they increase the difficulty of the target's physical tasks by one step for one round. Action.
8	*Disruptive field (electronics) (2 Intellect points):* When you wish it, you disrupt devices within immediate range (no roll needed). All devices operate as if they were 3 levels lower while in range of your field. Devices reduced to level 0 or below do not function. Action.
9	*Gravity negation (2 Intellect points):* You float slowly into the air. If you concentrate, you can control your movement at half your normal speed; otherwise, you drift with the wind or with any momentum you have gained. This effect lasts for up to ten minutes. Action to initiate.
10	*Feed off pain:* Any time a creature within immediate range suffers at least 3 points of damage (after Armor subtraction) in one attack, you can restore 1 point to one of your Pools, up to its maximum. You can feed off any creature in this way, whether friend or foe. You never regain more than 1 point per round. Enabler.

navigating unfamiliar terrain, and identifying important contacts after arriving someplace new. Enabler.

Polyglot. You are practiced in speaking up to four other languages of your choice. Enabler.

Tier 2: Diplomat. You are trained in all tasks related to pleasant social interaction and persuasion. You're also trained in tasks related to detecting falsehoods. Enabler.

Always Learning. You gain 3 new points to divide among your stat Pools however you wish. Enabler.

Tier 3: Due Diligence. After a ten-hour recovery task, choose one skill that you believe will clearly help you reach a particular goal. You are trained in tasks related to achieving that goal if you can spend at least an hour going over research materials or otherwise practicing the skill. Enabler.

Tier 4: Command (3 Intellect points). Your audible command, backed by your sheer force of will and charisma, targets a creature within short range that can understand you. An affected creature attempts to carry out your command as its next action. The command can't inflict direct harm on the creature or its allies, so "Commit suicide" won't work, but "Flee" might. In addition, the command can require the creature to take only one action, so "Unlock the door" might work, but "Unlock the door and shoot whoever you see on the other side" won't. If you also have the Fast Talk special ability, you can string two commands together that require the target to take two actions over the course of two rounds. Action.

Tier 5: Calm (3 Intellect points). Through reasoned discourse, appeals to sanity and the common good, and other entreaties, you prevent a target within long range from attacking anyone or anything for one round. If you also have the Enthrall special ability, a target remains calm for one minute after you use this ability if it or its allies are not attacked. Action.

Fast Talk, page 46

Enthrall, page 45

Music is a beast. Your instrument is the whip. And you're the beast tamer

Plays A Deadly Instrument GM Intrusions: *Instruments break. Instruments can be stolen. Instruments can be dropped or forced out of a musician's hand.*

Tier 6: Call in Favor (4 Intellect points). Lots of people owe you favors, even those employed by or allied with a foe. When you call in a favor successfully, an affected target of level 3 or less within short range does what he can to help you out of a specific fix in a way that minimizes their risk of revealing their divided loyalties to their employer or other allies. For example, they might untie you, slip you a knife, leave a cell door unlocked, and so on. Each additional time you attempt to use this ability on the same target, the difficulty increases by one step. Action.

PLAYS A DEADLY INSTRUMENT

Music is a beast. Your instrument is the whip. And you're the beast tamer. The beast roars at your practiced command, shaking the hearts and stirring the minds of all who hear and see you perform. The sound is what's important, but so is the instrument you use to produce it. And yours is a one-of-a-kind customized special edition appliance for producing mind-blowing performances. There's no other instrument like it. One minute you might be jamming to stir the hearts of your allies to battle, and the next minute using that same instrument to tear out your enemy's throat.

Connection: Choose one of the following.

1. Pick one other PC. They're a good player, but if you could teach them a few of your tricks, they might really excel.

2. Pick one other PC. In the past, they taught you a few tricks in customizing your instrument.

3. Pick one other PC. This character doesn't seem to like your music.

4. Pick one other PC. You think they suspect that you were involved with marauders or other criminals. Whether you were or not is up to you.

Additional Equipment: One portable musical instrument of your choice that is modified or reinforced so that it could also be used as a mundane melee or ranged weapon. For example, the bow of your stringed instrument might also serve as a sword. Your reinforced iron flute as a baton or blow gun or your guitar might also fire pistol rounds. You also have tools for keeping your instrument in repair and in tune, which is a must, especially if you use your instrument in a fight.

Minor Effect Suggestion: Your music affects that foe so much that they're shaken and use their next turn to flee.

Major Effect Suggestion: Your music affects that foe so much that they can't help but hum the tune they heard you play in stressful situations.

Tier 1: Musical Performer. You are trained in playing a musical instrument of your choice, such as a guitar, flute, or violin. You are also practiced in using that instrument—or some component of that instrument—as a light or medium weapon. Enabler.

Musical Interlude. After a target has willingly listened to you play your music for at least one round while outside of combat, the difficulty of your first attack against that foe is decreased by one step. Enabler.

Tier 2: Inspirational Performance (1 Intellect point). Through your musical performance, you inspire your allies. While you play, your allies within short range modify the difficulty of one—and *only* one—of the following task types (your choice) by one step to their benefit: defense tasks, attack tasks, or tasks related to any skill that you are trained or specialized in. Alternatively, you can demoralize your foes, in which case while you play, your foes within short range modify the difficulty of one of the following task types (your choice) by one step to their detriment: defense tasks, attack tasks, or tasks related to any skill that you are trained or specialized in. Action.

Tier 3: Musical Defense. While your musical instrument is in your hand or hands, you are trained in Speed defense tasks. Enabler.

Virtuoso. You are specialized in playing your musical instrument. If you are already specialized, you instead add +1 to any die roll related to playing music with your instrument. Enabler.

Tier 4: Instrument Upgrade. You further customize your instrument, granting it one additional unique attack mode from the following list.

Firebreathing (5 Intellect points). When you wish it, your instrument produces a stream of blazing fire for up to ten minutes. You can use the fiery display to visually enhance your performance by drawing attention to yourself, or as an action to attack up to

three creatures standing next to each other within short range (making a separate attack roll for each target). A successful attack inflicts 4 points of damage. Enabler.

Song of Shock and Awe (5+ Intellect points). You blast a fan of lightning out from your instrument to short range in an arc that is approximately 50 feet (15 m) wide at the end. This discharge inflicts 4 points of damage. If you apply Effort to increase the damage rather than to decrease the difficulty, you deal 2 additional points of damage per level of Effort (instead of 3 points), and targets in the area take 1 point of damage even if you fail the attack roll. Action.

Automatic Instrument (5 Speed points). Your instrument sprays projectiles everywhere, attacking every creature in an immediate area within short range. You must make attack rolls against each target. You inflict 4 points of damage on targets you hit. Action.

Tier 5: Mind-blowing Performance. You can use this ability in one of two ways. Either your ongoing musical performance keeps the attention of all NPCs that hear you for as long as you play, or your performance inspires all NPCs (of your choosing) that hear it to function as if they were one level higher for the next hour. Action.

Tier 6: Deadly Instrument. You deal 2 additional points of damage with your instrument when you use it as a weapon, including when you use an attack granted by Instrument Upgrade. Enabler.

Dirge (5 Might points). If you strike a foe of level 3 or lower with your musical instrument, you kill the target instantly. Action.

PLAYS TOO MANY GAMES

A lifetime spent playing games has gifted you with a strong desire to win, and keen reflexes built from long hours of practice. When you open the rulebook, pick up the cards, or grab the game controller, your mastery is evident in your confident manner. You know things most people will never learn, or even dream that it's possible to learn by playing games. In fact, many dismiss you as someone that doesn't know the real world, having sunk yourself in meaningless pursuits. To some extent, maybe. But lessons, reflexes, and strategies you've learned by playing too many games have applications in the real world, where people who don't play enough games toil and live their dreary lives.

You might be slight and wiry, still young. Or comfortable and wider, having enjoyed many snacks while you play more sedentary games. Gamers come in all shapes and sizes.

Connection: Choose one of the following.

1. Pick one other PC. You have been friends with this character for as long as you can remember and often heed their advice and guidance.

2. Pick one other PC. That PC consistently beats you in one of your favorite games,

even though they don't practice like you. You're a bit miffed, but try not to show it.

3. Pick one other PC. You beat that PC in a game where money was on the table. They still haven't paid you, but you know that they are good for it eventually.

4. Pick two other PCs. They have a game where they ask you to play more and more difficult versions of one of your favorite games. Whether you play along is up to you.

Additional Equipment: You have a custom game controller (or if in a setting where video games don't exist, a custom version of your game, such as a set of cards, dice, or a deluxe board game).

Minor Effect Suggestion: The difficulty of your next task, or that of an ally, is reduced by one step, either in the real world or in the game you are playing.

Major Effect Suggestion: You or an ally can take an immediate extra action, either in the real world or in the game you are playing.

Tier 1: Game Lessons. You've played so many games that you've picked up some real knowledge. Choose any two noncombat skills. You are trained in those skills. Enabler.

Gamer. Pick any one style of game such as real-time strategy games, games of chance in the style of poker, roleplaying games, and so on. You can apply an asset to a task related to playing that style of game once between each recovery. Enabler.

Tier 2: Zero Dark Eyes. Some people's eyes are degraded by constantly playing games. And maybe that'll still happen to you, but not yet. You're still young and instead of degrading, your vision is actually better thanks to all your practice. You can see in very dim light as though it were bright light. You can see in total darkness as if it were very dim light. Enabler.

Resist Tricks. You're trained in solving puzzles and recognizing tricks from years of game playing. Enabler.

Tier 3: Sniper's Aim. By dint of almost constant practice playing games that simulate making ranged attacks, your hand-eye coordination is off the chart. You have an asset on all ranged attacks. Enabler.

Plays Too Many Games GM Intrusions: *Missed attacks strike the wrong target. Equipment breaks. Sometimes people react negatively to someone who has lived most of their life in imaginary game worlds.*

Tier 4: Mind Games (3 Intellect points). You use lies and trickery, mockery, and perhaps even hateful, obscene language against a foe that can understand you. If successful, the foe is stunned for one round and cannot act, and it is dazed in the following round, during which time the difficulty of its tasks is increased by one step. Action.

Practiced Player. You gain 3 new points you can immediately add to your Intellect Pool. Enabler.

Tier 5: Gamer's Fortitude. Sitting and playing a game for twelve hours straight is not something most people can do, but you've figured it out. Once after each ten-hour recovery, you can transfer up to 5 points between your Pools in any combination, at a rate of 1 point per round. For example, you could transfer 3 points of Might to Speed and 2 points of Intellect to Speed, which would take a total of five rounds. Action.

Tier 6: Reframe the Game. To win, sometimes you must dig deep and find a little extra fortitude. In addition to your normal recovery rolls each day, you can—at any time between ten-hour rests—recover 1d6 + 6 points to your Intellect Pool. Action.

Gaming God. Any time you use Effort on an Intellect action, add one of the following enhancements to the action (your choice):
- +2 to the roll.
- +2 to damage.
- Automatic minor effect.

Enabler.

RESIDES IN SILICON

Your mind exists in a mechanical drone no larger than a grapefruit. You either evolved artificial intelligence on your own or exist as the uploaded personality of a human mind. You can hover about and sense the world with electronic senses, or interface directly with networked systems. You're more fragile than your companions, but your ability to scan and analyze reality is second to none, and as you grow more practiced, you learn to eventually create brief duplicate instances of your consciousness that you can use to infect enemy machines and networked systems.

Your mechanical body is probably a hovering sphere the size of a human fist, leaking digital light from external circuits and scan ports.

Connection: Choose one of the following.
1. Pick one other PC. They found and activated you in the ruins of some past conflict you can't clearly recall.
2. Pick one other PC. Until you developed sentience (or remembered your uploaded mind), they deployed you as a scanning tool.
3. Pick one other PC. They helped upload your mind into a drone when your original body failed. You're not sure if you're thankful or resentful about how things turned out.
4. Pick one other PC. They knew who you were and what you did before you were uploaded.

Additional Equipment: Your own mechanical body.

Minor Effect Suggestion: The difficulty of the next action you attempt is decreased by one step.

Major Effect Suggestion: You dart behind your foe's ally, and the foe attacks its ally instead of you.

Tier 1: Ghost in the Machine. Your mind exists within a miniature quantum digital chip embedded in a tiny hovering mechanical drone about 5 inches (13 cm) in diameter. You retain your Speed Pool, Intellect Pool, and special abilities (work with your GM if an ability provided by your descriptor or type requires additional adaptation). Your Might Pool is reduced by 5 points. As a probe, you have a limited ability to affect the physical world, but you do have manipulators and can activate cyphers. You move by levitating to a maximum height of 6 feet (2 m) over the ground (unless in a weightless environment, in which case you can move freely). The difficulty of all physical tasks (other than fine manipulation) is increased by two steps. Most mental tasks, including qualifying attacks granted by your type, are not penalized. Because of your size, foes often ignore you, and you're hard to hit: the difficulty of stealth tasks and defense tasks is decreased by one step. Finally, when you descend three steps on the damage track and would normally be dead, there's a chance you can be repaired by someone with the right tools who succeeds on a difficulty 7 Intellect task in robotics.

Interface. By directly plugging an optical filament into another mechanical device, you can identify it and communicate with it.

Resides in Silicon GM Intrusions: Drones are hurled a long distance in a detonation. Anti-intrusion digital protection attacks are triggered during an interface attempt. A hacker attempts to take control of the drone.

This communication doesn't grant you any special abilities (see Controlling Interface). Enabler.

Illumination (1 Intellect point). You can project bright light in a cone that extends a short distance. Enabler.

Tier 2: Scan and Analyze (3 Intellect points). You can analyze objects and areas within immediate range to learn a surprising amount of information from tiny scraps of evidence. To do so, you must spend one minute scanning an object or area. Once you finish scanning, you can discover up to three pertinent pieces of information about the object or area, possibly clearing up a lesser mystery and pointing the way to solving a greater one. The GM will decide what you learn and what the level of difficulty is to learn it. (For comparison, pulling a partly degraded piece of stored data from a derelict robot is a difficulty 3 task for you.) One minute to scan.

Tier 3: Controlling Interface (5+ Intellect points). You interface with another machine and control it as if it was your body for one hour. The target must be level 2 or lower. To interface with a resisting machine, you must succeed on a physical attack. Once you have established control, you sense what the machine senses. You can allow it to act freely or override its control on a case-by-case basis. Instead of applying Effort to decrease the difficulty, you can apply Effort to increase the maximum level of the target. Thus, to control a level 5 machine (three levels above the normal limit), you must apply three levels of Effort. When the effect ends, the machine has no record of having been controlled or anything it did while under your command (unless you wish it to record such things). Action to initiate.

Tier 4: Machine Improvement. You gain 6 new points to add to your Intellect Pool. Enabler.

Tier 5: Network Injection (5 Intellect points). When you have access to an interlinked communication web, you can inject your consciousness into it. Once you do, you can spend one minute to identify and attempt to communicate with any or all machines that are also connected directly or wirelessly within 1 light minute (0.1 astronomical

units) of your location. You can ask one basic question about the machines or anything happening near them and receive a simple answer. For example, while in an area with many machines, you could ask "Where is the missing spacecraft called *Hyperdrive*?" and if the craft is within 1 light minute of you, one or more machines will probably provide the answer. While you communicate with the system, your drone body is inactive, and you are unaware of what is happening to it or in its vicinity. One minute to initiate.

Tier 6: Another Instance of You (6 Intellect points). When you have access to an interlinked communication web or a willing machine, you can inject another instance of your consciousness into it that lasts up to one hour. The additional instance of you has your abilities but performs all tasks as a level 5 creature. The instance lasts until its health is depleted, an hour elapses, you use this ability again, or the host system is destroyed. Action to initiate.

REVELS IN TRICKERY

Whether you're a performer, thief, sorcerer, warrior, or simple wanderer, you delight in charming, fooling, confounding, and surprising others. Some of your tricks are meant to delight and entertain. Others are useful for getting out of tight corners and confusing your foes. Even if you're a good-hearted trickster, you've likely accidentally hurt or confused your friends, so you try to avoid making them the target of your antics. But some say you're destined to betray everyone and everything, though you regard the concept (and the personification, if any) of fate as just another trick.

You probably wear a garment with several concealed pockets from which you can produce hidden coins and other oddments of guile.

Connection: Choose one of the following.

1. Pick one other PC. You're jealous of their finery.

2. Pick one other PC. You suspect that they are cursed, but you don't know if you should be more afraid for them or of them. Perhaps if you perform tricks for them, you'll discover their true nature.

3. Pick one other PC. You once tricked them so completely that they attacked and hurt you, thinking you were a foe. You've healed, but both of you are still wary of each other.

4. Pick one other PC. You tricked them into thinking that you are someone that you're not, and now it's been so long, you're not sure if you should reveal the truth.

Additional Equipment: A disguise of your choice.

Minor Effect Suggestion: Your foe loses track of you and moves just out of immediate range before realizing their error.

Major Effect Suggestion: Your foe is confused by your antics. On its next turn, it attacks one of its allies instead of you, before realizing the truth.

Tier 1: Legerdemain (1 Speed point). You can perform small but seemingly impossible tricks. For example, you can make a small object in your hands disappear and move into a desired spot within reach (like your pocket). You can make someone believe that they have something in their possession that they do not (or vice versa). You can switch similar objects right in front of someone's eyes. Action.

Opportunist. You have an asset when you attack a creature that has already been attacked at some point during the round and is within immediate range. Enabler.

Tier 2: Impersonate (2 Intellect points). You alter your voice, posture, and mannerisms, whip together a disguise, and have an asset on an attempt to impersonate someone else, whether it is a specific individual (Yanir of the city watch) or a general role (a city watch person). Action to initiate.

Wit or Menace. Choose whether you're trained in pleasant social interactions (including persuasion) or negative social interactions (including coercion and intimidation).

Tier 3: Poke and Run (3 Speed points). When you attack a creature that has eyes, the difficulty of the attack is increased by one step. If you hit, the creature has trouble seeing for the next hour, and you can move or attempt to hide as part of the same action. Tasks the creature performs that rely on sight are modified by one step to its detriment during this period. Action.

Tier 4: Calm (3 Intellect points). Through jokes, song, or other art, you prevent a foe from attacking anyone or anything for one round. Action.

Tier 5: Trap Trick. You are trained in creating simple traps, especially varieties of deadfalls and snares using natural objects from the environment. You can create a trap in under a minute. When you lay a trap, decide whether you want to hold the victim in place (a snare) or inflict damage (a deadfall). Next, attempt an Intellect-based task with a difficulty of 3 (for a snare) or a difficulty equal to the number of points of damage you want to inflict (for a deadfall). For example, if you want to inflict 4 points of damage, that's a difficulty 4 task, though your training reduces the difficulty. On a success, you create your trap, which is considered level 3 for avoiding detection before it is sprung and for a victim trying to struggle free (if a snare). If you are trained in stealth, disguise, or similar tasks, the trap is considered level 4 for these purposes; if you are specialized, level 5. A minute's worth of actions.

Tier 6: Fake-Out (8 Intellect points). You're not hurt at all! Choose to regain all points in a Pool, ascend one step on the damage track, throw off any ongoing effect (like curse, sleep, or turned to stone), or change a failed die result to a 20 (you can't change the result if you roll a natural 1, unless you also have Wrest From Chance). Once you use this ability, it is not available again until after you make a ten-hour recovery roll. Enabler.

RULES THE SEA

You have been given—or you've seized for yourself—a growing mastery over the waters of the world. That mastery isn't absolute, but it does allow you to shape water, thrive within its cool and nourishing grasp, and speak with the denizens of the deep as a potential ally. Whether they will one day truly look upon you as the ruler of the sea depends on how you comport yourself as you gain power to yourself, and whether or not someone else already claims that title.

You probably wear tight-fitting clothing that allows you to move quickly through the water. Your garments might be blue or green, perhaps with a crashing wave motif.

Connection: Choose one of the following.

1. Pick one other PC. This character has been your friend for a long time, and you have learned how to confer your power to breathe underwater while they are next to you.

Rules The Sea GM Intrusions: *A denizen of the sea takes offense. No open water is to be found. Water becomes polluted from unrelenting waste.*

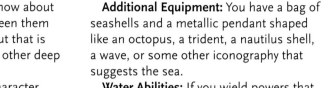

2. Pick two other PCs. You know about an important connection between them that even they don't know about that is somehow related to the sea or other deep waters.

3. Pick one other PC. That character knows a secret about your past that is tied to your ability to manipulate water and talk with denizens of the sea. That character hasn't yet shared the secret, and it's up to them whether they ever will.

4. Pick one other PC. The first time you met that character was when they and a friend were drowning in some kind of accident. You saved the PC but failed to save the friend.

Additional Equipment: You have a bag of seashells and a metallic pendant shaped like an octopus, a trident, a nautilus shell, a wave, or some other iconography that suggests the sea.

Water Abilities: If you wield powers that would normally use force or other energy, they use water instead. For example, a blast of energy might create a wave of water that crashes down on your target.

Also, if you wish, you can swap an ability gained from your type for the following.

Create Water (2 Intellect points). You cause water to bubble up from a spot on the ground you can see. The water flows from that spot for one minute, creating about 1 gallon (4 liters) by the time it stops.

Minor Effect Suggestion: You can take an extra action. You may use this action only to move or perform a movement-related activity.

Major Effect Suggestion: The difficulty of any Speed defense action you take before the end of the next round is reduced by one step.

Tier 1: Strength of the Sea. You gain 3 new points to divide among your stat Pools however you wish. If you're away from open water for longer than one day, these points fade. They return within two rounds of you fully submerging yourself in water. Enabler.

Water Adapted. You can see, breathe, and survive underwater even at great depths, and are trained in swimming tasks. Enabler.

Knowledge of the Sea. You are trained at tasks to identify aquatic creatures and geography. Enabler.

Tier 2: Sea Talk (2+ Intellect points). You can convey a basic concept or ask a simple question to a creature that lives underwater and cannot speak or understand speech, and the creature can provide you with a basic answer. If you apply a level of Effort and succeed on an interaction task, the affected creature performs a favor for you, though usually will refuse one that risks its life. Action.

Tier 3: Power of the Sea. You gain 3 new points to divide among your stat Pools however you wish and +1 to your Speed Edge. If you're away from open water for longer than one day, these points and the extra Edge fade. They return within two rounds of you fully submerging yourself in water. Enabler.

Healing Waters. You are sustained by the sea. When you spend time at least half-submerged in water, you can regain 1 Might point per round and must give your full concentration to the process each round, to a maximum number of points equal to your tier. You can use this ability again after your next recovery roll. Action to initiate; action each round to regain Might.

Tier 4: Wave of Destruction (6+ Speed points). You produce a churning wave of water that crashes forward a short distance in an arc that is approximately 50 feet (15 m) wide at the end. This turbulent force inflicts 4 points of damage. If you apply Effort to increase the damage rather than to decrease the difficulty, you deal 2 additional points of damage per level of Effort (instead of 3 points), and targets in the area take 1 point of damage even if you fail the attack roll. If you use this ability while standing in or submerged in water, either on land or in the water, you can use this ability with a level of Effort for free, which doesn't count against your normal Effort limit. Action.

Tier 5: King of the Sea. You gain 3 new points to divide among your stat Pools however you wish and an additional +1 to your Speed Edge. If you're away from open water for longer than one day, these points and the extra Edge fade. They return within two rounds of you fully submerging yourself in water. Enabler.

Current Rider (5 Speed points). For ten minutes, while moving through water, you can swim a long distance each round and still take an action. Alternatively, you can create a bubble of air an immediate distance across and move it and all its contents (possibly including yourself) a short distance each round as your entire action each round for 10 minutes. Action to initiate or create.

Tier 6: Tsunami (6+ Speed points). You create a wall of turbulent water up to 2,500 square feet (762 sq. m) in size, shaped as you wish. The wall of water is a level 7 barrier. Anyone attempting to swim or pass through the wall automatically takes 10 points of damage. The wall lasts for one hour. Alternatively, you can create a moving wall of water (a tsunami) by applying levels of Effort. Each level of Effort you apply when you create the water wall gives it the impetus to move a short distance before collapsing. If you apply multiple levels of Effort, the tsunami sweeps forward a short distance each round, before finally collapsing. Creatures caught up in the moving wave must succeed on a Speed defense task or take 8 points of damage. Action to create.

RUNS AWAY

You don't always run away, but it's your first instinct. It's saved you more than a few times. Being cautious is the best policy, and you've developed it into something of an art form. If someone is going to put up their defenses that person is you. Once a new danger is adequately assessed (from a safe perspective), you'll probably deal with it. You're no coward; you just want to be the one to decide when to engage an enemy.

You probably prefer comfortable clothing with neutral tones that allow you to run easily and if necessary, hide.

Connection: Choose one of the following.

1. Pick one other PC. In the recent past, while running away from an active threat, you accidentally left that character to fend for themselves. They survived, but just barely. It is up to the player of that character to decide whether they resent you or have decided to forgive you.

2. Pick one other PC. Recently, they accidentally (or perhaps intentionally) put you in a position of danger. You're fine, now, but you're wary around that character.

3. Pick one other PC. From your perspective, they seem even more nervous around a specific idea, person, or situation than yourself. Through your measured approach to caution, you would like to teach them how to be more comfortable with their fears.

4. Pick one other PC. They are skeptical that you're thoughtful in your caution and chuckle when you explain how being judicious saves lives. They might have even called you a coward once.

Additional Equipment: You have a pair of new running shoes that fit perfectly.

Minor Effect Suggestion: You can attempt a stealth task at any point before the end of the next round.

Major Effect Suggestion: You can take an extra action. You can use this action only

Runs Away GM Intrusions: *Quick movements sometimes lead to dropped items, slipping on uneven ground, or going the wrong way by accident.*

to move a short distance or to attempt a stealth action, or move an immediate distance and attempt a stealth action.

Tier 1: Go Defensive (1 Intellect point). When you wish, while in combat, you can enter a state of heightened awareness of threat. While in this state, you can't use points from your Intellect Pool, but you gain +1 to your Speed Edge and gain two assets to Speed defense tasks. This effect lasts for as long as you wish or until you attack a foe, or if no combat is taking place within range of your senses. Once the effect of this ability ends, you can't enter it again for one minute. Enabler.

Tier 2: Speedy. You gain 3 additional points to your Speed Pool. Enabler.

Quick to Flee. You are trained in stealth and movement tasks. Enabler.

Tier 3: Running Speed. You move much farther than normal in one round. This means that as a part of another action, you can move up to a short distance so long as you do not move toward a foe. As an action, you can move a long distance or up to 200 feet (61 m) as a Speed-based task with a difficulty of 4 so long as you do not move toward a foe. Enabler.

Tier 4: Increasing Determination. If you fail at a noncombat physical task (pushing open a door or climbing a cliff, for example) and then retry the task, the difficulty is reduced by one step. If you fail again, you gain no special benefits. Enabler.

Speedier. You gain 3 points to your Speed Pool. Enabler.

Tier 5: Go To Ground (4 Speed points). You move up to a long distance and attempt to hide. When you do, you gain an asset on the stealth task to blend in, disappear, or otherwise escape the senses of everyone previously aware of your presence. Action.

Tier 6: Burst of Action (6 Speed points). You can take two separate actions this round, so long as one of those actions is to hide or to move in a direction that is not toward a foe. Enabler.

SAILED BENEATH THE JOLLY ROGER

You sailed with a crew of dread pirates for years. The high seas ran red with the blood of those you targeted, especially when they would not yield up the contents of their holds without a fight. Victims both deserving and undeserving went to watery graves thanks to you and your comrades. But that's in your past; you've decided to end your days as a pirate and join some other cause. The question is, will your past let you go so easily?

You probably wear a fashionable coat and might be bedecked with rings and other jewelry you garnered during your days as a pirate.

Connection: Choose one of the following.

1. Pick one other PC. That character knows that you were a pirate, even though it is a secret you've kept from the other PCs so far.

2. Pick one other PC. You believe that they are working as a bounty hunter or treasure hunter secretly interested in your past. The PC chooses whether or not this is true.

3. Pick two other PCs. They were pirates, however briefly, along with you.

4. Pick one other PC. You were part of a boarding crew that sunk the ship they were sailing on. You thought that the PC had drowned until they turned up recently. They don't recognize you, at least not yet.

Additional Equipment: You have a treasure map, though you're not certain what the treasure is.

Minor Effect Suggestion: Your foe is so intimidated by your prowess that it backs away, unwilling to attack. It can still defend itself.

Major Effect Suggestion: Your foe is terrified by your skill and flees.

Tier 1: Survivor. When you get hurt, you shake it off. You ignore the impaired condition of the damage track and treat the debilitated condition as impaired. Enabler.

Sailor. You are trained in tasks related to sailing and trained in the geography of islands and coastlines. Enabler.

Tier 2: Pirate Tactics. When your foe is weakened, dazed, stunned, moved down the damage track, or disadvantaged in some other way, the difficulty of your attacks against that foe is decreased by one step beyond any other modifications due to the disadvantage. Enabler.

Fearsome Reputation (3 Intellect points). You and those you ship with have earned a fearsome reputation in some parts. If your foes have heard of you, affected targets within earshot become afraid, and the difficulty of all attacks they make against you is increased by one step until one or more of them successfully inflicts damage on you or one of your allies, at which time their fear abates. Action.

Tier 3: Sea Legs. You have gotten used to rough seas and unexpected surges. You are trained in balance. Also, you ignore one step worth of increased difficulty from rough terrain (like that of a pitching deck during a battle or storm). Enabler.

Sharp-Eyed. Because you must always keep an eye out when you're sailing, you are trained in all tasks related to perception and navigation. Enabler.

Tier 4: Mobile Fighter (3 Speed points). As part of your attack, you can leap on or over obstacles, swing from ropes, run along narrow surfaces, or otherwise move around the ship (or any battlefield) at your normal speed as if such tasks were routine (difficulty 0). You can't use this ability if your Speed is modified from wearing armor. Enabler.

Tier 5: Lost in the Chaos. When faced with several foes at once, you have developed tactics for using their numbers against them. When two or more foes attack you at once in melee, you play one off the other. The difficulty of Speed defense rolls or attack rolls (your choice) against them is reduced by one step. Enabler.

Tier 6: Duel to the Death (5 Speed points). Choose a target (a single individual creature that you can see). You are trained in all tasks involving fighting that creature. When you successfully attack that target, you inflict +5 damage or +7 damage if the creature is engaging someone else instead of you. You can only duel one creature a time. A duel lasts up to one minute, or until you break it off. Action to initiate.

SCAVENGES

You're a scavenger, or as some call you, a "scav." You do what you must in order to survive in a world that wants you dead. That means lots of hiding and running away. You have to stay on the move to scavenge for food and water. You rarely know where you'll

next lay your head, nor how safe the place you finally choose will be. But you have a knack for turning junk into needful things, and in locating especially prized items. You have faith that one day, your skills will transform your life and lead to a better tomorrow. But until then, you sift the ruins for useful junk.

You probably wear clothes scrounged from the ragged remains of fashions from before the apocalypse.

Connection: Choose one of the following.

1. Pick one other PC. This character helped hide you once when you were sick, saving you from a group of marauders.

2. Pick one other PC. For some reason, that character has bad luck with items you craft from junk. They tend to break, do something other than what they're supposed to do, and sometimes even explode in that character's hands.

3. Pick one other PC. That character is especially taken with your junk-scavenged crafts, and when they use an item in a way that requires a roll, they add +1 to the result.

4. Pick one other PC. You found a dead body in the ruins that looked exactly like that character. What this could mean, you don't know; you haven't told that character of your find, at least not yet.

Additional Equipment: You begin the game with a bag of light tools, the tools needed to make your second-tier crafts and one physical item you can carry off the Useful Stuff Table.

Minor Effect Suggestion: For your target, the difficulty of the next task it attempts involving an item you crafted before the end of the next round is increased by one step.

Major Effect Suggestion: You have an asset on the next roll you make within the next hour using an item you crafted.

Tier 1: Post-Apocalyptic Survivor. You are trained in stealth and Might defense tasks. Enabler.

Ruin Lore. You are trained in scavenging, which means you're more likely to find useful things, and junk that can potentially be turned into useful things in the ruins of what came before. Enabler.

Tier 2: Junkmonger (2 Intellect points). You are trained in crafting two kinds of items using scavenged junk. If you have scavenged (or have otherwise obtained)

Useful Stuff Table, page 76

Scavenging, page 74

Scavenges GM Intrusions: *An item made with recycled junk breaks. Someone shows up claiming the useful item or piece of junk scavenged belongs to them. A recycled cypher explodes.*

Junk Table, page 76

Crafting, Building, and Repairing, page 217

at least two pieces of junk in different categories (electronic, plastic, dangerous, metallic, glass, or textile), you have the materials you need to craft a new item in one of your areas of training (unless the GM deems otherwise).

Tier 3: Survivor's Advantage. Scavenging is dangerous business, especially when you've got to compete with other survivors. When your foe is knocked down, weakened, dazed, stunned, moved down the damage track, or disadvantaged in some other way, the difficulty of your attacks against that foe is decreased by one step beyond any other modifications due to the disadvantage. Enabler.

    Lucky. Why are you alive when so many others are dead? Might just be that you're lucky. You add 3 points to your Pools. Enabler.

Tier 4: Know Where to Look. Whenever the GM obtains a result for you on the Useful Stuff Table, you get two results instead of just one. If the GM is using some other method to generate rewards for finding valuables in the ruins, you should gain double the result you would otherwise obtain. Enabler.

Tier 5: Recycled Cyphers. All cyphers you use function at one level higher than normal. If given a week and at least ten items of junk from the Junk Table, you can tinker with one of your cyphers, transforming it into another cypher of the same type that you had in the past. The GM and player should collaborate to ensure that the transformation is logical— for example, you probably can't transform a pill into a helmet. Enabler.

Tier 6: Artifact Scavenger (6 Intellect points + 2 XP). You've developed a sixth sense for searching for the most valuable items in the wasteland. If you expend the time required to succeed on two scavenging tasks, you can exchange all the results you would otherwise obtain for a chance to gain an artifact of the GM's choosing if you succeed on a difficulty 6 Intellect task. You can use this ability at most once per day, and never within the same general area. Activity requires several hours.

SERVES AND PROTECTS

You're a cop. It's a hard job, one that's often thankless, especially when bad apples among your number abuse their authority. But you take it seriously. It's your

Serves and Protects GM Intrusions: *The gun jams. The car runs out of gas. A suspect decides not to cooperate. A witness reacts badly to seeing the police badge.*

job to enforce the law, protect people and property, and keep the peace. Investigating crimes means questioning witnesses and suspects. Often, hard questions are all that's required to get someone to confess. With your badge and your commanding presence, you're perfect for the job.

While on duty, you're in uniform, display your badge prominently, and carry a gun on your belt. When off duty, you wear civvies but still usually carry your gun and badge.

Connection: Choose one of the following.

1. Pick one other PC. That character was once a cadet who trained under you, but they've now gone their own way.

2. Pick one other PC. You know they spent several months behind bars, but you're not sure for what.

3. Pick one other PC. They're an old friend who hates the fact that you're a cop and sometimes tries to get you to quit.

4. Pick one other PC. You know there's a warrant for them on record, probably for unpaid parking fines (though you're not sure). You've chosen not to question them about it, but you could change your mind.

Additional Equipment: Police uniform and duty belt (containing handcuffs, radio, holster, and flashlight), a badge, a gun (medium ranged weapon) and a baton (light melee weapon).

Minor Effect Suggestion: The next time you attempt to command the same foe, the difficulty of the task is decreased by one step.

Major Effect Suggestion: The foe either surrenders or is influenced by your ability for twice as long as normal.

Tier 1: Badge. You're an officer of the law and have a badge, even when you're off duty or on sabbatical. When you show it, your badge and your air of authority together give you an asset for all interactions with law-abiding citizens, but this could increase the difficulty of interactions with scofflaws by one step. Enabler.

Practiced With Guns. You are practiced with using guns and suffer no penalty when using them. Enabler.

Tier 2: Command (3 Intellect points). Calling on your authority as a vested officer of the law, you issue a simple command to one target, who attempts to carry out your command as its next action if it can

---

> ## BADGE
>
> Having a real badge requires ongoing employment by a police department. That said, you could be on a sabbatical, taking a leave from active duty, or simply on vacation for several weeks each year without fear of losing your standing. If your police badge is confiscated for any reason and you use a facsimile to gain the benefit of having a badge, there's a chance that someone will recognize it as a fraud (though most NPCs will be fooled).

---

hear and understand you. The command can't inflict direct harm on the target or its allies, so "Commit suicide" won't work, but "Get down" or "Get out of here" might. In addition, the command can require the target to take only one action, so "Unlock the door" might work, but "Unlock the door and run through it" won't. Action.

Driver. You are practiced with all tasks relating to driving a car. Enabler.

Tier 3: Cool Under Fire. You are trained in Speed defense tasks. Enabler.

Police Training. You are trained in stealth, perception, and picking locks. Enabler.

Tier 4: Rapid Attack (3 Speed points). Once per round, you can make an additional attack with your gun. Enabler.

Tier 5: Commanding Presence (2 Intellect points). You can use this ability in one of two ways: first, your words keep the attention of all NPCs within short range who can hear and understand you. This lasts for as long as you speak, up to one minute, but only if the NPCs aren't attacked during that time. If your words are meant to distract the NPCs from noticing nearby activity, the difficulty of any perception tasks performed by the NPCs is modified by one step to their detriment. If you also have the Enthrall special ability, you can target all NPCs within long range who can hear and see you.

Second, your words can instead inspire all friendly NPCs of your choosing who can hear and understand you. After speaking to them for a few minutes, for the next hour, they function as if they were one level higher. Action to initiate.

Enthrall, page 45

Serves in an Elite
Military Squad
GM Intrusions: A
weapon jams. An
enemy anticipates the
plan. Friendly fire. A
commanding officer takes
a dislike to the character.

Tier 6: Never Fumble. If you roll a natural 1 when attacking with your gun, you can ignore or countermand the GM's intrusion for that roll. You can never be disarmed of your gun; nor will you ever drop it accidentally. Enabler.

SERVES IN AN ELITE MILITARY SQUAD

You belong (or once belonged) to a specially trained military unit. You work with others in your unit like parts in a well-oiled machine. Alone, you are competent, but together, you can accomplish more than any of you could manage alone. You probably take orders from a commanding officer. However, if you've somehow become separated from the command structure, you and your squad-mates continue to act as a group, because you know that your chances of survival are higher if you can all stay and work together when things become most difficult.

You probably wear some kind of military uniform similar to that worn by your squad-mates.

Connection: Choose one of the following.

1. Pick one other PC. That character seriously hurt a fellow squad-mate in an altercation, and possibly even killed them. You're not certain if the character was totally in the right for their part in the fight.

2. Pick one other PC. They once lent you an extra box of ammunition, which made all the difference in a firefight. You still owe them a favor in return.

3. Pick one other PC. You once carried them for miles on your back when they were wounded. Because they suffered a head wound in the incident, you're not sure they remember the incident.

4. Pick one other PC. That character, who is not a squad-mate, confided in you that they hate "jack-booted thugs" who serve in the military and is glad you're not one.

Additional Equipment: Medium rifle and combat uniform.

Minor Effect Suggestion: The target is confused, causing it to stumble and drop whatever it's holding.

Major Effect Suggestion: The target is stunned, and loses its next action.

Tier 1: Coordinated Action. If two or more allies with this special ability work together to accomplish a task, even if one or both are not trained in that task, an asset is provided as if the squad members were all trained. Enabler.

Wirelessly Linked. Technology ensures that you can always communicate with your allies who also have this special ability, no matter where they are located. The GM may determine that certain locations block the signal (such as within sealed bunkers designed to prevent just such sorts of communication). Enabler.

Tier 2: Specialty. The squad shines when every member has a different specialty. Choose the tier 1 focus ability or abilities from another focus from the list of foci provided by your GM. This is your specialty in your squad (or one of your specialties; your type abilities may also represent your specialty). Enabler.

Tier 3: Weapon Proficiency. You can choose from one of two benefits. Either you are trained in using standard issue military weapons, or you have the Spray ability (which costs 2 Speed points). If a weapon can fire rapid shots without reloading (usually called a rapid-fire weapon, such as the automatic pistol), you can spray multiple shots around your target to increase the chance of hitting. This move uses 1d6 + 1 rounds of ammo (or all the ammo in the weapon, if it has less than the number rolled). The difficulty of the attack roll is decreased by one step. If the attack is successful, it deals 1 less point of damage than normal. Enabler (being trained in using standard issue military weapons) or action (Spray).

Tier 4: Force Multiplier. If two or more allies with this special ability work together to accomplish a task, one of you can take an extra action. The squad members determine

If at least two people in a group of characters don't take Serves in an Elite Military Squad, some of the abilities granted by the focus will not be available.

who takes the extra action; however, the same character can't be designated to take the extra action granted by this ability on consecutive rounds. For example, if three squad members are all attacking the same enemy, an alternating squad member takes the extra action provided by this ability from one round to the next. That extra action is probably to make an additional attack but doesn't have to be. Enabler.

Tier 5: Weapon Specialist. You can choose from one of two benefits. Either you are trained in using standard issue military weapons (or specialized if you are already trained), or you have the Arc Spray ability, which costs 3 Speed points. If a weapon can fire rapid shots without reloading (usually called a rapid-fire weapon, such as the automatic pistol), you can fire your weapon at up to three targets (all next to one another) as a single action. Make a separate attack roll against each target. The difficulty of each attack is increased by one step. Enabler (being trained in using standard issue military weapons) or action (Arc Spray).

Tier 6: Good Soldiers Never Die. When you would normally die, you instead fall unconscious for one round and then awaken. You immediately gain 1d6 + 6 points to restore your stat Pools and are treated as if impaired until you rest for ten hours. If you die again before you take your ten-hour recovery roll, you are truly dead. Enabler.

TOUCHES THE SKY

The storm smells like life to you; like love. Electricity charges the air, dances across your skin, and connects you to the wind, the weather, and the sky. You issue commands through that connection, and the weather listens. The winds curl to your desire; they lift you, protect you, and give you the power to summon storms or break them apart. An electrical storm, a blizzard, or when your mastery reaches its zenith, even a tornado is something you can call up and loose upon the world.

You probably wear sleek clothing designed to stay out of your way when high winds roar past you. Flaring coats, cloaks, and capes can look dramatic, and they may be for you, too, if you train yourself in managing the excess fabric.

Touches the Sky GM Intrusions: *An ally is accidentally struck by forking lighting. An unexpected grounding effect inflicts damage. The weather is seeded by a much smaller effect, and a storm grows out of control.*

Connection: Choose one of the following.

1. Pick one other PC. You can't affect that PC with your focus abilities, though you don't know why.

2. Pick one other PC. You recently discovered that if they stand near you when you use your first-tier Hover ability, they too lift into the air. They must remain within short range of you to retain the effect, and it lasts only for as long as you hover yourself.

3. Pick one other PC. Their parents (or other loved ones) were killed in a freak storm. When they discovered your connection to the weather, they didn't know how to react. They either feel anger toward

you, or hope you can help provide some answers; it's up to them.

4. Pick one other PC. Something about them makes controlling the weather harder. When they stand near you, your focus abilities cost 1 additional Intellect point.

Additional Equipment: You wear an iron amulet taken from a lightning rod that sometimes crackles with electricity. Whoever holds it (if you willingly give it into their possession) is immune to your weather abilities.

Weather Abilities. If you wield powers that would normally use force or other energy, they instead use various effects generated by extreme weather. For example, a blast of energy could be a wind blast, a blast of blizzard cold, or a small bolt of lightning. Also, if you wish, you can swap an ability gained from your type for the following.

Zap (2 Intellect points). You attack a foe within short range with an electrical discharge that inflicts 4 points of damage and dazes your target so that the difficulty of its next action is increased by one step. Action.

Minor Effect Suggestion: The target is dazed, and the difficulty of their next action is increased by one step.

Major Effect Suggestion: The target is stunned, and loses their next action.

Tier 1: Hover (1 Speed point). You float slowly into the air. As your action, you can concentrate to remain motionless in the air or move up to a short distance, but no more; otherwise, you drift with the wind or with any momentum you have gained. This effect lasts for up to twenty minutes. Action to initiate.

Tier 2: Wind Armor (1 Intellect point). When you wish it, a cyclone of wind surrounds your body for ten minutes that gives you +1 to Armor and an additional +2 to Armor against physical projectile weapons specifically. While the cyclone is active, you feel no discomfort from the wind, and you can interact with other creatures and objects normally because the wind flow automatically diverts to enable such interaction. Enabler.

Tier 3: Windrider (4+ Intellect points). You summon winds that pick you up and allow you to fly for one minute at a rate of up to a long distance each round. You can't carry

A character who Touches the Sky might be a god of weather in a mythological setting, a caped crusader in a superheroes setting, or mortal who serves the divine in a fantasy setting.

other creatures with you normally, unless you apply Effort. For each level of Effort you apply, you can bring one ally of about your size with you through the air. You can also increase the duration of the effect by one minute per level of Effort applied. Action to initiate.

Tier 4: Break Storm (4 Intellect points). You can disperse a natural storm over the course of a few rounds. If the storm is particularly large, you disperse only a portion of it a few miles in radius. If the storm is supernatural or magical, you suppress the effects of the storm within a protective bubble of wind that surrounds you and any creatures standing next to you for one hour. Action to initiate.

Tier 5: Cold Burst (5+ Intellect points). You emit a blast of cold in all directions, up to short range. All within the burst take 5 points of damage. If you apply Effort to increase the damage rather than to decrease the difficulty, you deal 2 additional points of damage per level of Effort (instead of 3 points), and targets in the area take 1 point of damage even if you fail the attack roll. Action.

Tier 6: Control Weather (10 Intellect points). You change the weather in your general region. If performed indoors, this creates minor effects, such as mist, mild temperature changes, and so on. If performed outside, you can create rain, fog, snow, wind, or any other kind of normal (not overly severe) weather. The change lasts for a natural length of time so that a storm might last for an hour, fog for two or three hours, and snow for a few hours (or for ten minutes if it's out of season). For the first ten minutes after activating this ability, you can create more dramatic and specific effects, such as lightning strikes, giant hailstones, twisters, hurricane-force winds, and so on. These effects must occur within 1,000 feet (305 m) of your location. You must spend your turn concentrating to create an effect or to maintain it in a new round. These effects inflict 6 points of damage each round. Action.

TRANSCENDS HUMANITY

You aspire to become something greater than you are now. You want to transcend humanity and become posthuman either through biological alteration, nanomachine enhancement, or both. After you achieve that goal, you'll set your evolved mind to new challenges. Maybe you'll solve war, death, or some other intractable issue humans can't even conceive of ever solving.

Connection: Choose one of the following.

1. Pick one other PC. You can't seem to affect them with your abilities in any way.

2. Pick one other PC. When that PC holds your hand, you gain +1 to your Intellect Edge.

3. Pick one other PC. You've had a vision that, sometime in the future, they'll be directly responsible for accelerating your evolution, though the details of *how* remain hazy.

4. Pick one other PC. Sometimes when foes attack you and miss, their attacks hit that character instead, and vice versa. It's not something you can consciously control.

Posthuman Ability: When you call on special abilities from your type that would normally use force or other energy, they instead use the power of your evolved mind. This alteration changes nothing except the ability's origin.

Minor Effect Suggestion: A foe is held in place for the next round by the power of your evolved mind.

Major Effect Suggestion: Your mental ability breaks a weapon, shield, or piece of armor the target was using.

Tier 1: Self-Improvement. You gain 6 new points to divide among your stat Pools however you wish. Enabler.

Tier 2: Mind Reading (4 Intellect points). You can read the surface thoughts of a

Transcends Humanity GM Intrusions: *Regular people can become suspicious or afraid of posthumans. Supporting a mind capable of quantum manipulation is draining, leading to episodes of extreme hunger, trembling, and fainting.*

creature within short range, even if the target doesn't want you to. You must be able to see the target. Once you have established contact, you can read the target's thoughts for up to one minute. If you or the target move out of range, the connection is broken. Action to initiate.

Tier 3: Force at Distance (4+ Intellect points). You temporarily bend the fundamental law of gravity around a creature or object up to twice your mass within short range. The target is caught in your telekinetic grip, and you can move it up to a short distance in any direction each round that you retain your hold. A creature in your grip can take actions, but can't move under its own power. Each round after the initial attack, you can attempt to keep your grip on the target by spending 2 additional Intellect points and succeeding at a difficulty 2 Intellect task. If your concentration lapses, the target drops to the ground. Instead of applying Effort to decrease the difficulty, you can apply Effort to increase the amount of mass you can affect. Each level allows you to affect a creature or object twice as massive as before. For example, applying one level of Effort would affect a creature four times as massive as you, two levels would affect a creature eight times as massive, three levels would affect a creature sixteen times as massive, and so on. Action to initiate.

Tier 4: Pyrokinesis (4 Intellect points). You cause a creature or flammable object you can see within short range to catch fire. It is an Intellect attack. The target takes 6 points of ambient damage per round until the flames are extinguished, which a creature can do by dousing itself in water, rolling on the ground, or smothering the flames. Putting out the flames takes an action. Action to initiate.

Tier 5: Reshape Matter (7 Intellect points). You can reshape objects on a molecular level. You can create something from nothing, or affect and transform a single object (no larger than you).

If creating a new object, you can create any item you choose that would ordinarily have a difficulty of 5 or lower (using the crafting rules). Once created, the item lasts for a number of hours equal to 6 minus the difficulty to create it. Thus, if you create a

set of sturdy manacles (difficulty 5), those manacles would last for one hour.

If you are using this ability to reshape an object already in existence, the difficulty is the level of the finished object +1, and it requires concentrating on the object for one minute per level of the finished object. You can also attempt to damage an existing object in the same way; inflicting 10 points of damage if you are successful. Action to create or deal damage. One or more minutes to reshape.

Tier 6: Higher State of Existence (8 Intellect points). You have begun the process of transcending normal matter through manipulation of the quantum field. You can change your phase state for up to one minute at a time. When you do, you can't affect or be affected by normal matter or energy. Only mental attacks and special quantum field disrupting energies, devices, or abilities can affect you, but likewise, you can't attack, touch, or otherwise affect anything physically.

On the other hand, you can use your mental abilities while out of phase. Each time you do, there's a chance that the strain causes you to drop out of your phased state (if you roll an odd number on an attack roll). If this occurs, you can spend another action to become phased again if the duration of your original phase isn't complete. Action to initiate.

WALKS THE WASTELAND

Most people want to hide from the devastation, or just curl up and die rather than face a hostile world. Not you. You're determined to see what's out there, to survive, and more than that, to thrive. It's that, or let the radioactive rats get you.

You probably don't spend a lot of time on your appearance, given that you wear the cobbled-together clothing and bits and pieces of armor you're able to scavenge from the ruins. Appearance doesn't matter; actions do.

You're likely not much of a talker. You're a doer.

Characters with this focus are sometimes called scavengers. Sometimes they were soldiers, mercenaries, or others that had some basic survival training, but other times they are just people who decide to hope when everything looks darkest.

If you already have Control Weather from the sixth-tier adept list or some other source, you can expand the range of dramatic and special effects, so that they can occur up to 1 mile (1600 m) from you.

Sixth-Tier adept, page 36

Walks the Wasteland GM Intrusions: Even if the PC is a survivor, sometimes their equipment or weapons fail. Bandits of the wasteland are attracted by the commotion (of some other encounter). An area is unexpectedly contaminated with intense radiation.

Crafting, page 217

Connection: Choose one of the following.

1. Pick one other PC. This character seems an able survivor, but in your mind, they seem to be at the end of their rope. You're constantly trying to convince them to keep trying, go the distance, and survive for a better tomorrow.

2. Pick one other PC. You feel very protective of this character and don't want to see them harmed.

3. Pick one other PC. This character comes from the same place you do, and you knew each other as children. Whether that place exists any longer is something you and that character should decide.

4. Pick one other PC. You found this character almost dead in the wastes. You rescued them, nursed them back to health, and kept them safe until they were back on their feet. Whether they feel embarrassment, gratitude, or something else is up to them.

Additional Equipment: If you wish, you can ask the GM to swap an ability gained from your type for an artifact called an enviroscanner.

Minor Effect Suggestion: You restore 2 points to your Might Pool.

Major Effect Suggestion: The difficulty of your next action is decreased by two steps.

Tier 1: Survivor. You are specialized at finding food and water in places where such things are difficult to find. This doesn't just mean out in the wilderness. Even in the confines of an unfriendly encampment, a bombed-out ruin, or even a radioactive wasteland, you might find enough sustenance to get by. Enabler.

Weapon at Hand. If you find a weapon you're not practiced in using, you're treated as if practiced in using it after just a few hours of operating it. Enabler.

Tier 2: Defender (2 Intellect points). You know that to survive this world, you can't go it alone. Choose a nearby ally. That character becomes your scavenging partner. You are trained in all tasks involving finding, healing, interacting with, and protecting them. You can have only one character so designated at a time. Action to initiate.

Hardy. You have eaten your share of spoiled food and irradiated water, and survived. Whether that's because you've adapted or because you were just tougher than the rest is anyone's guess. You're trained in all Might defense tasks. Enabler.

Tier 3: Hit Them Where It Hurts (3 Speed points). There are two kinds of apocalypse survivors; the quick, and the dead. Once per round, you can make an additional attack against the same target if your first attack hit. Enabler.

Apocalyptic Stare. You've seen it all and survived, though not unscathed. Your demeanor is of someone that shouldn't be trifled with; you are trained in all tasks related to intimidation. Enabler.

Enviroscanner, page 79

If more than one PC has the Survivor ability, normal rules for helping other characters apply if the PCs work together.

Helping, page 211

Tier 4: Tough As They Come. Lying bleeding in the dirt isn't an option for a survivor. Your ten minute recovery roll takes one action instead, so that your first two recovery rolls take one action, the third takes one hour, and the fourth takes ten hours. Enabler.

Push on Through (2 Might points). You ignore the effects of terrain while moving for one hour. Enabler.

Tier 5: Pain Only Makes You Stronger. Well, at least it doesn't weaken you as quickly as others. You ignore the impaired condition of the damage track and treat the debilitated condition as impaired. Enabler.

Tier 6: Using What's Available (4 Intellect points). If you have the time and the freedom to scrounge for everyday materials in your environment, you can fashion a temporary asset that will aid you once to accomplish a specific task. For example, if you need to climb a wall, you could create a climbing device; if you need to break out of a cell, you can find something to use as a lockpick; if you need to create a small distraction, you could put together something to make a loud bang; and so on. The asset lasts for a maximum of one minute, or until used for the intended purpose. One minute to assemble materials; action to create asset.

WAS FORETOLD

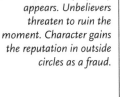

Was Foretold GM Intrusions: *An enemy described in prophecy appears. Unbelievers threaten to ruin the moment. Character gains the reputation in outside circles as a fraud.*

Whether you were once a normal person or always a little special, you now enjoy—or possibly dread—a growing reputation as the "chosen one." Chosen to do what might not be so clear. Perhaps you were living a normal life, only to discover that something might be special about you when you survived an accident or an attack that killed everything else in the area. A piece of ancient text identifies you by your distinguishing features, and claims that your involvement in a future crisis might save or doom the world. An enigmatic mystic comes into your life, and trains you in esoteric methods that unlock

your potential. Whatever your route to ascendance, you wish that being the chosen one wasn't wrapped in so much mystery and enigma.

Depending on your level of acceptance of your special status, you either dress to blend in, or you wear loud and elaborate fashion that makes it clear that you are someone of importance.

Connection: Choose one of the following.

1. Pick one other PC. The character believes your intervention once cured someone close to them of a fatal condition. You're not sure you did, or if the condition just went into remission.

2. Pick one other PC. You were a drunk or otherwise lost to questionable practices until this character plucked you out of the gutter and cleaned you up. You began to accept your status after that.

3. Pick one other PC. You made up a mental exercise designed to give this character respite from anxiety during trying situations, but you now fear unanticipated long-term side effects.

4. Pick one other PC. You're pretty sure that one of your off-hand statements from when you were younger and concerned with consequences is responsible for starting them spiraling into a bad situation they faced. The PC might know this, or they might just vaguely remember you from long ago.

Additional Equipment: Some distinguishing birthmark, tattoo, or talisman that always seems to find you again even if lost or stolen.

Minor Effect Suggestion: You learn something secret about the target.

Major Effect Suggestion: Foes within sight are dazed for one round after you use an ability. During this time, the difficulty of all tasks they perform is modified by one step to their detriment.

Tier 1: Something About You. Others recognize there is something different about you, something that makes them more amenable to paying attention to your desires. The difficulty of all tasks related

An enigmatic mystic comes into your life, and trains you in esoteric methods that unlock your potential.

to interaction are decreased by one step. Enabler.

Knowing. You are trained in one area of knowledge of your choice. Enabler.

Tier 2: Destined for Greatness. You enjoy uncanny luck as if something was watching over you and keeping you from harm. When you would otherwise descend a step on the damage track, make an Intellect defense roll versus the difficulty set by the level of the foe or effect. If you succeed, you do not descend that step. If the step was because you went to 0 points in a Pool, you are still at 0 points; you just don't suffer the negative effects of being impaired or debilitated. If you would otherwise descend the final step on the damage track to death, a successful defense roll keeps you at 1 point in one Pool, and you instead remain debilitated. Enabler.

Tier 3: Overcome All Obstacles (3+ Intellect points). Those who stand against you do so to their peril and eventually shrink away in your presence. When you focus on a particular foe within long range, the target suffers 2 points of Intellect damage (ignores Armor) each round for one minute or until the target can throw off the effect. This ability can only be active on one target at a time. You can apply Effort to increase damage during the first round, and for any one round in which you apply Effort and expend another action. Action to initiate.

Tier 4: Center of Attention (5+ Intellect points). A literal (or metaphorical, depending on the genre) beam of pure radiance descends from on high and spotlights you. All creatures you choose within immediate range of you fall to their knees and lose their next action. Affected targets cannot defend themselves and are treated as helpless. Action.

Tier 5: Show Them the Way (6+ Intellect points). Your presence overwhelms a creature you can touch and ask to aid you. Essentially, you control the actions of the target for up to ten minutes who fails to defend against your presence. The target must be level 3 or lower. Once you have established control, you maintain control through verbal instruction. You can allow the target to act freely or override control

on a case-by case basis. Instead of applying Effort to decrease the difficulty, you can apply Effort to increase the maximum level of the target. Thus, to affect a level 5 target (two levels above the normal limit), you must apply two levels of Effort. When the effect ends, the creature vaguely remembers doing your will, but it's as blurry as a dream. Action to initiate.

Tier 6: As Foretold in Prophecy. You accomplish something that proves that you are truly the chosen one. The difficulty of the next task you attempt is reduced by three steps. You can't use this ability again until after you've taken a one hour or a ten-hour recovery action. Action.

WEARS POWER ARMOR

You possess an amazing suit of super strong iron-alloy armor powered by advanced technology, including a power source that either runs on advanced micro-fission or perhaps even a fusion power unit. The suit was likely once fitted for mass military deployment during an earlier war, but you've customized the fit, so it fits well enough. The power armor grants several abilities that far outstrip those of a normal person.

Your power armor suit is distinctive, covering you from head to foot in its protective embrace. The suit might still bear the insignia of the military force or mercenary unit that originally commissioned its creation, though you may have given it a custom paint-job that reflects your personality and esthetic.

Tier improvements come about because you are constantly tinkering with your armor, making improvements, customizing, and adding additional components that you acquire along the way.

Connection: Choose one of the following.

1. Pick one other PC. That character helped you find and refurbish the suit.

2. Pick one other PC. You accidentally stepped on that character while wearing your power armor and broke their foot. It's healed up, but sometimes you think you can still detect a limp.

3. Pick one other PC. Something about that character seems to interfere with your armor, usually in a fashion that temporarily shorts out your armor.

Wears Power Armor GM Intrusions: Your armor won't come off. Your armor acts under its own power. Your armor suffers a momentary power loss. NPCs are scared by the visage of your power armor.

Some characters have abilities that grant them additional effects against helpless targets.

4. Pick one other PC. They know the code that will eject you from your armor, whether you're willing to come out or not.

Additional Equipment: Power armor (as described in tier 1), a set of tools appropriate for tinkering with your power armor.

Armor Abilities: When you perform special abilities provided by your type that would normally be produced by you, they are instead produced by your armor. For example, your Onslaught attack produces a beam of force, but when you use it, the effect appears to manifest from a special projector on your armor. This alteration changes nothing other than the power's origin.

Minor Effect Suggestion: Your armor's systems learn from your successful actions. You gain a +1 bonus to rolls involving a similar task (such as making attacks against the same foe or operating the same device).

Major Effect Suggestion: Your power armor performs better than expected, and you gain a +2 bonus to Speed defense rolls for one round.

Onslaught, page 31

Tier 1: Spectacular Armor. Your suit is effectively medium armor (+2 to Armor); however, you suffer no Speed penalties for wearing it. Also, your suit grants other benefits: it provides breathable air for up to eight hours and a comfortable environment even in bitter heat, cold, or underwater to a depth of 4 miles (6 km); and it allows you to see in the dark up to a short distance. Getting into the suit requires an action (and, of course, access to your suit). Enabler.

Armored Might. While wearing your special suit, you gain 3 points to your Might Pool. Enabler.

Tier 2: Heads-Up Display (2+ Intellect points). Your armor comes with systems that help you make sense of, analyze, and use your weapons in your environment. When you trigger this ability, you gain an asset on one attack roll as the suit perfectly outlines foes and steadies your aim, regardless of whether you're making a melee or ranged attack.

Alternatively, you can use the heads-up display to magnify your vision, increasing your vision range to 5 miles (8 km) for two rounds. If you apply one level of Effort, you can also see through mundane materials (such as wood, concrete, plastic, and stone) to a short distance in false color images. If you apply two levels of Effort, you can see through special materials (such as solid lead or other substances) to an immediate distance in false color images; however, the GM might require you to succeed at an Intellect-based task first, depending on the material blocking your armor's sensors. Enabler.

Tier 3: Plate Reinforced Armor. You gain +1 to Armor (for a total of +3 to Armor) while wearing your power armor. Enabler.

Tier 4: Force Blast. You figure out how to project blasts of pure force from the gauntlets of your power armor. This allows you to fire a blast of force that inflicts 5 points of damage with a range of 200 feet (61 m). There is no cost for you to use this ability. Action.

Tier 5: Field Reinforced Armor. You gain +1 to Armor (for a total of +4 to Armor) while wearing your power armor. Enabler.

Tier 6: Masterful Armor Modification.
Choose one of the following modifications to make to your armor. If you choose to make a different modification later, you can do so, but you must expend 2 XP each time, and substitute the updated modification for the previous modification.

Jet-Assisted Flight (3+ Might points). You modify your power armor to allow you to blast off the ground and fly for one minute at a time. For each level of Effort applied, you can increase the duration by an additional minute. Action.

Improved Field Reinforcement. You gain +1 to Armor (for a total of +5 to Armor) while wearing your power armor. Enabler.

Cypher Pod. The power armor provides an insulated pod in which you can carry one additional cypher than your cypher limit normally allows. Enabler.

Drone (3 Intellect points). A level 4 drone no larger than 1 foot (30 cm) on a side launches from your armor for one hour, flying up to a long distance each round. The drone accompanies you and follows your instructions. It has manipulators, allowing it to attempt to accomplish physical tasks. You'll probably make rolls for your drone when it takes actions. A drone in combat usually doesn't make separate attacks but helps with yours. On your action, if the drone is next to you, it serves as an asset for one attack you make on your turn. If the drone is destroyed, you must expend another 2 XP to rebuild it or choose another Masterful Armor Modification. Action to initiate.

WEARS SPURS

Some call you a vigilante, others call you a villain. It depends on whether you're more concerned with helping others or just yourself. Either way, you're someone who tends to act without the consultation or approval of authorities to accomplish what you think needs to be done. Often enough, that's fighting outlaws and desperados. Whether that's because you can't stand to see evil flourish or because you see them as competition is up to you. Either way, you can ride like the wind, shoot like Annie Oakley, and drink like Wild Bill Hickok and still never lose a game of cards.

You probably wear a duster, a wide-brimmed hat, a kerchief you can pull up around your mouth to keep down the dust, and expensive cowboy boots complete with spurs.

Wears Spurs GM Intrusion: *A posse from another town shows up looking for a gunman matching the character's description. A game of cards causes tempers to flare. Someone wearing a mask engages the character in a duel.*

Cyphers, page 340

There's a lot of truth in the old saying about running away and living to fight another day.

Connection: Choose one of the following.

1. Pick one other PC. They once challenged you to draw after an argument, but you declined. It's up to you both whether you're still angry with each other or have forgiven and forgotten.

2. Pick one other PC. You winged them once when practicing your shooting. You're a much better shot, now.

3. Pick one other PC. You both helped bring in a felon wanted in four states and split the reward evenly.

4. Pick two other PCs. They came to you because they hoped you might be interested in putting together some kind of gang to ride west.

Additional Equipment: Access to a horse or similar mount (level 2), six-shooter (medium pistol), spurs for your boots.

Minor Effect Suggestion: Your horse kicks the target, knocking the target prone.

Major Effect Suggestion: Your horse (or your bullet) strikes your target in a limb, making that limb useless for the next minute.

Tier 1: Rider. You are trained in all tasks related to riding a horse, including care and feeding, healing, and otherwise seeing to your mount's needs. If you use your action to urge your mount to take an action—such as jumping a ravine—the task is one step less difficult. Enabler.

Ride and Shoot. You can make an attack with a light or medium ranged weapon and attempt a riding task—such as urging your mount to jump a ravine—as a single action. Enabler.

Tier 2: Home on the Range. You are specialized in finding food and water in places where such things are difficult to find. This doesn't just mean out in the wilderness. Even in a boomtown where everyone is offering some kind of service to miners hoping to strike it rich, you might find enough sustenance to get by without having to pay for it. Enabler.

Quick Hands. Not many people can get the draw on you. You are trained in initiative tasks. Enabler.

Tier 3: Shoot Them Down (2 Speed points). You know how to kill quickly. When you hit with a ranged attack using a pistol, you deal 4 additional points of damage. You can't make this attack in two consecutive rounds. Action.

Tier 4: Hold Your Whiskey. You are trained in Might defense tasks. Also, if you've had a few drinks (enough to make normal people staggering drunk), you can act without penalty, and moreover, gain an asset to Intellect defense tasks and intimidation tasks. Enabler.

Tier 5: Bullet in Time. If you attack with your pistol from a hidden vantage, with surprise, or before an opponent has acted, the difficulty of your attack is reduced by two steps. On a successful hit with this surprise attack, you inflict 4 additional points of damage. Enabler.

Tier 6: Shoot to Kill (5+ Speed points). With a swift and sudden draw from your holster, you shoot a foe in a vital spot. If the target is level 3 or lower, it is killed outright. Instead of applying Effort to decrease the difficulty, you can use it to increase the level of the target you affect; each level of Effort applied increases the effective level by 1. Action.

WONDERS

The world is a big place. The way that leaf looks, how your dog's fur is so soft, a rainbow, pictures taken from planets like Mars and Jupiter; everywhere you turn, something new and interesting waits for you to dig in and take a look. Time after time, when you take the time to scratch the surface and ask some questions, you learn something new. When you wonder about something, often enough, what you learn is wonderful.

Your sincere appreciation for everything around you makes some people love you for your genuine earnestness. Though a few find your outlook annoying, you don't mind.

Wonders GM Intrusions: *Some creatures are interminable grouches and will not be swayed by wonder, a sense of awe, or sincerity. Sometimes the character asks a question and discovers a terrible secret instead of a wondrous one.*

You merely wonder what it is about them that makes them so sour.

Connection: Choose one of the following.

1. Pick one other PC. You were childhood friends. As you became more enamored of it all, they descended into more of an angry acceptance of life. You worry they don't see the world as you do.

2. Pick one other PC. You can see that the character needs some advice on how to appreciate life to its fullest. You're not sure if they are ready to hear it yet.

3. Pick one other PC. They seem to delight in new experiences and learning new things as much as you. When you help them, or they help you with a noncombat task, an asset is gained even if neither of you are trained in accomplishing that task.

4. Pick one other PC. The character was once your mentor, but you felt you learned everything you could from them and moved on. You are still friends.

Additional Equipment: A compass.

Minor Effect Suggestion: Your foe is distracted by your question and leaves their defenses down; the difficulty of the next attack made against them is reduced by one step.

Major Effect Suggestion: Intuition flares, and you can ask the GM one question about what you're looking at.

Tier 1: Asks the Question (1 Intellect point). You can pose a question so insightful to a creature that can see and understand you that it distracts it so that it loses its next turn and increases the difficulty of the target's Speed defense roll by one step for one round. If you choose to continue asking questions to the same target after the first in order to keep it pondering for longer than one round, you must use Effort each time. Action.

Learning. Always asking questions eventually provides answers. You are trained in one noncombat skill. Enabler.

Tier 2: Stands in Wonder (3 Intellect points). You get caught up in a scene, the intricacies of an object, or even in the wonder inherent in a particular person. When that happens, you notice things others do not. You can ask the GM one question related to a person, place, or thing you are currently looking at and gain information you didn't already know (if any is to be had). Action.

Tier 3: Enriched Mind. You add 5 points to your Intellect Pool. Enabler.

More Learning. You are trained in one noncombat skill. Enabler.

Tier 4: Power of Wonder. You gain +1 to your Intellect Edge and are trained in Intellect defense rolls. Enabler.

Tier 5: Smarter Every Day. You add 5 points to your Intellect Pool. Enabler.

Tier 6: Transmit Wonder to Others (5 Intellect points). You can affect others with your sense of wonder and peculiar way of looking at the world. When you do, you speak with such wonder and sincerity that you and allies who hear you find the difficulty of the next task they attempt within the next round decreased by one step. If the task they attempt is related to the subject of your wondrous description, the difficulty of the attempted task is decreased by two steps.

WORKS FOR A LIVING

No one ever expected great things from you. Whether because you had no choice in the matter, or because you saw what needed doing, you started working early in life, learning as you went. Whether it's putting in fences, installing electrical wiring, putting up houses, or mining asteroids, you work for a living. What's more, you take great satisfaction in it, and in a job well done.

You probably wear clothing suited to hard work, which might be overalls, a jumpsuit, or some kind of work uniform.

Connection: Choose one of the following.

1. Pick one other PC. You suspect they look down on your chosen profession. They must choose whether that's true or not.

2. Pick one other PC. In your opinion, this character could use some instruction in basic knowledge related to your expertise.

3. Pick one other PC. That character reminds you of a fellow worker you knew a while ago. You can't help but like them.

4. Pick one other PC. This character owes you a fair bit of money.

Additional Equipment: Set of tools suitable for basic electrical, plumbing, and carpentry tasks.

Minor Effect Suggestion: You draw on your experiences and reduce the difficulty of your next action by one step.

Works For A Living
GM Intrusions: *Repairs sometimes fail. Wiring can be tricky to decipher and still carry an electrical charge. Some people are rude to those who work for a living.*

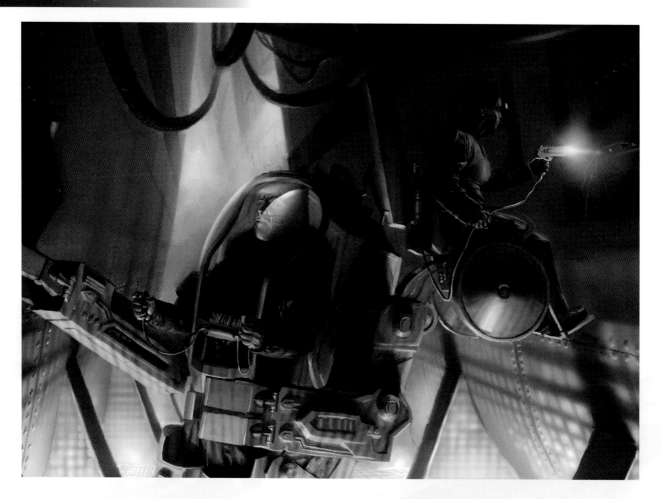

Major Effect Suggestion: You can make a free, no-action recovery roll.

Crafting, Building, and Repairing, page 217

Tier 1: Handy. You work for a living and are trained in tasks related to carpentry, plumbing, and electrical repair. Your knowledge in these realms also gives you an asset to craft entirely new items within your spheres of knowledge and the limits of possibility within the setting. Enabler.

Muscles of Iron, page 40

Tier 2: Muscles of Iron (2 Might points). For the next ten minutes, the difficulty of all Might-based actions other than attack rolls that you attempt are reduced by one step. If you already have Muscles of Iron, the effect of this ability lasts one hour instead of ten minutes. Enabler.

Eye for Detail, page 41

Tier 3: Eye for Detail (2 Intellect points). When you spend five minutes or so thoroughly exploring an area no larger than a typical room, you can ask the GM one question about the area, and they must answer you truthfully. You cannot use this ability more than one time per area per twenty-four hours. If you already have Eye for Detail, you can use this ability twice in the same area in the same twenty-four hour period instead of just once. Enabler.

Tier 4: Capable. Hammering, digging, repairing, and other physical labor has made you stronger. You gain 3 new points to add to your Might Pools. Enabler.

Tough It Out. Working for a living has toughened you over time. You have +1 to Armor against any kind of physical damage, even damage that normally ignores Armor. Enabler.

Tier 5: Expert. People who want things fixed right the first time call you. Instead of rolling a d20, you can choose to automatically succeed on a task you're trained in. The task must be difficulty 4 or lower, and it can't be an attack roll or a defense roll. Enabler.

Tier 6: Self-Improvement. A life spent working for a living has its own rewards. You gain 6 new points to divide among your stat Pools however you wish. Enabler.

Part 2
FANTASTICAL GENRES

CHAPTER 3

POST-APOCALYPTIC

*Science Fiction,
page 250*

Fantasy, page 236

Post-apocalyptic literature, movies, and games are a subgenre of science fiction that focuses on the dystopia that follows the fall of civilization. Strictly speaking, post-apocalyptic stories take place after the end of the world. At least, the end of the world for most people. Players take the role of the survivors (or their descendants) trying to persevere in the face of immense hardship. Popular post-apocalyptic scenarios include those set after nuclear war, in the aftermath of a zombie plague, in the months and years following an alien invasion, or after the environment collapses in the face of human overpopulation. Other ways the world could end include a massive meteorite strike, the long-awaited robot-uprising, a powerful solar flare that burns out the world's power grids and communications, or even something as prosaic as a global disease pandemic.

CREATING A POST-APOCALYPTIC SETTING

For a post-apocalyptic story to have long-term interest, the world can't be completely dead. Other people are necessary to interact with, help, and compete against for limited resources. A wealth of food, parts, and other supplies should be available so that survivors can live long enough to establish something more long-term. Other threats should also manifest—rival survivors, mutant abominations, wild creatures, aliens, disease, poisons, and yes possibly even zombies—depending on the post-apocalyptic world you want to create.

Creating a post-apocalyptic setting is almost cheating because you can start with the world as it is now, with its current technology, its history, and all the rest, before ruining it with an apocalypse of your choosing.

Alternatively, you could decide that the apocalypse comes much earlier in the history of the real world, or much later. You

might even decide that the apocalypse that defines your setting occurs in another world entirely, perhaps in a fantasy world where the gods all suddenly and inexplicably go extinct.

However, if you stick with the real world as your baseline, consider these additional advantages that you gain. Maps are the biggest benefit. All the maps of the real world are useful as maps of your fictional post-apocalyptic world with just a few modifications. Add a crater here, a shanty-town there, and maybe a crashed jet-airliner or another oddity, and voila, you've created a high-fidelity map in just minutes.

Another advantage of starting with the real world is that it sets a baseline for designing the post-apocalyptic cultures, wildlife, plant-life, architecture, and so on. It's easy to make a major and memorable encounter using something like a bear, even if it's a zombie bear or radioactive bear, or just a huge freaking bear facing off against characters armed with their fists and sticks.

Your players might start a game a little more invested in the setting if they're already familiar with a few of the locations and history, even if those locations are ruined, and the history is forgotten by most of the characters. To the players, it's "home." Setting a shootout in a fictional version of a now-ruined nearby supermarket, library, or coffee-house will be all the more visceral because the players will be able to imagine it as clearly as if they'd been there themselves. Because they probably have.

Even if your baseline is the real world, you've chosen to run your game after some kind of apocalypse. That means that many encounters and situations faced by the PCs should be colored by that event. Thus, the aforementioned shootout in the grocery store should contain a post-apocalyptic twist. Maybe there's a berserk android in aisle seven, a wounded mutant in the stock-room, or a radiation hazard associated with a particular food item.

Gods of the Fall—a Cypher System game setting—describes a post-apocalyptic fantasy world where all the gods died out.

In some post-apocalyptic settings, GMs may wish to offer players the chance to play as robots or androids. This can be accomplished by using the Artificially Intelligent descriptor.

Artificially Intelligent, page 256

RUNNING A POST-APOCALYPTIC GAME

It's easy for characters to find motivation in a post-apocalyptic game. Unlike most other settings, the character's most basic needs can't be assumed to be met. Even the most basic physiological needs, like air, water, and food, might be an issue from one day to the next. Thus, scavenging in supermarkets, gas stations, abandoned homes, and warehouses is likely to be an activity that characters must often do, at least as they begin their careers in the world's aftermath. More guidance for this activity is discussed under Scavenging.

In addition to meeting their base physiological needs, characters need to locate a place of safety. Finding a location free of radiation, zombies, disease or poison, killer robots, or rival groups of hungry survivors is a must. It's likely that only after these basic needs are met (or a strategy for meeting these needs over the long-term is developed) will characters become motivated by goals that apply in other genres, such as saving the innocent, finding the missing heir, defeating the marauders, exploring for monetary gain, and so on.

If you're looking for inspiration, don't be afraid to steal plots from post-apocalyptic stories and games you like. Long-running series and popular games provide a wealth of possible ideas, both in grand campaign arcs and for individual encounters. A single episode that describes a relatively small story can make a great session. If an ally falls down into a ruined structure or needs medicine to recover from sickness, if all the food is stolen, or if a shelter previously thought to be secure is overrun with an external threat, players will react viscerally and become invested.

WASTELAND THREATS

The environment itself is riddled with dangers in many post-apocalyptic scenarios. It's nearly a defining characteristic of the genre. Getting from point A to point B isn't assured because the bridge might be out, the road could be choked with dead vehicles, mutant ants might be living beneath part of the pavement, or a radiation storm could set in. Or the characters could just blunder into a poisoned swamp. These plus a few additional hazards you could throw at the PCs are presented hereafter. Choose one or roll when you need a threat to throw at your players; if a particular entry on the list doesn't match your conception of the apocalypse, ignore it and use something else. As described under Scavenging, attempts to find a safe place to hole up could also require a roll on the Wasteland Threat Table.

CUSTOMIZING YOUR AFTERMATH

My post-apocalyptic game has mutants and killer robots. Maybe even aliens and super-science items. But Shanna's post-apocalyptic game attempts far more realism because she wants to focus on the challenges of simple survival in a ruined world. A wide continuum of post-apocalyptic scenarios is possible. The threats, useful items, and creatures described and referred to in this chapter attempt to span that continuum. If you're running a "realistic" game, ignore results that you dislike, don't choose them, or modify them so that they make sense in your scenario. For instance, a realistic version of psychic lichen might simply be lichen that gives off an invisible spore that results in a similar sleepiness.

SCAVENGING

Characters in a post-apocalyptic setting must usually spend part of each day scavenging for supplies or a place of safety. Generally speaking, characters must spend two to four hours searching through the rubble and ruins before succeeding. Finding enough food for a group of characters to eat for one day is a difficulty 5 Intellect task. Finding a place of relative safety to regroup and rest is also difficulty 5. Characters who succeed on either one of these also get to roll up to once each day on the Useful Stuff table and three times on the Junk table.

Found food often takes the form of canned, processed, dried, or otherwise preserved goods from before the apocalypse, but sometimes it includes fresh

Finding enough food for a group of characters to eat for one day is a difficulty 5 Intellect task. Finding a place of relative safety to rest is also difficulty 5.

WASTELAND THREAT TABLE

1	**Radioactive crater (level 3):** Inflicts 3 points of ambient damage per round and drops character one step on damage track each day the character fails a difficulty 5 Might defense task.	
2	**Radioactive storm (level 3):** Treat as a radioactive crater, but one that moves.	
3	**Exposed electrical wiring (level 5):** inflicts 5 points of damage per round of contact and character is stunned and unable to take their next action until they succeed on a difficulty 5 Might defense task.	
4	**Dilapidated infrastructure, minor (level 3):** The floor gives way beneath a character who falls 30 feet (9 m) on a failed Speed defense roll, taking 3 points of ambient damage and dropping one step on the damage track.	
5	**Dilapidated infrastructure, major (level 5):** The building, underpass tunnel, or cave collapses or the bridge over which the vehicle is passing crumbles. Characters suffer 5 points of damage, and on a failed difficulty 5 Speed task are buried under suffocating rubble until they can escape or are rescued.	
6	**Abomination cave (level 2):** They were people once, or their ancestors were. Now they're dangerous threats best avoided.	*Abomination, page 127*
7	**Toxic spill (level 5):** Sticky orange goo busts from rusted ancient barrels. Characters who fail on a Speed defense task are caught and held in place until they can escape the morass, and suffer 5 points of damage each round they remain stuck.	
8	**Quantum singularity (level 6):** Attempts to change the past to avert the apocalypse have consequences, including these points of unstable space-time; characters who fail an Intellect defense task are teleported a short distance in a random direction and possibly several hours forward in time.	
9	**Roach infestation:** These insects the size of dogs have truly come into their own now that they've grown in stature and intelligence. They have little use for survivors, except as food.	*Roach, page 81*
10	**Unexploded ordnance:** Either a level 5 explosive that can inflict 5 points of damage to all creatures and objects within short range, or much less likely, a level 10 unexploded pocket-nuke that could kill everything in a several-mile radius and is likely radioactive to boot.	
11	**Killer Robot depot (level 6):** Designed by robots to kill humans, killer robots may be what caused the apocalypse in the first place.	*Killer robot, page 148*
12	**Superstorm (level 6):** With the climate destabilized, storms of unprecedented strength sometimes blow, creating windstorms and tornados that inflict up to 6 points of damage each round victims remain exposed.	
13	**Choking pollution (level 4):** Asbestos and other substances once safely bound up in the infrastructure is loose, sometimes as clouds of dangerous particulate matter inflicting 4 points of damage per round for three rounds as on a failed Might defense roll.	
14	**Animate vegetation (level 4):** Kudzu got a lot worse in the aftermath; creatures that fail a Speed defense roll take 4 points of damage each round from strangulation and vine constriction until they can escape.	
15	**Poisoned waters (level 5):** Whether it's water flooding a structure, a stream, a swamp, or a lake, drinking it inflicts 5 points of damage per round for three rounds on a failed Might defense task, and 2 points of damage per round for three rounds merely for getting wet on a failed Might defense task.	
16	**Psychic lichen (level 4):** Psychic lichen gently attacks the minds of nearby creatures, causing them to grow tired and nap if they fail an Intellect defense roll. If not awakened, the dozing body serves as food for a new psychic lichen colony.	
17	**Stinging insects (level 2):** These wasps are the size of eagles and inflict 2 points of Speed damage (ignores Armor) with a sting attack. When a swarm of 3 or more attack, they act as a single level 4 creature with a sting that inflicts 4 points of Speed damage (ignores Armor)	
18	**Bear, grizzly:** level 5; health 20; Armor 1; A regular bear can be terrifying in many situations.	*Marauder, page 156*
19	**Bear, radioactive:** level 5; health 20; Armor 3 from carapace; radioactive bite maul attack inflicts 5 points of damage and on failed Might defense task, stuns target so that targets loses its next action.	
20	**Marauder patrol (level 4):** Whether on scavenged trucks or motorcycles, or riding on mutant pigs bred as war mounts, a marauder patrol is bad news.	*War pig: level 3; grant rider an asset on melee attacks or can make a separate tusk attack when rider attacks*

fruits and vegetables found growing wild or cultivated by other survivors. Safe places to hole up include homes, RVs, offices, apartments, or any location that can be secured and defended and isn't radioactive, poisoned, or overrun with hostile creatures.

The difficulty of succeeding at finding food and water and finding a safe place varies by location and by how many days the characters have already spent in one location. Each week characters spend at the same location increases all scavenging difficulties by one step and requires that the characters succeed on a new task to determine if the place they're staying is still safe. The result of failing to find food and water is obvious. If PCs fail on the task of finding (or keeping) a safe place, the characters' presence is noticed by hostile forces, or they face a result from the Wasteland Threat Table.

Useful Stuff: Food, water, and a safe place to rest are the most important finds, and are the basis of each scavenging task. But other obviously useful stuff is often found along with these basic requirements. When a group of characters successfully finds either food and water or a safe place, the GM can roll for them on the Useful Stuff Table up to once per day. If it's the first day the characters have searched in a particular area, each character might find something useful, but in succeeding days, a group normally only gets a single roll to find useful stuff.

Useful stuff also includes a "loot" entry. Loot includes collectible coins from before the apocalypse such as silver dollars and gold eagles. It also includes jewelry and artwork that survived the disaster and related material that can be used as currency or barter when characters find other survivors or arrive at a trade-town.

Items found on the Useful Stuff table are generally expensive or exorbitant items (except for firearms, which start in the expensive category).

Junk: Characters who find food and water also find lots of junk. Characters are free to ignore that junk, but some characters might have a use for what they find, especially characters with the Scavenges focus. All characters gain up to three results of the Junk Table each time they successfully scavenge for food or a safe place to stay if they want to do so. Sometimes junk can be fixed, but more often it can be disassembled and used as parts to create something else.

Cyphers, page 340

Currency and Prices, page 182

USEFUL STUFF TABLE

01–10	Tools (provide an asset to tasks related to repair and crafting)
11–20	Medicine (provide an asset to one healing related task)
21–25	Binoculars
26–35	Chocolate bar or similarly sought-after candy or snack
36–45	Textbook (provide asset to knowledge related task)
46–50	Coffee or tea
51–55	Gun or rifle with ten shells or bullets
56–60	Flashlight
61–65	Loot
66–70	Gasoline (2d6 × 10 gallons)
71–75	Batteries
76–80	Functioning vehicle (sedan, pickup, motorcycle, etc.)
81–85	Generator
86–90	MRE cache (food and water for 6 people for 1d6 weeks)
91–95	Ammunition cache (100 shells or bullets for 1d6 different weapons)
96–97	Helpful stranger (level 1d6 + 2, stays with PCs for a week or two)
98–99	Cypher (in addition to any other cyphers the GM awards)
00	Artifact (in addition to any other artifacts the GM awards; see end of this chapter)

JUNK TABLE

1	Electronic junk (stereo, DVD/Blu-ray player, smartphone, electric fan, printer, router, etc.)
2	Plastic junk (lawn furniture, baby seat, simple toys, inflatable pool, etc.)
3	Dangerous junk (paint, rat poison, solvents, industrial chemicals, etc.)
4	Metallic junk (car bodies, old play sets, grills, empty barrels, frying pan, etc.)
5	Glass junk (vases, windows, bowls, decorative pieces, etc.)
6	Textile junk (coats, pants, shirts, bathing suits, blankets, rugs, etc.)

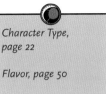

SUGGESTED TYPES FOR A POST-APOCALYPTIC GAME

Role	Type
Survivor	Explorer with stealth flavor
Heavy	Warrior
Dealer	Speaker
Trader	Speaker with skills flavor
Sage	Explorer with knowledge flavor
Evolved	Adept

Character Type, page 22

Flavor, page 50

Types, page 90

SUGGESTED FOCI FOR A POST-APOCALYPTIC GAME

Doesn't Do Much
Drives Like A Maniac*
Entertains
Fights Dirty
Governs*
Hunts Nonhumans
Lives in the Wilderness
Looks for Trouble

Masters Defense
Masters Weaponry
Moves Like a Cat
Murders
Mutates*
Needs No Weapon
Never Says Die
Plays a Deadly Instrument*

Scavenges*
Serves In An Elite Military
    Squad*
Walks The Wasteland*
Wears Power Armor*

*New in this book

SUGGESTED CREATURES AND NPCS FOR A POST-APOCALYPTIC GAME

Abomination*
Cannibal*
CRAZR
Devolved*
Elite soldier*
Fusion hound*
Gamma spiker*

Giant rat
Giant spider
Glowing roach
Guard
Mad creation*
Marauder*
Robot mimic*

Scrap drone
Thug
Vat reject
Wardroid

*New in this book

Creatures, page 126

Some GMs believe that zombies should also be on any list of post-apocalyptic creatures.

Creatures, page 274

Zombie, page 333

OTHER CREATURES AND NPCS FOR A POST-APOCALYPTIC GAME

Crazy loner: level 3, deception and attacks
    as level 5
Gamma snake: level 4; bite inflicts 5 points
    of Speed damage (ignores Armor)
Innocuous rodent: level 1

Mongrel dog: level 4
Survivor, sickened: level 3, interaction and
    knowledge tasks as level 2
Survivor, typical: level 3

ADDITIONAL POST-APOCALYPTIC EQUIPMENT

In a post-apocalyptic setting, the following items (and anything else appropriate to the setting) might be available in trade from other survivors, or in the rare trade-town. Items found on the Useful Stuff table are generally expensive or exorbitant items (except for firearms, which start in the expensive category).

INEXPENSIVE ITEMS

Weapons	Notes
Knife	(rusty and worn)
Light weapon	(won't last long)
Wooden club	

Armor	
Animal hide	
Light armor	smell raises stealth tasks difficulty by 1 step

Other Items	
Candle	
Duct tape	Useful and ubiquitous
Plastic bag	Useful and ubiquitous (won't last long)

MODERATELY PRICED ITEMS

Weapons	
Handaxe	Light weapon
Knife, multipurpose	Light weapon, and asset to small repair tasks
Machete	Medium weapon

Armor	
Leather jacket	Light armor

Other Items	
Backpack	
Bag of heavy tools	
Bag of light tools	
Bedroll	
Bolt cutter	
Climbing gear	Asset for climbing tasks
Cricket bar	Ground-cricket protein bar feeds two people for one day
Crowbar	
First aid kit	Asset for healing tasks
Gas mask	Breathable air for four hours
Handcuffs	
Padlock with keys	
Portable lamp	
Rope	Nylon, 50 feet (15 m)
Sleeping bag	

EXPENSIVE ITEMS

Weapons

.22 pistol	Light weapon, short range
.22 rifle	Light weapon, long range
.45 pistol	Heavy weapon, short range
9mm pistol	Medium weapon, short range
Grenade	Explosive weapon, inflicts 5 points of damage in immediate radius
Hunting rifle	Medium damage, long range
Shotgun	Heavy weapon, immediate range

Armor

Riot gear	Medium armor

Other Items

Radiation detector	
Nightvision goggles	
Radiation tent	Prevents radiation damage for three days
Radiation pill (pack of 5)	Asset for defense tasks vs. radiation effects for twelve hours

POST-APOCALYPTIC ARTIFACTS

Artifacts in a post-apocalyptic game include still working technology from before the war that is not widely available, as well as cobbled-together pieces of tech that can weaponize previously prosaic items. If the apocalypse was related to some kind of alien invasion, artifacts would obviously include even stranger items.

AUTODOC

Level: 1d6

Form: Backpack-sized plastic module from which clamps, forceps, scalpels, and needles can extend

Effect: When strapped to a target (or when someone wearing the autodoc is damaged), the autodoc activates and restores 1 point to a target's Pools per round for ten rounds or until the target is fully healed, whichever happens first.

Depletion: 1 in 1d10

ENVIROSCANNER

Level: 1d6

Form: Forearm mounted computer tablet

Effect: This multifunction device can receive radio transmissions, automatically map locations the wearer has visited, play various forms of media, keep voice and written records, and provide an asset to any task related to interfacing with other computerized systems or machines. Also, the wearer can scan for specific materials, toxic traces, and life forms within short range.

Depletion: 1 in 1d10 (check per use of scanning function)

MILITARY EXOSKELETON

Level: 1d6 + 1

Form: Articulated metal struts with deformable padding and straps for custom fit to a human frame

Effect: For one hour per use (when the exoskeleton is powered on), the wearer has +1 Speed Edge and +1 Might edge.

Depletion: 1 in 1d10

ROCKET FIST

Level: 1d6 + 2

Form: Metal gauntlet with flaring rocket exhaust nozzles

Effect: If the user activates the fist as part of an attack, the punch gains a rocket assist. If the attack is successful, the fist inflicts additional damage equal to the artifact level and throws the target back a short distance.

Depletion: 1 in 1d10

ROCKET-PROPELLED GRENADE

Level: 1d6 + 3
Form: Tube with sight and trigger
Effect: The user can make a long-range attack with a rocket-propelled grenade that inflicts 7 points of damage to the target and every creature and object next to the target.
Depletion: 1 in 1d6

TERAHERTZ SCANNER

Level: 1d6 + 1
Form: Visor fitted with bulky electronics
Effect: By emitting terahertz and long-range infrared light, this device allows a user to see a short distance through most interior walls of standard structures, through normal clothing, and into normal bags and briefcases. Only stone or concrete more than 6 inches (15 cm) thick prevents a scan. Regardless, images are black and white and fuzzy, and lack fine detail.
Depletion: 1 in 1d20

A terahertz scanner visor utilizes the same technology as is used in airports on Earth, but it is far more portable thanks to the relentless advance of technology.

RACIAL DESCRIPTORS

In a post-apocalyptic setting, some GMs may want to offer races affected by the disaster.

MORLOCK

You lived your life deep underground in artificial bunkers, hidden from the world's destruction and the brutal scavengers that live above. As a morlock, you have a keen mind for the technology salvaged from the before-time. In fact, every morlock comes of age by fitting a piece of morlock technology to its body to provide enhancement and extend its life. Which means that you are part flesh, and part machine. Your skin is pale as milk, except where it's been replaced with strips of metal and glowing circuits.

You have the following characteristics:

Enhanced Intelligence: +2 to your Intellect Pool.

Cyborg Body: +2 to your Might Pool and to your Speed Pool.

Partially Metallic: +1 to Armor.

Repair and Maintenance: As an entity of both living flesh and humming machinery, recovery actions you make require that you first succeed on a difficulty 2 repair task as part of your recovery action. On a failure, the recovery action is not used; however,

the normal rules for retrying apply, and you must use Effort on a new action if you wish to try again. If you wish, you can increase the difficulty of the repair task to gain bonus points back to your Pools. Every point you raise the difficulty of the task above 2 translates into a bonus point you gain back to your Pools if you succeed.

Morlock Prejudice: The difficulty of all positive interaction tasks is increased by one step.

Initial Link to the Starting Adventure: From the following list of options, choose how you became involved in the first adventure.

1. The PCs found you in a collapsed subterranean tunnel.

2. The other PCs encountered you exploring underground, and you convinced them to allow you to accompany them.

3. You were exiled from the morlock communities, and needed help on the surface.

4. The only way to save the morlock community you hail from is to venture to the surface to find an ancient mechanical part needed to repair a failing ancient system.

ROACH

You are born of a race of evolved insects once called "cockroach," but that is far in the past. Radiation and forced evolution have radically increased your size, shape, and ability to think. Your exoskeleton mimics the shape of a human being, though not perfectly. When you move about human society, shadows and cloaks are your ally if you wish to pass unnoticed. When those of your kind are discovered, it usually goes poorly for someone. You, however, have a wandering spirit and seek to explore the fallen world and find a new way forward.

You have the following characteristics:

Scuttler: Your Speed Edge increases by 1.

Sense by scent: You can sense your environment even in total darkness.

Cling: You can move an immediate distance each round on walls or clinging to the ceiling.

Carapace: +1 to Armor.

Glide: You can extend small wings from your carapace that grant an asset in jumping tasks, and allow you to fall up to a short distance without taking damage.

Skill: You are trained in disguise tasks.

Inability: You are susceptible to disease and poison. The difficulty of resisting disease or poison is increased by one step.

Inability: You mimic a human, but are not as fierce. The difficulty of tasks involving combat— including attack and defense rolls—is increased by one step.

Insect Prejudice: The difficulty of all positive interaction tasks is increased by one step.

Initial Link to the Starting Adventure: From the following list of options, choose how you became involved in the first adventure.

1. The PCs didn't realize what you were when they asked for your help.

2. You've managed to hide your roach ancestry so well; everyone thinks you are like them.

3. You are the last of your kind.

4. You have a secret agenda, and the PCs were gullible enough to let you come along.

CHAPTER 4

MYTHOLOGICAL

The mythological genre is a subgenre of fantasy. Fantasy features magic (or magic under a different name, like "psionics") in the setting. Magic allows characters to accomplish things they normally couldn't. But the mythological genre takes that concept and turns it up a notch. Instead of portraying mortals in a made up magical world, characters in the mythological genre play in a setting of real world myth, possibly one penned by Homer (The Iliad and the Odyssey), Aesop (the fables saved by the historian Herodotus), Aeschylus (Prometheus Bound, Agamemnon, The Libation Bearers, and The Eumenides), Euripides (The Trojan Women, The Bacchae, Medea, Helen, Andromache, Electra, Heracles), Sophocles, (Oedipus, Electra, and Antigone), and many more Greek playwrights. Of course, myths other than those inspired by the Greeks are entirely suitable for the mythological genre. For instance, the stories told of the Norse gods are just as rife with interpersonal conflict as those told about the Greek gods;

witness how one Marvel comic franchise has spun those stories into mythological gold.

A defining characteristic of mythological fantasy revolves around the active presence of gods in the world, and how their plans affect regular people. Which means that characters in a mythological setting will not only have the opportunity to interact with divine beings; they may even *be* divine beings.

Note that just because the mythological genre has its origin in the far past, the genre could easily be set in the modern world, with gods secretly (or not so secretly) dwelling among us. Some amazing examples of this concept include American Gods by Neil Gaiman and The Percy Jackson and the Olympians books by Rick Riordan. But far future settings that include ancient mythological beings are also something that fiction has done well: examples include the enduring Brother to Demons, Brother to Gods by Jack Williamson and the amazing Dan Simmons books Ilium and Olympos.

CREATING A MYTHOLOGICAL SETTING

Almost everything true for creating a fantasy setting is true for creating a mythological one. Examples of fantasy settings in the real world are rife. (If you're reading this, it's likely you've played a fantasy RPG.)

The difference in a mythological setting is one of tone, focus, and theme.

But before we explore theme, you need to figure out who your main mythological figures are. Is it Zeus and other associated entities? Gods from a different mythological pantheon, or gods you make up yourself? Whatever the case, your next step is to determine what associations these various NPC gods have between them, what each of them wants, and how far each might be willing to go to get it. What powers can they draw on? Who are their enemies? Remember that not all mythological entities are gods; some might be devastating monsters.

Once you know who the major divine entities are, you can determine the status

of your world. Is it at peace or on the verge of war? For instance, consider the Greek Titanomachy, where the older generation of gods (the Titans) were cast down in a series of wars by the newer generation of gods (the Olympians). A theme that might emerge in such a setting is one of perseverance, or the importance of standing up for what's right, or perhaps the inevitable end that faces all things.

When our mythological setting book called *Gods Of the Fall* was written, the theme that developed was simple: though the world is broken, hope remains. The arbiters of that hope are the PCs.

Now that you have a theme don't let all your work go to waste. Recognize that an overt theme might be asking too much of the players to live up to unless you provide explicit, in-world help. If you want your game to unfold according to your theme, players need easy tools to help them understand their role. A great tool in a mythological setting is the concept of prophecy. Prophecies from gods of Fate and

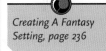

Creating A Fantasy Setting, page 236

Destiny (or from the Oracle in Delphi) can give the PCs what they need.

For instance, if your theme is "the importance of perseverance" you might develop a series of prophecies that speak of enduring pain, offering redemption even for the wicked, helping the weak to survive, and so on.

What would the prophecies be in your mythological world?

RUNNING A MYTHOLOGICAL GAME

Running a mythological game probably means embracing high-powered PCs and equally impressive NPCs. If you're going to let PCs parlay with gods or even *become* gods, they need some power. Using the power shifts (or "divine" shifts and accompanying dominions as is suggested in *Gods of the Fall*) is one way to gradually ramp characters into godlike relevance. If you're using power shifts, increasing the difficulty to 15 instead of 10 is something to consider. What was impossible for mortals is not for divine entities. If you do this, creature levels should also be able to rise above 10.

If you're running your mythological game in a larger fantasy setting, clearly defined roles for good and evil are expected. However, if you're mashing up your mythological game in a modern or sci-fi setting, figuring out which divine NPCs and creatures are good and which are evil might be part of the fun. For instance, a god of the ancient world transposed to the modern setting who doesn't learn to change with the times is probably nothing less than a horrific monster.

In a standard fantasy game, the expectation for PCs doesn't usually demand anything other than a willingness to go on adventures, explore strange places, and in high-minded groups, to oppose evil and help the downtrodden, though sometimes characters are more concerned about how much gold and treasure they accumulate. Which is great for standard fantasy.

A mythological game assumes that the stakes the PCs are ultimately playing for are of extreme importance. The fate of the world itself may eventually come into the balance. Tales of what the PCs do will eventually become the myths in a later age. If the PCs succeed in the quests presented to them, they'll become names that are never forgotten. All of which means that the adventures created for mythological games should always have some tie to the much larger epic narrative; an individual adventure can be a small story, but it should be clear that the creatures fought, the clues found, or some other elements have ties to something far larger.

For example, if the PCs find themselves defending a mother in childbirth who comes under attack by wave after wave of increasingly hostile creatures, those creature shouldn't simply be marauding orcs or hungry wolves. In a mythological game, those creatures are probably called by an unseen god jealous of the unborn child. This unseen power seeks to prevent the birth of a potential competitor. The links to this unseen power may not be apparent when the attacks first start, but PCs should be able to untangle the connection by the time they succeed on their task.

SUGGESTED TYPES FOR A MYTHOLOGICAL GAME

Types, page 22

Flavor, page 50

Role	Character Type (all have access to power or "divine" shifts)
Champion	Warrior flavored with abilities that enhance dominance and endurance
Defender	Warrior flavored with abilities that protect other PCs and NPCs
Destroyer	Explorer flavored with abilities that enhance combat, stealth, and ranged attacks
Reconciler	Adept flavored with abilities that exert mental and spiritual influence over foes
Savior	Speaker flavored with abilities that enhance healing, magic, and aiding others
Shaper	Adept flavored with knowledge skills and magic

84

SUGGESTED FOCI FOR A MYTHOLOGICAL GAME

Abides in Stone
Awakens Dreams
Bears a Halo of Fire
Blazes with Radiance
Builds Robots†
Carries a Quiver
Casts Spells
Changes Shape*
Channels Divine Blessings
Commands Mental Powers
Consorts with the Dead
Controls Beasts
Controls Gravity
Crafts Illusions
Crafts Unique Objects
Defends the Weak
Employs Magnetism
Entertains
Exists in Two Places At
   Once
Exists Partially Out of
   Phase
Explores Dark Places
Fights Dirty
Fights with Panache

Finds the Flaw in All
   Things*
Focuses Mind Over Matter
Fuses Flesh and Steel†
Gazes into the Abyss*
Grows to Towering Heights
Howls at the Moon
Hunts Nonhumans
Hunts Outcasts
Hunts with Great Skill
Infiltrates
Keeps a Magic Ally*
Leads
Lives in the Wilderness
Looks for Trouble
Makes Prophecy*
Masters Defense
Masters the Swarm
Masters Weaponry
Metes Out Justice
Moves Like a Cat
Murders
Needs No Weapon
Never Says Die
Operates Undercover

Performs Feats of Strength
Rages
Revels in Trickery*
Rides the Lightning
Rules the Sea*
Sees Beyond
Separates Mind From Body
Shepherds Spirits
Siphons Power
Slays Monsters
Solves Mysteries
Speaks for the Land
Stands Like a Bastion
Throws With Deadly
   Accuracy
Touches the Sky*
Travels Through Time
Was Foretold*
Wears a Sheen of Ice
Wields Two Weapons at Once
Works Miracles

*New in this book
† Reskin focus for fantasy
   setting if appropriate

SUGGESTED CREATURES AND NPCS FOR A MYTHOLOGICAL GAME

Abomination*
Assassin
Chimera
Demigod
Demon
Devil
Djinn
Dragon
Dream sallow
Elemental
Fallen angel
Ghost
Ghoul
Giant
Giant rat

Giant snake
Giant spider
Goblin
Golem
Guard
Hydra*
Mad creation*
Marauder*
Mechanical soldier
Occultist
Ogre
Orc
Priest*
Shadow elf
Skeleton

Soldier*
Soldier, elite*
Statue
The Minotaur*
Thug/bandit
Typhon*
Vampire
Wendigo
Werewolf
Witch
Wizard, mighty
Zombie

*New in this book

OTHER CREATURES AND NPCS FOR A MYTHOLOGICAL GAME

Gargoyle: level 3; flies a short distance each round; Armor 5; battering fist or wing attacks inflict 5 points of damage

Giant crab: level 6; Armor 4; two pincer attacks as a single action inflict 6 points of damage and holds prey

Harpy: level 3; flies a long distance each round; attacks by snatching and dropping victims from a height

Oracle: level 2, predicting future events using obscure phrases open to interpretation as level 8

Siren: level 4; swims a short distance each round; song entrances victims who hear that can't resist

Two-headed snake: level 2, two bites as a single action inflict 2 points of Speed damage (ignores Armor)

White stag: level 5, Speed defense and stealth tasks as level 8; runs a long distance each round

MYTHOLOGICAL ARTIFACTS

SPEAR OF FATE

Level: 12

Form: Large spear intricately carved with divine symbols

Effect: This spear functions as a normal weapon of its type. It is so well crafted and carved with magic runes of such power that it never misses. No attack roll is necessary for the wielder to hit with it. If a PC rolls in hopes of achieving a special effect but gets a 1, the spear still hits the target (though a GM intrusion is still appropriate). If the user defeats an enemy with the spear, the wielder learns a secret about the defeated foe related to a topic the wielder names.

Depletion: 1 in 1d20

STORM HAMMER

Level: 12

Form: Medium hammer with oversize head

Effect: This hammer functions as a normal weapon of its type and the difficulty of attacks made with it is decreased by one step. Also, the wielder can make a long-range lightning attack on a target and all creatures within immediate range of the target that inflicts damage equal to the artifact level. Alternatively, every other round they can throw the hammer at a single foe within long range, inflicting double the artifact level in damage. Once thrown, the hammer returns to the wielder. The wielder can activate the hammer and gain the ability to fly a long-range each round while holding it. This ability lasts for ten minutes. Finally, the wielder can use the hammer to travel between alternate dimensions they have previously visited.

Depletion: 1 in 1d20

SWORD OF DEATH

Level: 13

Form: Greatsword with night-black blade

Effect: This sword functions as a normal weapon of its type. In addition, it instantly kills any level 1 or level 2 creatures it hits. To kill more powerful creatures, instead of applying Effort to decrease the difficulty of the attack, the wielder can apply Effort to increase the maximum level of the target. Thus, to instantly kill a level 5 target (three levels above the normal limit), the wielder must apply three levels of Effort. The souls of creatures killed by the weapon are stored in the blade.

Depletion: 1 in 1d20

THUNDERBOLT

Level: 13

Form: A sizzling bolt of lightning

Effect: This weapon functions as a normal spear, but holding it requires a wielder to succeed on a difficulty 5 Intellect ask to avoid taking 7 points of electricity damage each round for two rounds. The difficulty of attacks made with it is decreased by one step. In addition, the wielder can make a long-range lightning attack on a target and all creatures within immediate range of the target that inflicts damage equal to the artifact level. Once thrown, the bolt returns to the wielder, ready to be used the next round.

Depletion: 1 in 1d20

RACIAL DESCRIPTORS

In a mythological setting, some GMs may want players to be able to choose more extreme racial options. Below are a couple possibilities.

HELBORN

Demons of the underworld sometimes escape. When they do, they can taint human bloodlines. Things like you are the result of such unnatural unions. Part human and part something else, you are an orphan of a supernatural dalliance. Thanks to your unsettling appearance, you've probably been forced to make your own way in a world that often fears and resents you. Some of your kin have large horns, tails, and pointed teeth. Others are more subtle or more obvious in their differences—a shadow of a knife-edge in their face and a touch that withers normal plants, a little too much fire in their eyes and a scent of ash in the air, a forked tongue, goatlike legs, or the inability to cast a shadow. Work with the GM on your particular helborn appearance.

You gain the following characteristics.

Devious: +2 to your Intellect Pool.

Skill: You are trained in tasks related to magic lore and lore of the underworld.

Helborns are sometimes called cambions.

Cambion, page 129

Incombustible: +3 to Armor against damage from fire only.

Helborn Magic: You are inherently magical. Choose one tier 1 ability from the list of foci for a mythological game provided by your GM. You gain that ability as part of your helborn heritage.

Inner Evil: You sometimes lose control and risk hurting your allies. When you roll a 1, the GM has the option to intrude by indicating you lose control. Once you've lost control, you attack any and every living creature within short range. You can't spend Intellect points for any reason other than to try to regain control (a difficulty 2 task). After you regain control, you suffer a −1 penalty to all rolls for one hour.

Inability: People distrust you. The difficulty of any task you attempt to persuade or deceive is increased by one step.

Initial Link to the Starting Adventure: From the following list of options, choose how you became involved in the first adventure.

1. You were nearly beaten to death by people who didn't like your look, but the PCs found and revived you.

2. The PCs hired you for your knowledge of magic.

3. Every so often you get visions of people trapped in the underworld. You tracked those people down and found the PCs who'd never visited the underworld. Yet.

4. Your situation at home became untenable because of how people reacted to your looks. You joined the PCs to get away.

GIANT

You stand at least 12 feet (4 m) tall, and tower over everyone around you. Whether you are a full-blooded giant or merely have giant heritage from large ancestors, you're massive. Always large for your age, it only became an issue once you reached puberty and topped 7 feet (2 m) in height, and kept growing from there.

You have the following characteristics:

Tough: +4 to your Might Pool.

Mass And Strength: You inflict +1 points of damage with your melee attacks and attacks with thrown weapons.

Breaker: The difficulty of tasks related to breaking things by smashing them is reduced by one step.

Inability: You're too large to accomplish normal things. The difficulty of tasks related to initiative, stealth and fine manipulation of any sort (such as lockpicking or repair tasks) is increased by one step.

Additional Equipment: You have a heavy weapon of your choice.

Initial Link to the Starting Adventure: From the following list of options, choose how you became involved in the first adventure.

1. You fished the PCs out of a deep hole they'd fallen into while exploring.

2. You were the PC's guide in the land of giants and stayed with them afterward.

3. The PCs helped you escape a nether realm where other giants were imprisoned by the gods.

4. You protected the PCs from sight by hiding them behind your bulk when they were on the run.

Suggested Foci For a Mythological Game, page 85

CHAPTER 5

FAIRY TALE

Modern, page 244

The fairy tale genre is a predecessor of the fantasy genre, historically speaking. Folklore featuring elves, giants, goblins, trolls, dragons, knights, mermaids, witches, and similar elements are the basis of the fantasy genre that sets heroes of a magical medieval world against just such foes. Fantasy stories and games often presume that such creatures are quite real and that they're something anyone with any sense and education, within the context of that fantasy world, knows as real and dangerous, if hopefully far away.

However, the power of a fairy tale—or a game set in a fairy tale inspired setting—is that magic, magical creatures, and enchanted forests bigger on the inside than outside are presumed to be nothing more than stories made to entertain or frighten adults and children. Thus, when a talking animal or a house on legs is encountered, they are truly amazing and fantastical, as opposed to something that might be expected.

Which argues that to pull off a fairy tale adventure or campaign, a GM might want

to present the game in a modern setting. In a modern setting, characters have regular jobs that don't normally involve hunting goblins or exploring ancient ruins. This means that when the moths take shape and become the cloak of a princess of summer come to beg a favor or steal a child, or the house grows legs and runs away one morning, player characters will be rightfully amazed (and probably somewhat terrified).

CREATING A FAIRY TALE SETTING

You could easily have fairy tales in other times and settings, but for our purposes in this chapter, we'll deal with a default setting in the modern day. The PCs are probably normal people, not secret agents or special investigators.

Whatever the setting, the main thing to remember when preparing to run a fairy tale themed game is that it's desirable to invoke a sense of wonder rather than fear. A sense of enticement, of yearning, and the promise of a release from the everyday problems that plague us. What does it matter if your

internet provider has jacked up your bill yet another $20 a month when the stray cat on your patio begins to talk about the land of moonbeams, fairy gold, and music that will shiver a soul with everlasting delight?

Of course, every good story—and game—requires a complication, problem, or threat to overcome, otherwise, what's the point? In a fairy tale, the odd, furry, magical little creatures you've discovered to be responsible for stealing your shoes might actually turn out to be just the nicer cousins of an altogether more vicious version that will also steal the beating heart out of your chest, if given half the chance.

That's when a fairy tale game threatens to become a game of horror. Indeed, horrific elements should be part of a fairy tale. But to retain the style, horror should not predominate. For every erlking, cryptic moth, or troll encountered, players should be dazzled and aided by a helpful fairy, a prince of summer, to a talking cat or rabbit that knows secrets of all sorts. And as is described in the chapter dealing with horror,

Of an old King in a story
From the grey sea-folk I have heard
Whose heart was no more broken
Than the wings of a bird.

And three tall shadows were with him
And came at his command;
And played before him forever
The fiddles of fairyland.

—G. K. Chesterton

if everything is terrifying, then nothing is. If the thrill of wonder fails to find the PCs more than just on their initial introduction to the game, view it as an opportunity to try again.

If you're looking for inspiration in creating a modern fairy tale adventure or campaign, we recommend you start with a variety of

Horror, page 257

works by master tale-spinner Neil Gaiman. Of particular note, check out Coraline, Neverwhere, and the Ocean at the End of the Lane. You can also watch an animated version of Coraline. Other things to watch for fairy tale inspiration include The Neverending Story (story by Michael Ende, directed by Wolfgang Petersen), Pan's Labyrinth (written and directed by Guillermo del Toro), Labyrinth (screenplay by Terry Jones, directed by Jim Henson), and Nocturna (directed by Adrià Garcia & Víctor Maldonado). You should also watch at least the first season of the show Once Upon A Time.

Other RPGs also provide great inspiration. As with stories and movies, there are too many to list them all here, but if you have a chance, take a look at Mouse Guard (by Luke Crane, based on the graphic novel series by David Petersen) and A Red & Pleasant Land (by Zak Smith).

RUNNING A FAIRY TALE GAME

Retaining a fairy tale esthetic is difficult. You've got to maintain mood and atmosphere at all times. Consider these tips.

Give the players time to develop their characters before they meet the talking cat, the strange little man selling singing chocolate mice, or a raccoon wearing clothing and glasses on the street corner. Let them get attached to the characters, at least a little, so that when those PCs see something wondrous, the players will be thrilled.

Be evocative, by using both your descriptive language to paint the picture of what players see, and your body language and gestures. For example, if you're describing a faerie forest, don't simply tell them that they see a faerie forest. Instead, as you gesture up and with wide eyes, tell the players something like "The forest canopy stretches high overhead, alight with drifting motes of firefly light like drifting stars. The air is bracing and smells of the cool night, peppermint, and thunderstorms. From afar, a music like harps and violins gambols, somehow suggesting a great midnight feast taking place someplace deeper within the press of golden trees."

Fairy tale games are often one-shot sessions or a short arc of a few sessions. They are very difficult to run as long-term campaigns, but it's possible. If that's what you want, remember that you need to keep

alive wonder and reward at the same pace as characters discover the dark side of fairy tales. Gifts of golden armor or magic beans should follow characters fighting back forces of the Unseelie court busy making baby-stealing plans in the modern world.

NATURE OF FAERIE

Faerie (also called by many other names) is a dimension of magic separate from but closely parallel to the mundane world. Whether Faerie is just a collective term for thousands of separate curled up dimensions hidden in corners, in closets, or at the center of forests, or it's one continuous realm that overlaps the real world where it's thinnest doesn't matter. It's a place those with open hearts can find by following a way between tall trees (or looming library shelves) to a place where everything is different. Where elves walk, nymphs dance, unicorns gallop, and both natural growths and built structures become vast and enchanting.

Humans don't tend to do well in such a world if they stay too long, as the sensory input is just hard on the nervous system. But fey creatures depend upon it, like plants to the light. A fey creature too long cut off from its land of origin (or its stream, hill, or burrow) slowly becomes mortal and then dies.

When a fey creature is cut by silvered or cold-forged weapons, they temporarily lose the sustaining benefit of their connection to Faerie. This severed connection usually disrupts a fey creature's ability to heal. A silvered weapon is one that either contains silver as part of an alloying process, has silver inlay, or has been coated in dusting of silver powder (which usually only lasts through a single fight). In truth, many items are cold-forged in the modern era, while many others are not. We suggest that any hand-forged item containing iron could be considered a cold-forged weapon for harming fey creatures. Thus, most bullets and other modern items wouldn't be treated as cold-forged by this definition, but some would fit the bill.

FAIRY TALE WONDERS

The Fairy Tale Wonders table is a way you can quickly generate simple delights, and greater wonders appropriate to a fairy tale esthetic. This table is to be used about as often as the table that follows—the Fairy

FAIRY TALE WONDERS TABLE

1 **Inheritance:** A letter in a golden envelope arrives in the mail or is found in the attic addressed to a character, letting them know they have inherited a large chest. When found, the chest might contain a faerie artifact and hints as to the character's faerie ancestry.

2 **Musical marvel:** The character finds a musical instrument that allows them to play perfectly (while using that instrument) even if they've never studied that instrument before.

3 **Adventure mouse:** An enchanted mouse leads the characters to a clue they need to get on with their adventure.

4 **Friend indeed:** A princess of summer learns of the character's plight, and in the guise of a friendly reporter, lawyer, or police officer, extracts the characters from a difficult situation with charm so intense it seems supernatural (and it probably is).

5 **Faerie path:** The character finds a secret for getting across town using a "shortcut" that turns an hour's drive in traffic to a five minute walk down a sunny garden path.

6 **Cup of many liquids:** Whatever mundane consumable liquid the character wishes for appears in this small cup; coffee, tea, hot chocolate, brandy, and so on.

7 **Faerie luck:** Tiny human figures with wings flit overhead, wave and smile, and wish the characters a good day. For the rest of the day, the character has a sense of luck and happiness, and an asset on all noncombat tasks attempted.

8 **Nightmarket:** A door to a previously unknown market held at night, staffed by all manner of beings—and several talking animals dressed as people—selling the kinds of goods one might find at a flea market, farmer's market, and in a few cases, a magic shop.

9 **Faithful companion:** A huge shaggy dog shows up with something the character lost in its mouth. (Ask the character to make up something that they lost.) The dog might continue to follow that character, especially if the character cares for it.

Shaggy Dog: level 3; intelligent but doesn't speak

10 **Hat of perfection:** The character finds a hat that seems to go with everything they wear and provides an asset to all interaction and disguise checks. A label on the hat brim reads "Property of the King of Good Endings."

11 **Alluring goal:** A floating castle is sometimes glimpsed at sunrise, but only the characters can see it.

12 **Treasure in an egg:** Among the eggs in a birds nest is found one solid gold egg.

13 **Talking portrait:** A portrait on the wall animates and the person depicted tells a story, which might simply be a story of their life, but could also be a warning, or directions to someplace else.

14 **Magic bookstore:** A book shop opens on the corner where amazing books whose titles are new to characters (and are not found anywhere else) can be bought and perused.

15 **Bonus room:** The character has a dream where they find another room in their house that looks out onto a faerie forest. Upon waking, the room proves to be real.

16 **Mysterious benefactor:** Something amazing happens for the character—they get a book deal, win the lottery, find something thought lost, or similar, after which a silver card smelling of cloves arrives with the message "You're welcome. ~M."

17 **House with legs:** A house across the street stands up on hairy legs, moves a few feet to the left, and settles again, apparently once again as normal as ever.

18 **Flowered jetstream:** A person wearing a long cape flies overhead on what appears to be a broom. Flowers of all varieties drift down in their wake.

19 **Gingerbread winds:** A strong wind blowing in from east smells of gingerbread, sugar, and wonderful baking things. If followed to its source, a small home is discovered where a fey baker is at work, and willing to share their creations.

20 **Candyfall:** When the storm front rolls in, candy wrapped in golden, copper, and silver foil drops from the clouds.

Tale Threats table. If wonders don't beckon to the PCs who step off the path most traveled, why would they leave their jobs as accountants, biologists, journalists, and so on just to be eaten by trolls or be imprisoned forever in a fairy tower? Most of these wonders should be presented as GM intrusions.

FAIRY TALE THREATS

The Fairy Tale Threats table provides more dangers you throw at your PCs playing in a setting where the unexpected can lead to dire repercussions almost as often as wonders. The results are not meant to be the major story arc, though you could probably spin some of them out to serve that purpose. Most of these threats should be presented as GM intrusions.

FAIRY ARTIFACTS

Artifacts in the fantasy setting and magic items in others games focused on fantasy gaming would also be suitable for a fairy tale setting. However, every fairy tale artifact should come with some quirk that sets it apart from simple "wand of fire" or similar item. Come up with your own or roll a quirk from the table.

CARVING KNIFE OF SHARPNESS

Level: 1d6 + 1
Form: Knife (light weapon)
Effect: This weapon functions as a normal weapon of its kind. When the wielder gets a special major effect when attacking, they can choose to lop off one of the target's limbs.
Depletion: 1 in 1d20

SOULFUL FIDDLE

Level: 1d6 + 2
Form: Fiddle apparently made of bone
Effect: This instrument acts like a normal instrument of its kind. If the wielder is trained in its use and plays an appropriate tune, those within short range who can hear it must succeed or fall asleep, become amenable to suggestion, follow the fiddle player in a light trance, or take some similar action. Effects last no more than ten minutes.
Depletion: 1 in 1d20

The GM determines the effect of a lost limb; however, a fairy creature can withstand lost limbs with far more aplomb than a mortal creature will display in a similar situation.

FAIRY ARTIFACT QUIRK TABLE

1	Is sometimes invisible.
2	Cries like a baby if jostled.
3	Becomes cold as ice to the touch and steams condensation when danger threatens.
4	Contains a secret compartment which invariably holds a chunk of rock broken from a what might be a strange jade sculpture.
5	Also serves as a key to some magically locked doors and chests.
6	Bites owner for 1 point of damage with tiny teeth if jostled.
7	Always muttering and complaining, though useful warnings and other information can sometimes be gained.
8	Jealous of any other cyphers, artifacts, or beautiful objects in the wielder's life.
9	The "painting" of a princess of summer on the object sometimes leaves it, robbing the artifact of power.
10	Causes flowers to grow wherever it is stored or set down.

VICIOUS TANKARD

Level: 1d6 + 2
Form: Hefty ale tankard carved of stone
Effect: In addition to serving as a convenient means to drink a variety of liquids, the tankard can be used as a medium weapon that inflicts +2 damage (for a total of 6 points of damage) if the tankard was previously topped off with good ale or spirits. Anyone who picks up the tankard is practiced in using it in this fashion. Surprisingly, using the tankard as a melee weapon does not cause more than a modicum of good ale or spirits to slosh out.
Depletion: 1 in 1d20 (check per fight)

MIRROR OF FARSIGHT

Level: 1d6 + 3
Form: A medium mirror with elaborate frame
Effect: Answers one question per day, but usually not directly.
Depletion: 1 in 1d20

FAIRY TALE THREATS

1. **Wild Hunt (level 5):** Baying and screeching, a pack of hounds (level 2) carries a sledge through the sky driven by an antlered entity. (Treat as a prince of summer.) The hunt notices characters who fail a difficulty 3 Speed-based task to find cover.

2. **Unexpected eclipse:** A strange different moon, briefly interposes itself between the region the characters inhabit and the sun. Midnight scrabblers ooze out of hard surfaces and attack until the eclipse fades after about a minute.

3. **Trolls:** A couple trolls emerge from the alley, under the overpass, or from the heart of the forest looking to fill their bellies.

4. **Cursed trap (level 4):** A chest, spell, or found object transfers the character bodily to a fairy tower where they are imprisoned unless they succeed on a difficulty 4 Intellect-based task.

5. **Feral trees:** Awakened trees attack those who do not know the proper passwords or who are not accompanied by a fey friend.

6. **Razorblade butterflies:** What at first seems to be a delightful mass of colorful butterflies flitting through the field is revealed as threat as creatures are afflicted with hundreds of tiny cuts from the fluttering wings.

7. **Item with a mind of its own:** An object gained during the adventure—be it a cypher, a faerie artifact, or a letter that must be delivered to the Queen Under the Hill—awakens to limited mind and movement, and decides it likes to play hide and seek.

8. **Gingerbread winds, dire:** A strong wind blowing in from east smells of gingerbread, sugar, and wonderful baking things. If followed to its source, a small home is discovered where a fey baker is at work, willing to share their creations. But the baker is secretly a cannibal.

9. **Angry noble:** A prince(ss) of summer takes an interest in the characters and begins to work against them.

10. **Greedy wall:** level 4; Armor 3; victims within immediate range of this graffiti-and-art-covered wall must succeed on an intellect defense task or be drawn into the wall and become themselves one more piece of art. Trapped creatures gain one additional attempt to escape. Otherwise, they must be freed, or the wall must be destroyed.

11. **Masquerade, dire:** Fancy invitations on ebony paper with scarlet ink arrive inviting the PCs to a masquerade ball. However, an evil witch is behind the summons.

12. **Blight:** A faerie wood, path, or another area the PCs have become attached to sickens and begins to die. It might be a curse, or perhaps goblins have taken up residence beneath the ground, poisoning it.

13. **Allergic to magic:** The character reacts unexpectedly to the appearance of a fey being, a spell, a faerie artifact, or similar and must succeed on a difficulty 4 Might defense task or fall into a deep sleep of indeterminate length.

14. **Wish upon a star (level 5):** A falling star of green fire streaks down and impacts; PCs who fail a Speed defense task suffer 5 points of damage and must deal with the antagonistic fey creature that steps out of the crater.

15. **Angry ants:** Whispering insults, obscenities, and slurs, angry ants surge up from the ground and attempt to pull the PCs down.

16. **Falling house:** A house on legs stumbles, and the PCs must succeed on a difficulty 4 Speed defense task or suffer 8 points of damage and, on a failed difficulty 6 Might defense task, become buried under the rubble.

17. **Spoken curse:** An entity curses the character(s). Is it a real curse, or just a passing threat? Only time will tell.

18. **Trapped:** When the characters attempt to use the magic door or exit they expect will take them either home or to some safe spot, they discover it no longer works, or instead takes them into a dank dungeon where a cruel shadow elf waits.

19. **Three blind mice, see how they run:** A slidikin with a carving knife of sharpness attacks the characters.

20. **Inevitable dragon:** A dragon learns of the PCs, first investigating them in human shape under false pretenses, before deciding how it will ambush them and take all their treasures for itself.

Prince of summer, page 146

Midnight scrabbler, page 143

Troll, page 95

Feral tree, page 95

Razorblade butterflies, page 95

Witch, page 330

Goblin, page 297

Angry ants, page 95

Shadow elf, page 313

Slidikin, page 315

Dragon, page 287

Carving knife of sharpness, page 92

RACIAL DESCRIPTORS

In a fairy tale setting, GMs may want changelings and pixies to be mechanically different from humans. Below are some possibilities for how this might work.

CHANGELING

You grew up in the normal world but discovered—or perhaps you knew all along—that you weren't really who everyone thought you were. That's because when you were still very young, the child whose name you have now was stolen, and you were put in its place. Abandoned by your people and distrusted by the mundanes who sense your otherworldliness, you are prone to falling into deep funks. However, you are just as adept at pulling yourself out them when the situation demands it. If nothing else, you're supremely adaptable.

You have the following characteristics:

Innovator: +4 to your Intellect Pool.

Face-taker: When you expend 2 XP, you can change your appearance over the course of one minute to look like someone else of about your size who you've had direct contact with or from whom you have a piece of hair, flesh, or object they handled often. You lose the ability to return to your previous look unless you have the same components at hand for that previous look to initiate the change.

Changeable: When you fail at a task, you can change the way you go about achieving it and roll twice on the second attempt and take the higher result. For example, instead of trying to convince the officer you are in the office after dark on legitimate business, you might elect to flee.

Skill: People never know what to think about you. You are trained in deception.

Inability: Your fluid nature leaves you less resistant to physical threats. The difficulty of any Might defense task is increased by one step.

Fragile: When you fail a Might defense roll to avoid damage, you take 1 extra point of damage.

Additional Equipment: You have an amulet with a strange symbol on it, the only link you have with your past, however enigmatic.

Initial Link to the Starting Adventure: From the following list of options, choose how you became involved in the first adventure.

1. The PCs discovered you weren't quite human, but by then you were already friends.

2. You wanted to find your place of origin, and the PCs offered to help you find it.

3. Everything was fine until "faerie hunters" turned up at your home and tried to kill you, and succeeded with your family. You gathered the PCs to help you track down the murderers.

4. You helped the PCs deal with a small infestation from Faerie.

SUGGESTED FOCI FOR A FAIRY TALE GAME

Foci appropriate for crime and espionage, and childhood adventure settings might also be appropriate for a fairy tale setting.

Calculates the Incalculable
Changes Shape*
Commands Mental
    Powers
Consorts With the Dead
Crafts Unique Objects
Doesn't Do Much
Eliminates Occult Threats*
Entertains
Explores Dark Places
Fell Through A Rabbit
    Hole*
Fights Dirty
Figures Things Out*
Finds The Flaw in All
    Things*
Focuses Mind Over
    Matter
Governs*
Helps Their Friends*

Howls at the Moon
Hunts Outcasts
Hunts With Great Skill
Infiltrates
Interprets the Law
Is Hunted by Moths*
Is Idolized by Millions
Is Licensed to Carry
Leads
Learns Quickly*
Likes to Break Things*
Lives in the Wilderness
Looks for Trouble
Masters Weaponry
Moves Like a Cat
Murders
Needs No Weapon
Never Says Die
Negotiates Matters of Life
    and Death*

Operates Undercover
Plays Too Many Games*
Runs Away*
Sees Beyond
Serves In An Elite Military
    Squad*
Separates Mind From Body
Slays Monsters*
Solves Mysteries
Throws With Deadly
    Accuracy
Was Foretold*
Wields Two Weapons at
    Once
Works For A Living*
Works the Back Alleys
Wonders*
Works the System
Would Rather Be Reading
*New in this book

Character Focus, page 90

Chapter 12: Modern, page 244

Suggested types and additional equipment for a contemporary fairy tale setting are the same as in a modern setting, so refer to Chapter 12: Modern in the Cypher System Rulebook for that information.

SUGGESTED CREATURES AND NPCS FOR A FAIRY TALE GAME

Assassin
Cambion*
Crime boss
Cryptic moth*
Detective
Djini
Dragon
Erlking*
Faerie*
Ghost
Giant

Giant rat
Giant snake
Giant spider
Goblin
Guard
Mad creation*
Midnight shambler*
Mokuren
Nuppeppo
Occultist
Priest*

Prince(ss) of summer*
Professor*
Secret agent
Shadow elf
Shoe thief*
Slidikin
Soldier
Thug/bandit
Werewolf
Witch
*New in this book

OTHER CREATURES AND NPCS FOR A FAIRY TALE GAME

Most fey creatures of level 2 or higher regain 1 point of health per round while above 0 unless wounded by silvered or cold-forged weapons.

Angry ants: swarm as a level 1 creature; constant whispering insults, slurs, obscenities; those physically attacked must also succeed on a difficulty 3 defense task or be stunned and lose their next turn

Feral tree: level 3; Armor 3; rooted in place; lashing branches attack up to three characters as a single action and on a failed Might defense task, hold the victim in place until they can escape

Nymph: level 3, stealth and positive social interactions as level 6

Pixie: level 2, stealth and finding lost items as level 6

Razorblade butterflies: level 1; swarm as a level 3 creature able to attack all creatures in an area an immediate distance across

Talking Cat: level 1, knowledge tasks as level 7

Troll: level 6; claws inflict 7 points of damage and grabs victim until escape; grabbed creature takes 10 points of damage per round; trolls regain 3 points of health per round

Reversals and lying NPCs are common in fairy tale adventures.

CHAPTER 6

CHILDHOOD ADVENTURE

Horror, page 236

Science Fiction,
page 250

Childhood adventure books, television shows, and movies are a genre that often mix elements of horror or science fiction. But the focus of the genre is on the kids, usually in the range of eleven to seventeen years of age, who encounter strange and unexplained happenings, who must then do something about it. Childhood adventure distinguishes its young characters as active heroes, not victims. Normally, protecting children is a common motivating influence for adult characters in all kinds of stories and games. By focusing on the child as the protagonist instead, a reader, viewer, or an RPG game player gains a real sense that the stakes are somehow higher.

Popular childhood adventure scenarios include children finding and aiding a misunderstood alien, children dealing with the aftermath of a disaster in the absence of all the adults who are dead or missing, or children fending off the attacks of some kind of horrific monster that adults believe to be imaginary. Many other childhood adventures are possible, and fiction is

littered with them. One of the most popular follows the exploits of Harry Potter and his friends as he learns of his wizarding background and begins instruction in the magical arts, courtesy of J. K. Rowling.

In fact, childhood adventure stories are so popular that literature has its term for the genre: Young Adult fiction (usually abbreviated to YA fiction).

CREATING A CHILDHOOD ADVENTURE

In many cases, childhood adventures in RPGs don't make long-term campaigns, but instead serve as short-term experiences where players try something new, or at least something they don't normally do: play as a teenage (or pre-teen) character.

Childhood adventures have their biggest impact on players if the setting is somewhat familiar. Which means that a blend of modern with some science fiction, fantasy, or horror is the most popular. By using the modern world as the basis for a childhood

adventure, the GM doesn't need to spend too much time doing basic worldbuilding.

The task before the GM is instead that of devising an overarching plot that'll challenge players. But as mentioned, the novelty of playing as children, all by itself, can go a long way, all on its own. When you're a kid, the importance of schoolwork, being home before dark, and watching after a younger sibling takes on additional import. When the GM throws in a monster in the basement, a face in the window, or a dream that everyone shares, seeing the threat through a child's eyes is part of the charm.

One way to create a childhood adventure is to make sure you're aware of all the previous art to draw inspiration and a sense of priorities and mood from. For starters, watch the eight episode miniseries Stranger Things by the Duffer Brothers, the movies Super 8 by J. J. Abrams, E.T. by Melissa Mathison (screenplay) and Steven Spielberg (director), and The Goonies by Chris Columbus (screenplay), Steven Spielberg (story), and Richard Donner (director). Then read some

childhood adventure fiction, this includes both the previously mentioned Harry Potter and the Sorcerer's Stone by J. K. Rowling and the classic To Kill A Mockingbird by Harper Lee. If you've got the time and the interest, continue with A Wrinkle In Time by Madeleine L'engle, The Lion, The Witch, and the Wardrobe by C. S. Lewis, The Golden Compass by Philip Pullman, and so many more.

RUNNING A CHILDHOOD ADVENTURE GAME

A major theme of childhood adventure is simple: kids helping kids. Sure, kid PCs might also help their parents, their mentors, and so on. But helping your friend who's being haunted, who is lost, who is different, and who is missing is a great place to start.

Another theme is how kid PCs deal with the issues facing them either without the notice of the adult world or in the face of outright disbelief and claims of "imaginary friends" and similar from adults who kids finally relate their problems to. Some

> *Kid protagonists might require a patron or mentor to help them accomplish goals that can only be accomplished in the adult realm.*

parents simply don't have time to listen to their child describe what is immediately assumed to be just a story. Others will listen and pretend to go along with a tall tale of monsters in the garden shed, but they don't actually believe it. Pretty soon, kid PCs must realize they've got to take care of the problem on their own.

That said, kid protagonists might require a patron or mentor to help them accomplish goals that can only be accomplished in the adult realm. For instance, in the Danny Dunn series (Danny Dunn and the Homework Machine; Danny Dunn, Time Traveler; Danny Dunn, Invisible boy; and so on), the protagonists rely to a greater or lesser extent on Professor Euclid Bullfinch as their patron. A professor makes a great patron, but other NPCs could accomplish similar tasks. An uncle who's a soldier. An older sibling who's a priest. Maybe even an aunt who's secretly a witch.

Kids also need a "safe" place to plan their adventures. This could be as simple as a friend's mom's basement, with a handy supply of pizza wheels, potato chips, and soda laid in by that friend's mother. A treehouse, a room at school set aside for the debate team, a shed that a friend's dad said the kids could use, or even a secret meeting place in an abandoned opera house at the center of town could also serve. What's important is that kids should feel somewhat safe in their secret base, at least most of the time. You might include one scenario where the base is under attack, but that should be the exception. Kids need a fallback or the childhood adventure you're

running risks turning into something much more harrowing and bleak. This might be just fine, if it suits your tastes. After all, the movie Pan's Labyrinth by Guillermo del Toro depicted a kind of childhood adventure, though your interpretation of what was going on can go one of two ways.

Finally, kids need some means of getting around. In many cases, bicycles are perfect. Not only because they allow the characters mobility, but because of what they represent: freedom. Bicycles don't require asking a parent or older sibling for a ride; they allow kid PCs to be autonomous, at least within a limited range. In a more urban environment, kids probably have subway passes, or in a setting that isn't a throwback to the 80s, maybe a ride-sharing app pre-installed on their smartphones by their parents.

CHILDHOOD ADVENTURE THREATS

The Childhood Adventure Threats table provides more dangers to throw at your PCs playing as kids. These dangers can be incidental to the larger plot or help you generate a larger plot. They're not meant to *be* the major story arc, though you could probably spin some of them out to serve that purpose. Most of these threats should be presented as GM intrusions. If you are rolling for results instead of choosing, ignore or change results that don't fit your game. For instance, if the PCs are dealing with a science fiction-inspired alien, ignore the results that suggest that ghosts or killer clowns come after the characters.

Professor, page 157

Soldier, elite, page 158

Priest, page 157

Witch, page 330

CHILDHOOD ADVENTURE THREATS

Bully, page 100

1	**Bullies in the alley:** Three bullies ambush one or more of the PCs at an unexpected location or time.
2	**Freak storm (level 1):** Inflicts 1 point of ambient damage per minute each minute the character fails a difficulty 3 Might defense task; reduces vision and chills characters, threatening worse with prolonged exposure.
3	**Rotten board (level 3):** While exploring the haunted house, old farm, or similar structure, a rotten board plunges PC into basement inflicting 3 points of damage on a failed difficulty 4 Speed defense roll.

4 **Bicycle breakdown:** One of the characters' bikes throws a chain, requiring a difficulty 3 Intellect task to repair it.

5 **Detention:** A character is set up by an NPC child, who threatens to embroil the character in an altercation where a teacher or other authority figure will be forced to step in and punish the offenders with detention, a truancy violation, or an unexpected trip home.

6 **Sinister authority figure:** A principle, a police officer, a mysterious man in a suit with a government badge, or some other authority figure takes an interest in the character(s) and begins to work against them.

7 **Bad dreams:** One PC suffers from a series of debilitating nightmares, and must succeed on a difficulty 3 Intellect defense task or be treated as dazed for several hours, during this time the difficulty of all tasks attempted by the character increases by one step.

8 **Unexpected roadblock:** Before the PCs can proceed, they are stopped by a parade blocking their path through town, a parent who demands that the PC finish their homework before leaving the house, a stolen bike, or some similar delay.

9 **Dilapidated house (level 4):** The old house, underpass tunnel, or cellar under the crazy old man's house collapses. Characters suffer 4 points of damage, and on a failed difficulty 4 Speed task are buried under suffocating rubble until they can escape or are rescued.

10 **Spiders:** Spiders of abnormal size infest this locked room, sub-basement, or subway tunnel.

11 **Ghost:** While investigating, a potentially "friendly" ghost appears before the PCs. It doesn't realize it's dead, and it might not be until later that the PCs realize the strange NPC who told them important information has been dead for thirty years.

12 **Dire circus:** Is the circus in town just a regular troupe of entertainers, or is one of the clowns secretly a killer?

13 **Missing parent:** One of the PCs' parents mysteriously goes missing. Is it related to the adventure they're already on, or unrelated? Did something bad happen, or did the parent's car just break down?

14 **Missing younger sibling:** As with a missing parent, a younger sibling doesn't show up when called. Are they over at a friend's house, or does the disappearance have something to do with the adventure the PCs are on? Either way, the PC is likely to be blamed, "You were supposed to be watching your sister!"

15 **Suspicious stranger:** The PCs realize that some guy in a white van is following them around, but trying to appear inconspicuous. Is he a random creeper, an agent of the organization the PCs have discovered as being involved in their adventure, or a detective hired by an estranged parent to keep tabs on one of the kid PCs?

16 **Accident:** A car threatens to barrel into a PC on a bike, or a car the PCs are getting a ride in suddenly blows a tire.

17 **Childhood illness:** One or more of the characters is struck down with a childhood illness like chickenpox, strep throat, or similar sickness for a couple days, during this time the difficulty of all tasks attempted by the character increases by two steps.

18 **Bees or wasps:** The PCs accidentally disturb a hive of stinging insects, that boil out of their hive and attack as swarm like a level 1 creature.

19 **Bear, black:** A black bear (escaped from the zoo or their natural environment) is disturbed while dumpster diving or investigating the garbage dump. The bear could be scared off but might be dangerous if not handled properly.

20 **Eggs:** The PCs find large eggs laid in some hidden spot. The eggs could be glowing alien eggs, dinosaur eggs, or something less dramatic, like ostrich or turtle eggs. If disturbed, whatever laid the eggs might come looking for the PCs.

Giant spider, page 297

Ghost, page 293

Killer clown, page 141

Bear, black: level 3, attacks as level 4

SUGGESTED TYPES FOR A CHILDHOOD ADVENTURE GAME

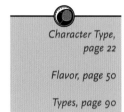

Character Type,
page 22

Flavor, page 50

Types, page 90

Role	Type
Finder	Explorer with stealth flavor
Delinquent	Warrior
Troublemaker	Speaker
Nerd	Explorer with knowledge flavor

SUGGESTED FOCI FOR A CHILDHOOD ADVENTURE GAME

Calculates the Incalculable
Doesn't Do Much
Entertains
Explores Dark Places
Fights Dirty
Figures Things Out*
Helps Their Friends*

Leads
Likes to Break Things*
Looks For Trouble
Moves Like a Cat
Plays Too Many Games*
Runs Away*
Solves Mysteries

Throws With Deadly Accuracy
Wonders*
Would Rather Be Reading

*New in this book

SUGGESTED CREATURES AND NPCS FOR A CHILDHOOD ADVENTURE GAME

Creatures, page 126

NPCs, page 152

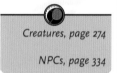

Creatures, page 274

NPCs, page 334

Bogeyman*
Detective
Erlking*
Faerie*
Giant rat
Giant snake
Giant spider
Ghost

Grey
Guard
Killer clown*
Mokuren
Occultist
Priest*
Professor*
Soldier*

Soldier, elite*
Thug
Vampire
Wendigo
Werewolf
Witch

*New in this book

OTHER CREATURES AND NPCS FOR A CHILDHOOD ADVENTURE GAME

Bully: level 2; health 8; verbal taunt attack dazes target who fails an intellect defense roll until target inflicts damage on or escapes from the bully

Crazy old neighbor: level 3, entertainment and deception tasks as level 5

Innocuous animal: level 1

Janitor, typical: level 3

Rabid dog: level 4; bite inflicts fear of rabies and if not treated, could lead to rabies

Teacher, typical: level 2, knowledge tasks as level 4

ADDITIONAL CHILDHOOD ADVENTURE EQUIPMENT

INEXPENSIVE ITEMS

Weapons	Notes
Kitchen knife	Light weapon (won't last long)

Other Items	
Band-aids	+1 on die roll for healing tasks
Basketball, baseball, soccer ball, etc.	+1 on die roll for positive interaction checks with other kids
Book of magic tricks	+1 on die roll for sleight of hand tasks after ten minutes of reference
Candy	+1 on die roll for positive interaction checks with other kids
Cheap flashlight	Provides light for several hours (won't last long)
Crayons	

Duct tape	Useful and ubiquitous
Journal and pen	
Jump rope	Useful when no rope is to be had
Permanent markers	
Plastic bag	Useful and ubiquitous (won't last long)

MODERATELY PRICED ITEMS

Weapons

Baseball bat	Light or Medium weapon
Hockey stick	Medium weapon
Wrist rocket	Light ranged weapon

Armor

Leather "letter" jacket	Light armor
Football equipment	Light armor

Kids find some things useful that adults might overlook

Other Items

Backpack	
Bedroll	
Compass	Asset to tasks involving navigation
Crowbar	
Energy bar	Feeds one person for one meal, but hunger remains
First aid kit	Asset for healing tasks
Fishing pole and lures	
Flashlight, rechargeable	Provides light for up to eight hours, recharges in one hour
Game (tabletop or video)	
Kite	
New sneakers	+1 to die rolls involving running, jumping, and climbing
Padlock with keys	
Portable lamp	
Rope	Nylon, 50 feet (15 m)
Scouting multipurpose knife	Asset to small repair tasks
Skateboard or rollerblades	with practice, rider can move a long distance each round
Sleeping bag	

EXPENSIVE ITEMS

Other Items

Bicycle	
Binoculars	
Smartphone or walkie-talkie	
Tablet computer or laptop	Asset to tasks involving finding things out

HANDLING PCS AS CHILDREN

The character creation process outlined by the *Cypher System Rulebook* creates fully competent, adult characters. To account for playing children, the GM could adopt one of the following optional rules.

OPTIONAL RULE: YOUNG ADULT ADJUSTMENTS

Young, page 13

Tiers Above Sixth, page 234

The Young descriptor described in Part 1 is one way to model a child PC. However, if *all* the PCs are playing children, the novelty of everyone having the same descriptor quickly wanes. One way to deal with this is to allow the PCs to make their characters normally, including choosing any descriptor that seems appropriate for their character, except for Young.

Then the PCs can apply the following adjustments to their characters, as appropriate to their age category.

AGE 9-13
Slight: -4 to your Might Pool
Vulnerable: Adults look out for you. You are trained in all pleasant social interactions with adults.

Inability: The difficulty of any Might-based task is increased by one step.
Inability: The difficulty of any task involving knowledge is increased by one step.

AGE 14-17
Youthful: -2 to your Might Pool
Inability: The difficulty of any task involving knowledge is increased by one step.

OPTIONAL RULE: TIER CAP

Standard Cypher System rules have six tiers of advancement (or even higher, if using the optional Tiers Above Sixth rule). However, some genres might not support that kind of power-up of character abilities. In particular, kids grow older and the campaign ends, or the game moves into another phase. For this reason, you should consider applying a tier cap of 3 to childhood adventure games with kids of up to thirteen years old, and a tier cap of 4 for childhood adventure games featuring PCs who are aged fourteen to seventeen.

The key to a great childhood adventure is to get the PCs invested in their characters. Roleplaying a youthful character might be a challenge to some, but it is well worth the extra work once everyone gets into the spirit

PART 3
GRITTY GENRES

CHAPTER 7

HISTORICAL

W ho says history is boring? Especially when you can bring what was past to life once more with exciting RPG scenarios starring your PCs. Historical games and fiction are based on actual historical events and set in a historical time and place. However, that doesn't mean there's no room for variation and surprise. Within the context of a game, anything could happen, starting with characters who may have never existed in *actual* history but whose presence helps tell a better story, or in the case of the PCs, allows your players to participate in something that was previously only relegated to history books.

A great historical RPG experience is one that balances authenticity with a compelling adventure plot. Given that lots of history fails to record all the people present at any given event, specific dialogue, and other actual minor details, the GM has a lot of leeway when balancing accurate historical events with elements created to make a particular adventure or campaign memorable.

HISTORINESS

"Historiness" is quality of seeming historical or evoking a historical feeling, even if it's not necessarily historical. If you're going for a strictly historical game, then replicating events from historical fiction may not be to your liking. That said, a gold mine of interesting setting options in fiction set in historical time exists. Consider the works of Jane Austen, Charles Dickens, or even William Shakespeare. Imagine a game weaving in and out of Pride and Prejudice, A Tale of Two Cities, or Macbeth.

You could go one step further, if you've decided strict historical games aren't for you by mixing fiction set in historical times with elements of horror or science fiction. Examples of this kind of fiction include Pride And Prejudice And Zombies by Seth Grahame-Smith, Penny Dreadful (the TV series), The League of Extraordinary Gentlemen comic, and Shades of Milk and Honey by Mary Robinette Kowal.

CREATING A HISTORICAL ADVENTURE

One of the draws of playing in a historical adventure is the thrill of "being there" when something important happens. Thus, in many cases, historical adventures in RPGs shouldn't be designed as campaigns, but instead serve as short-term experiences where players try something new, or at least something they don't normally do: play as figures involved in a momentous historical event.

Historical games should take cues from the closely related areas of historical fiction and historical re-enactment. The lessons of great historical fiction include the following.

- The GM should make sure to anchor the characters with problems or conflicts that connect them to the chosen time period; make sure PC backgrounds contain one relevant detail to the chosen historical setting.
- The GM shouldn't fall into the trap of assuming that just because history is often presented along with old paintings, drawings, or blurred black and white photographs, that history itself was drab. Dramatic events, surprising twists, and unexpected situations are just as likely in a historical adventure as any other kind.
- What's the point of a historical adventure if there is no suspense? Sure, everyone knows what happens by the end of any given historical battle, but the stories of individuals within those fights are not known. Will they live? Will they succeed in their mission? And what are the consequences? Think of all the war movies that have been filmed relying on that exact latitude to tell great stories.
- Make sure you know when the campaign ends. Maybe it's when the PCs successfully accomplish a specific task, but it might be externally timed to when a historical event takes place, whether they are attempting to offer aid, thwart it, or merely be aware of it as they attempt to do something that history hasn't recorded.

- Don't create more than you need to. Be ready to tell the PCs what they see and who they encounter when they are introduced to a historical location or person, but don't worry about things that the PCs are likely to never see. Yes, figure out what kind of currency is used, but getting a super-accurate list of prices just isn't necessary; the PCs will take your word for the cost of items, and for many other details. You're evoking a historical setting with your game, not writing a book report.

RUNNING A HISTORICAL GAME

Preparation is important in a historical game, and most of that entails choosing a historical period—or a specific historical event—to set your game. Given that all of history can serve, you won't lack for resources. Here are a few possibilities. Of course, the farther back you choose to set your historical game, the less information on specific events is available. On the other hand, that frees you up to get creative.

Once you choose the historical period and any special historical events you want to include in your adventure or campaign, direct your PCs to an appropriate set of foci. Alternately, you might decide to have your PCs play *as* historically significant figures, but if you do this, you may want to create their characters ahead of time. Most GMs will probably want to save historically significant individuals for use as NPCs.

PREHISTORY

If you're interested in exploring made up scenarios based solely on the fossil record, which includes dozens of different primates living in presumably primitive conditions, maybe this is the period for you. Though your mileage may vary, short scenarios like those told in pieces of fiction such as Quest for Fire and Clan of the Cave Bear could be entertaining.

CLASSICAL ANTIQUITY

Focusing on the history centered on the Mediterranean Sea, scenarios set in classical antiquity would include some element of ancient Rome or ancient Greece. During this time, Greek and Roman influence extended across Europe, North Africa, and the Middle East. Mashups with

the historical setting and the mythological setting could well include this time period.

People of ancient Greece had names like Aeschylus, Agape, Alexandra, Demetria, Diokles, Uripides, Heraclius, and Olympias.

People of ancient Rome had names like Aemiliana, Agrippa, Antonina, Augustus, Blasius, Brutus, Camilla, Cassian, Domitia, and Fabian.

ANCIENT EGYPT

This period runs from around 3100 B.C. to 332 B.C.—almost thirty centuries, until it was finally conquered by Alexander the Great. Ancient Egypt was the preeminent civilization in the Mediterranean world. The great pyramids of the Old Kingdom, the many hidden graves of great pharaohs, and the military conquests of the New Kingdom, this period and region is rife with game possibilities.

People of ancient Egypt has names like Aat, Addaya, Ahmes, Baskakeren, Bek, Cleomenes, Dedelion, Djedi, Duatentopet, and Hwernef.

SRI VIJAYA

In Southeast Asia, Sri Vijava was a city-state on the island of Sumatra in Indonesia that created a mighty trading empire that ruled the nearby seas from around 650 to 1377. The trade empire reached into Java, Kamjua, and even China. Rivalries also abounded, but this fortunate state was also a major vector for the spread of Buddhism.

People of Sri Vijaya had names like Balaputradewa, Dapunta, Indravarman, Rudra, Dharmasetu, Dharanindra, Samaragrawira, and Sumatrabhumi.

AMERICAN REVOLUTION

The American Revolution, taking place between 1775 to 1783, was a revolt against monarchy and set the stage for one of the most influential countries of the world to rise. Famous battles abound, including the Battle of Lexington, the Battle of Concord, and the Battle of Bunker Hill. The fledgling country's founding fathers penned the Declaration of Independence, drafted by Thomas Jefferson. A host of other important historical events occurred during this period, making it a period worthy of a historical RPG scenario.

People in America at the time of the revolution had names like Amity, Abner,

A fantastic look into the culture and reality of turn of the century exploration lies in the pages of The Lost City of Z: A Tale of Deadly Obsession in the Amazon by David Grann

Abraham, Aphra, Barnabas, Charity, Clement, Eli, Ester, and Hepzibah.

ANCIENT CHINA

There are numerous records of the many different dynasties that ruled China reaching back to at least 2070 B.C. and the Xia dynasty. If you'd like to create an adventure or campaign arc featuring emperors and Chinese dynasties, consider setting your game during the Han dynasty that lasted from 202 B.C. to 220 C.E.. This period is described as a golden age of Chinese history, thanks to a long period of stability and prosperity. At this time, Confucianism (a humanistic philosophy) was recognized and elevated as something all wise people attempt to follow. Math, writing, and other arts also saw rapid development.

People in ancient China had names like Ah, Ao, Bai, Buwei, Chao, Da, Fai, Guan, Ji, Kang, Lei, Lun, Qi, Wan, and Xin.

WORLD WAR II

It's possible that more books and movies have been created about this war than any other in-world history. Hitler, the Nazis, the Blitzkrieg, death camps in Germany, the bombing of Pearl Harbor, breaking the Axis code created with Enigma machines, and on and on. Creating a game where PCs are soldiers in a battle, agents in the field, scientists, diplomats, or some combination of all these would make an impressive campaign or an unforgettable one-shot.

People in America at the time of the Second World War had names like Magdalene, James, Evelyn, Donald, Dorothy, Ronald, Joyce, Marilyn, Walter, Billy, and Delores.

19TH CENTURY EXPLORATION

The 1800s and early 1900s were a time of major exploration. A short campaign where PCs are part of the exploration team for any one of these historical trips of discovery would be amazing. During this period of discovery, Darwin's second voyage on the HMS Beagle happened (1831-1836); Alfred Russel Wallace explored regions of the Amazon; David Livingstone explored the interior of Africa (1849–1855); many tried to find the North Pole and Robert Peary claimed he did in 1909; the South Pole was almost reached in 1841 by James Clark Ross, but it wasn't actually reached until 1909 by Roald Amundsen.

People in Europe during the 1800s had names like Albert, Agnes, Ambrose, Bess, Cole, Eudora, Jane, Lucas, Obediah, Nellie, Raymond, Ruth, and Stanley.

EDO PERIOD JAPAN

The Land of the Rising Sun enjoyed a long period of economic and cultural prosperity during the historical Edo period, which occurred between 1603 and 1868. The rule of the Tokugawa shogunate and Karou—essentially feudal governors and regional feudal lords, respectively—remained under the putative control of the Emperor, but the Shogun in Edo held the most power. Partly thanks to founder Ieyasu Tokugawa's forward-thinking policies and philosophies (developed from Confucian teachings), most Nihon natives had a chance to live comfortably and enjoy popular arts and culture that, in previous eras, were enjoyed only by the wealthy and powerful.

People of the Edo Period in Japan had names like Sakai, Toda, Yamaoka, Abe, Fujiwara, Okudaira, Sugawara, Hatakeyama, Sou, Chousokeabe, Reizei, Nikaidou, Shigenoi, Higashisanjou, and Hirano.

MEDIEVAL EUROPE

Many fantasy RPGs are described as "medieval" fantasy, but to run a historical medieval game, minus wizards, dragons, and kindly fairy godmothers, promises to be a far more gritty experience. That said, many misconceptions exist about what life was truly like in the Middle Ages. Luckily, internet resources being what they are, a little research will produce all manner of interesting facts, and maps of castles and countries for a medieval historical game to unfold.

People of medieval Europe had names like Adam, Agnes, Alice, Nicholas, Joan, Geoffrey, Margery, Gilbert, Ralf, Cecily, Henry, Isabella, and Roger.

AMERICAN OLD WEST

Gambling, train robberies, gangs of desperados, gold rush towns, and camping on the open range under the stars. All kinds of adventures are possible in the Old West for PCs who wants to wear spurs or who are wanted by the law.

People in America in the region and historical period broadly known as the "Old West" had names like John, Mary, William, Anna, James, Emma, George, Elizabeth, Charles, Margaret, Frank, Minnie, Joseph, and Ida.

Wears Spurs, page 67

Is Wanted by the Law, page 36

Crime and espionage, page 110

HISTORICAL ARTIFACTS

The concept of artifacts is probably inappropriate for a historical setting without some kind of supernatural, fantastical, or science fiction element. That said, objects of mystery such as the Antikythera mechanism (an ancient analog computer and orrery used to predict eclipses and other astronomical positions) reveal that both the ancient world—and by extension more recent historical periods—contained fascinating and useful objects that were anachronistic for their period. Most such artifacts were likely the creations of philosophers, lone geniuses, and similar figures. Of course, historical settings set very close to the present, such as a campaign involved with spying during World War II, would likely have access to artifacts similar to those presented in the crime and espionage genre chapter.

TIME TRAVEL GAMING

The material provided in the historical genre chapter is all completely applicable for a campaign revolving around time travel. Bouncing the characters around between World War II, the Renaissance, the 1930s and then back to ancient Greece can be fun and interesting, especially if the PCs are tracking down some kind of transtemporal problem or criminal (or attempting to loot history, like the movie Time Bandits). However, this, of course, requires a bit more prep on your part, because rather than researching just one historical setting, the GM must be prepared to allow the PCs to play in several historical periods, possibly more than one during a given play session.

For a time travel game, it's likely that PCs serve as operatives of some kind of transtemporal agency that's either pledged to protect time from saboteurs or pledged to create some sort of fork in time that wouldn't normally occur so as to improve the chances of the group's existence. Other possibilities exist, of course. A popular time traveling framing device is to serve as companions of a famous time lord whose name is an eternal mystery.

Time traveling PCs might eventually head into the future, whereupon the contents of the hard science fiction genre described in this chapter, and the science fiction setting described in the corebook also become useful for preparing for your adventures.

SUGGESTED TYPES FOR A HISTORICAL GAME

Role	Type
Constable (or night watchman)	Explorer with combat flavor
Detective	Explorer with stealth and skills and knowledge flavor
Knight	Warrior
Pirate	Explorer with stealth flavor
Tutor	Speaker
Merchant	Speaker with skills and knowledge flavor
Smith	Speaker with some warrior abilities and skills and knowledge flavor
Playwright	Speaker
Noble	Speaker with skills and knowledge flavor
Explorer	Explorer
Priest	Speaker

Types, page 22

Flavor, page 50

SUGGESTED FOCI FOR A HISTORICAL GAME

Calculates the Incalculable
Crafts Unique Objects
Descends from Nobility*
Doesn't Do Much
Entertains
Explores*
Explores Dark Places
Fights Dirty
Hunts Outcasts
Hunts With Great Skill
Infiltrates
Interprets the Law

Is Idolized by Millions
Is Licensed to Carry
Is Sworn To The Crown*
Is Wanted by the Law*
Leads
Lives in the Wilderness
Looks for Trouble
Masters Weaponry
Moves Like a Cat
Murders
Needs No Weapon
Never Says Die

Operates Undercover
Sailed Beneath the Jolly Roger*
Solves Mysteries
Throws With Deadly Accuracy
Wears Spurs
Wields Two Weapons at Once
Works the Back Alleys
Works the System
Would Rather Be Reading

*New in this book

SUGGESTED CREATURES AND NPCS FOR A HISTORICAL GAME

Assassin
Crime boss
Detective
Detective, master*
General

Guard
Marauder*
Occultist (with no magic)
Priest*
Professor*

Secret agent
Soldier*
Soldier, elite*
Thug/bandit

*New in this book

OTHER CREATURES AND NPCS FOR A SCIENCE FICTION GAME

Cat: level 1, Speed defense as level 3
Dodo: level 1
Dog: level 2, perception as level 3
Dog, guard: level 3, attacks and perception as level 4
Horse: level 3; moves a long distance each round

Merchant: level 1, haggling as level 3
Noble: level 2, pleasant social interaction as level 4
Rat: level 1
Serf: level 2, animal handling as level 3
Snake, poisonous: level 1, attacks as level 4
Warhorse: level 4; moves a long distance each round

ADDITIONAL HISTORICAL EQUIPMENT

In many historical periods, the default equipment described as Additional Fantasy Equipment is also available. If your historical setting moves much beyond the 17th century, add in additional select items from the items described under Additional Modern Equipment.

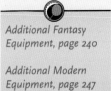

Additional Fantasy Equipment, page 240

Additional Modern Equipment, page 247

CHAPTER 8

CRIME AND ESPIONAGE

The crime and espionage setting is a specific section of the modern genre. A crime and espionage game enjoys many of the same benefits and has some of the same challenges that other modern games face. On the plus side, players can easily understand the context. They know what the internet is, the utility of a smartphone, what they can expect from law enforcement, and much more. This familiarity allows players to get into character more easily, in some ways. For the same reason, the GM has it easier—unless players and GMs let themselves get bogged down in checking facts, because everyone knows that information about how long it takes authorities to arrive after 911 is called is out there, just one more internet search away. Verisimilitude is key.

The particular subgenre of crime and espionage is one where most if not all the PCs are involved in some capacity with law enforcement, crime forensics, espionage, and (or) international spying. This means that for most players, personal familiarity

fails to bridge this gap. That is unless you're talking entertainment, which is replete with examples.

CREATING A CRIME AND ESPIONAGE SETTING

Since you're placing your crime and espionage game in the real world the only worldbuilding you need to do is to come up with—or elaborate on—the particular special agencies that will feature in your game.

Thus, if you're creating a game where PCs will be solving a series of potentially connected crimes, maybe you want them to be detectives, forensic specialists, and consultants associated with a particular police precinct. Alternatively, the PCs might be associated with an institute that is made up entirely of specialized consultants. On the other hand, maybe the PCs might own a detective agency.

Alternatively, if you want an espionage game, and spies are in the mix, the

infiltrating characters might be agents of a special department of a national government intelligence agency such as the FBI, FSB, CIA, DIA, NSA. Of course, remember that not all spying is sponsored by nation states. A lot of it is corporate spying, too, and many semi-secret organizations exist that sell their services to said corporate organizations.

As important as it is to determine the nature of the game you want and the agency or organization that your player characters will be part of, it's even more important to determine the central mystery or crime—or series of related mysteries and crimes—that will occupy your PC detectives, consultants, and spies. There are a few ways you can go, and they're not mutually exclusive.

As is popular on many crime drama shows, such as Bones, Law & Order, Castle, and Person of Interest, you could provide a series of crimes that the PCs must investigate and solve over the course of just two or three game sessions. However,

You could turn the usual expectation of a crime and espionage game on its head and have your characters be part of a criminal gang, the mob, or just a group that's on the wrong side of the law for perhaps very good reasons, even if those reasons don't impress the authorities.

some aspect of at least one of these crimes might be tied to an overarching story arc that reveals itself a little at a time over the course of several adventures. A criminal mastermind, like Sherlock's Moriarty, or True Detective's Yellow King. The campaign arc finale is likely one where the PCs finally discover their true nemesis, and hopefully bring that person or organization to justice.

If you're creating an espionage game, watch shows like Leverage, Burn Notice, Alias, and Blacklist. Lots of great movies come to mind, too. Too many to list, but consider many shows from the James Bond franchise, the Mission Impossible movies (and older shows), the Jason Bourne movies, the recent Man from U.N.C.L.E. (and older shows), and so on.

There's quite a bit of crossover when it comes to the kinds of individual games and connected campaign arcs. You might want to mix it up a bit by having one of the central game plots revolve around the PCs secretly having been double agents in their past, having the agency the PCs work for disavow them right in the middle of their mission, or have a war start that no one saw coming, complete with a deadly explosion. Maybe a nuclear explosion, if you're feeling like diverging a lot from the real timeline.

RUNNING A CRIME AND ESPIONAGE SETTING

One way to start a crime or espionage game is with a bang: introduce the PC investigators or spies to the problem immediately.

In a crime game, that probably means going to the scene of the crime, sometimes even a murder. Depending on the weapon used in a murder, the body itself becomes a clue. Gunshot wounds are easy—someone used a gun. But what about a body found with no blood? A corpse with crushed bones? A cadaver covered in mold? One with no skin? In addition to being shocking, figuring out the cause of death puts the PCs on their first steps toward solving the crime. Of course, the body may have been moved or damaged after death to hide the actual method of killing, but that's something for the PCs to discover with additional investigation.

In an espionage game, PCs might get a mission briefing from their handler or patron to get things rolling. Mission briefings tend to be slightly more useful than visiting a fresh crime scene, because some lower level investigators have presumably already compiled a list of clues, motives, photos of intended targets of assassination, and so on, and put all that in the briefing. The job of a PC spy is to follow up on the information provided, take out the enemy intelligence agent, and do so while retaining their cover.

In both cases, PCs should expect red herrings.

PCs either try to figure out who did the crime or stop the enemy secret mission before it can succeed. But smart criminals and clever spies try to throw off investigators and counterintelligence. As the GM, it's up to you to figure out what the criminals and spies do to accomplish that goal. They may actively set up a distraction, try to plant evidence on an otherwise innocent bystander, or just rely on the typical red herrings that often occur when investigators with imperfect knowledge try to piece together clues.

Crafting a good red herring involves making sure there is some truth to the evidence of *something* being not quite right with an innocent so that PCs feel like they're on the right track. For instance, the dead body may be known for sleeping

SUSPECT/INFORMANT TRAITS

1	**Nervous tic.** Pick one: Drums fingers, bites nails, cheek twitch, stammers, abdominal tensing, throat clearing.
2	**Obsequious.** Overly polite, rushes to comply with every request.
3	**Crude.** In language and metaphor, this person is crude, maybe on purpose, maybe naturally.
4	**Perfectly polite.** Seems like a normal, well-rounded person.
5	**Dressed to the nines.** This person looks amazing in their fashionable clothing and perfect haircut.
6	**Arrogant.** Can't believe the PCs would suspect them. "Do you know who I am?" No time to waste.
7	**Dead inside.** No apparent empathy for the victim of the crime or consequences of others' bad actions.
8	**Gossips constantly.** At first it seems like this person might have more leads, but nope. They're a gossip.
9	**Holier-than-thou.** Asks PCs if they've accepted the savior, doesn't trust PCs that don't share faith.
10	**Curious.** Constant questions about what else the PCs know related to the topic.
11	**Careful.** Thinks about answers, talks in measured tones, seems careful not to say too much.
12	**Fatalistic.** What's any of it matter? Seems fed up with life and permanently broken.
13	**Fixated.** Obsessed with some unrelated activity or hobby. Possibly fixated on conspiracy theories.
14	**Guilty, but of something else.** This person was involved in some previous illegal activity that no one ever found out about, but one unrelated to any the PCs may be investigating. Pick one: bribery, embezzlement, money laundering, insider trading, robbery, assault, spousal abuse, murder.
15	**Greedy.** Might be willing to talk, but only for some kind of consideration, financial in nature.
16	**Celebrity, minor.** Pick one: YouTube personality, mid-list novel author, d-list comedian/actor, game designer.
17	**Overly skeptical.** Not willing to believe what the PCs are telling them without overwhelming evidence, if then.
18	**Detached, possibly high.** Just kind of drifting through the interview, and life. Drugs possibly involved.
19	**Dying.** In chemotherapy, indicates (if asked) that doctors give them only two months to live.
20	**Slow.** Just not that bright, needs things spelled out, might not get it even then.

around. If it turns out the spouse has no alibi for the time of the murder, motive and opportunity are established. The spouse's obvious desire to not provide an alibi is the red herring. But further investigation shows that the spouse was up to something else slightly illegal or at least embarrassing (perhaps they were also involved in an out-of-wedlock coupling), and they just didn't want to say.

Creating a good red herring—especially in a game centered around solving crime—requires that an innocent NPC has a strong motive making them a good suspect as the murderer or the enemy spy. Simultaneously, make sure the PCs have the opportunity to meet another NPC who seems completely innocent because there's no apparent motive, opportunity, or other immediately obvious connection. But tiny clues here and there should eventually point to this NPC being the true person of interest, allowing the PCs to make the collar.

INTERVIEWING SUSPECTS/INFORMANTS

Either the PCs themselves identify a set of suspects, or they are given a likely set of suspects or informants in a mission briefing. For a game, you probably don't want to include more than three or at most four, since time is limited. Coming up with details of manner, personality, and interest for the suspects is your job, and you might find that easy enough. But to help you along your way, you can roll on the above table to quickly generate an NPC the PCs want to question. One of the suspects or informants the PCs end up talking to might be someone that helps them break the case or is the actual villain or at least the link that points the PCs to who they need to talk with next.

CAMPAIGN ARC

While a crime game may include one or two short mysteries to clear up, and a spy game some relatively quick intelligence gathering

runs to conclude, keep in mind the larger story, or campaign arc. And even if the PCs manage to jail a criminal mastermind or catch the master spy, that criminal could be out on bail in a few months or traded to a foreign power in return for spies being held there. Joaquín Escobar may have been captured, but he might be back on the streets or working as a double agent again sooner than the PCs realize.

Here are some other tips to consider. Detective and spy PCs run the risk of becoming entirely reactive. They wait for criminals to do something and then try to stop them. Indeed, the genre is set up that way; it's self-reinforcing. So, if you can occasionally find ways for the heroes to take actions that are more proactive, that's a nice change of pace. Maybe introduce elements to the game that are not entirely crime or spy-related, like personal business that must be dealt with, or opportunities to create their own department, agency, or organization.

TRADECRAFT

"Tradecraft" came to be a term associated with working as a spy during World War II. However, that association was cemented during the Cold War. Tradecraft includes several skills such as deception, infiltration, the ability to maintain a false cover identity, skills in ferreting information out of files or computer networks, and methods of hiding one's intrusion after the fact. Sometimes detectives (whether working for the police, or as private investigators) must also employ tradecraft when trying to solve cases.

Of course, it wouldn't be necessary to go to such lengths if criminals and enemy operatives weren't constantly working against characters trying to accomplish their goals. During the investigation, PCs face many challenges, such as those described in the Tradecraft Challenge Table. Use it when you need inspiration. Most of the elements noted on the table should be presented as GM intrusions.

But what about a body found with no blood? A corpse with crushed bones? A cadaver covered in mold? One with no skin? In addition to being shocking, figuring out the cause of death puts the PCs on their first steps toward solving the crime.

TRADECRAFT CHALLENGE TABLE

1	**Poisoned (level 4):** Inflicts 3 points of Speed damage for four rounds on a failed Might defense task.	
2	**Polonium poisoning (level 6):** Inflicts 5 points of Speed damage for six rounds on a failed Might defense task.	
3	**Double agent:** An NPC ally has been turned by an enemy criminal or foreign organization.	
4	**Interoffice politics:** Someone who seems unfit for the position replaces the PC's handler.	
5	**Falsely accused:** The characters are brought in for questioning regarding a serious offense leveled against them.	
6	**Equipment failure:** The radio, vehicle, microphone, GPS tracker, or some other piece of equipment important to the mission's success fails, and requires repair or replacement.	
7	**Cover questioned:** The character's cover identity comes into question, and some hard questions must be answered to assure those asking the questions that the PCs are who they pretend to be.	
8	**Media exposure:** The character is photographed or shown in a video that gets wide distribution, risking their investigation should anyone recognize them.	
9	**Hit squad:** An elite team of former military soldiers turned mercenary is hired to eliminate the characters.	*Elite soldier, page 158*
10	**Unexploded ordnance (level 5):** Explosive inflicts 5 points of damage to all creatures and objects within short range.	
11	**Secret agent:** An enemy secret agent tracks down the character or characters and tries to subvert their goals.	*Secret agent, page 338*
12	**Random police stop:** The local police force doing sobriety checks randomly selects the PCs (if they're driving) for questions. If characters are not driving, the police patrol accidentally encounters them.	
13	**Network compromised (level 6):** An enemy hacker has gotten into a PC's encrypted network and is in the process of learning their secrets. Do the characters even realize it?	*Hacker, page 154*
14	**Forged papers:** A forged arrest warrant threatens to put the PCs on ice unless they can prove they did no wrong (at least, not in this case).	
15	**Witness attacked:** A witness, informant, or other NPC with valuable information is brutally attacked, and is either dead or severely hurt and in a coma after the incident.	
16	**Serial killer:** An NPC who the characters interact with in some capacity is secretly a psychotic killer, but is also a master at keeping their homicidal activities secret, even as they begin to taunt the PCs via anonymous texts, emails, and social media posts.	
17	**Cover blown:** The PC's cover story is blown, and there's nothing for it but to deal with the aftermath.	
18	**In the wind:** A suspect the PCs were investigating becomes aware of the surveillance and goes to ground.	
19	**Body part found:** Either PCs find the body part of an NPC they were hoping to question, or a part of a body the PCs attempted to dispose of is found by authorities.	
20	**Captured:** The criminal gang or enemy operatives ambush the PCs at their base using sleep gas (level 6) and other tricks, hoping to bring them all in an unconscious state to the enemy headquarters for questioning.	

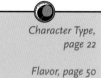

Character Type,
page 22

Flavor, page 50

SUGGESTED TYPES FOR A CRIME AND ESPIONAGE GAME

Role	Type
Detective	Speaker with skills and knowledge flavor
Forensic specialist	Explorer with skills and knowledge flavor
Criminal, reformed	Explorer with stealth flavor
Police officer	Explorer with combat flavor
Soldier	Warrior
Spy	Speaker with stealth flavor
Consultant	Speaker with Skills and knowledge flavor

SUGGESTED FOCI FOR A CRIME AND ESPIONAGE GAME

Calculates the Incalculable
Collects Bounties*
Conducts Weird Science
Crafts Unique Objects
Doesn't Do Much
Drives Like A Maniac
Eliminates Occult
    Threats*†
Entertains
Explores Dark Places
Fights Dirty
Finds The Flaw in All
    Things*
Governs*

Infiltrates
Interprets the Law
Is Idolized by Millions
Is Licensed to Carry
Leads
Learns Quickly*
Lives in the Wilderness
Looks for Trouble
Masters Weaponry
Moves Like a Cat
Murders
Needs No Weapon
Negotiates Matters of Life
    and Death*

Never Says Die
Operates Undercover
Serves In An Elite Military
    Squad*
Solves Mysteries
Throws With Deadly Accuracy
Wields Two Weapons at Once
Works For A Living*
Works the Back Alleys
Works the System
Would Rather Be Reading
*New in this book
†Only use if occult elements
    become part of setting

SUGGESTED CREATURES AND NPCS FOR A CRIME AND ESPIONAGE GAME

Assassin
Cannibal*
Crime boss
Detective
Detective, master*
General*

Guard
Hacker*
Marauder*
Occultist
Politician*
Priest*

Professor*
Secret agent
Soldier*
Soldier, elite*
Thug/bandit
*New in this book

OTHER CREATURES AND NPCS FOR A CRIME AND ESPIONAGE GAME

Businessperson: level 1
Clerk: level 1
Worker: level 2; health 8

Scorpion: level 1, Speed defense as level 2; attack inflicts 2 points of Speed damage and paralyzes for one minute

ADDITIONAL CRIME AND ESPIONAGE EQUIPMENT

In addition to all the equipment available to PCs described under Additional Modern Equipment in the *Cypher System Rulebook*, the following items are available. When items are used in a counter-surveillance capacity, assign a level from 1d6 to items to compare their efficacy, unless a PC user is involved directly.

EXPENSIVE ITEMS

Other Items	Notes
Hidden camera finder	Detects wired and wireless cameras in immediate range
Fingerprint kit	Opens to create fingerprint taking station
Sound amplifier	Captures sound up to 300 feet (91 m) away
Multichannel bug detector	Detects wired and wireless concealed microphones
Mini GPS tracker	Self-powered, encrypted beacon
Telephoto lens x 100	Comes with mount
Pen video camera	Provides asset to stealth tasks relate to making a secret recording
Concealed microphone	Self-powered, encrypted channel, record or transmit
Concealed camera	Self-powered, encrypted channel, stationary
Motion sensor	Creates audible or silent alarm
Cellular jammer	Jams cell and other radio traffic in short range
Card spoofer	Allows entry into many electronic locks requiring cards
Portfolio with hidden sleeve	Nearly impossible to find without knowing the secret of opening
Wireless keyboard detector	Reveals what's being typed on wireless keyboards within short range
SMS cracking package	Turn others' cell phones into bugs by application of known bugs
Rubber ducky	USB stick that allows hacker to input keystrokes on target computer
Keylogger	USB stick that allows all keystrokes on computer to be recorded
Mini-document scanner	Looks like a ballpoint pen
Drone	Transmits video and allows control within 300 feet (91 m)
Spy coin	Apparently normal coins with secret cavities for messages, poison, etc.

VERY EXPENSIVE ITEMS

Nightvision goggles	See in darkness as if in dim light
Spectrum analyzer	Gadget for detecting if a data connection is bugged

CHAPTER 9

HARD SCIENCE FICTION

The Fermi Paradox is the juxtaposition of high estimates for the existence of extraterrestrial life with the lack of any evidence for such life anywhere else in the universe.

What distinguishes the genre of hard science fiction from regular science fiction? Mainly, hard science fiction includes the perception of scientific accuracy. This means that a lot of the wilder aspects of science fiction are out because our current theories indicate that things like faster than light travel, UFOs and time travel may simply be impossible or beyond our capabilities ever to discover (for example extraterrestrial life).

What does that leave for hard science fiction to cover? A surprising amount. For the purposes of this genre chapter, hard science fiction might also be described as near future, which means that games that include advances in biotechnology that might improve health, intelligence, and longevity are on the table, possibly even up to the creation of "post" humans. Advances in computer processing and networking speeds means that the emergence of truly artificial machine intelligence, in all the ways that such an event could both aid society and threaten it, is a possible avenue

to explore in your games. And of course, hard science fiction often includes the colonization of the solar system, humanity's next "golden age" of exploration where we establish colonies on the Moon, Mars, and on dwarf planets in the asteroid belt, and possibly around the moons of Jupiter and Saturn. This serves as a fantastic game setting since it so greatly expands the canvas on which to create your narrative.

CREATING A HARD SCIENCE FICTION SETTING

Fashioning a futuristic science fiction setting takes some forethought. As just suggested, however, merely "evolving" current scientific trends forward a hundred or so years until man has colonized the solar system is a good start, even if your adventure is going to take place mostly on Earth, since it broadens both your possibilities and that of your players.

Next, you'll want to figure out the central theme of your game. You could focus on a

war between breakaway colonies—maybe Mars or a large corporation set up in the asteroid belt (the "Belt") decide they want independence. You could focus on the emergence of AI, incorporating the possibility of both wonderful uses of AI as well as "weaponized" uses for AI, not the least of which is the possibility of AI running amuck. A theme whose central story revolves around asteroid mining, deflecting an asteroid heading for Earth, or exploring an asteroid could be very interesting. Themes of more limited scope, such as attempting to get a malfunctioning spacecraft running again before it plunges into the sun or the atmosphere of Jupiter would also work well as one-shot adventures or short campaigns.

Many examples of hard science fiction are out there from to mine for concepts and ideas.

Solar System Colonization: The novel and TV series called the Expanse by S. A. Corey is a prime example of human colonization of the solar system, but many other examples exist, including the Mars trilogy by Kim Stanley Robinson, Cold as Ice and Dark As Day by Charles Sheffield, Mars (and other novels) by Ben Bova, and many more.

Rise of AI: A favorite movie and novel trope, examples can be found in the movies beginning with the classics 2001: A Space Odyssey based on the novel by Arthur C. Clarke. Other movie and TV examples of human AI emergence include Ex Machina, Terminator, Battlestar Galactica, A. I.. Artificial Intelligence, and more. Novels include Carnival by Elizabeth Bear, Accelerando by Charles Stross, Wake and other books in the WWW trilogy by Robert J. Sawyer, and more.

Advanced Biotech: Like the previous categories, too many stories about advanced biotech exist to list them all, so here are just a few (that don't overtly stray into horror). The movies Gattaca, Elysium, and Blade Runner. The novels Windup Girl by Paolo Bacigalupi, Blood Music and Darwin's Radio by Greg Bear, and the Rifter series by Peter Watts.

Sometimes hard science fiction asks readers to accept one element of the impossible along with other more scientifically grounded speculative fiction.

HARD SCIENCE FICTION THREATS

Asteroid miner, page 123

Guard, page 337

Assassin, page 335

1   **Solar flare (level 3):** A freak solar flare sends hard radiation sleeting through the character's vessel or location, affecting them and everyone nearby; inflicts 3 points of ambient radiation damage per minute each minute the character fails a difficulty 3 Might defense task; might lead to cancer if not treated later.

2   **Belligerent asteroid miner:** Four space-suited asteroid miners ambush one or more of the PCs at an unexpected location or time.

3   **Spacesuit issue:** One PC's spacesuit has a control malfunction, requiring a difficulty 3 Intellect task to repair it before the malfunction leads to a lethal outcome.

4   **Unexpected shake (level 5):** The spacecraft, station, vacuum habitat, or similar structure, convulses for not immediately obvious reasons, inflicting 5 points of damage on a failed difficulty 5 Speed defense roll and possibly leading to additional repercussions.

5   **Malevolent official:** A security officer, inspection official, habitat governor, or some other authority figure takes an interest in the character(s) and begins to work against them.

6   **Take them to the brig:** False charges (or real charges, if the PCs have conducted any illegal activities) means brig time for one or more of the characters if they submit to being led off by guards.

7   **Diplomatic event:** Is the diplomatic event the PCs have been invited to on the station a reason to celebrate, or an opportunity for an assassin hidden among the delegation to strike?

8   **Tunnel collapse (level 6):** The tunnel connecting two craft, subsurface moon tunnel, or spacecraft corridor collapses. Characters suffer 6 points of damage and on a failed difficulty 6 Speed task are either set adrift in the vacuum of space or are buried under sparking rubble until they can find some resolution, or die.

9   **Toxic reaction:** One PC suffers from a reaction to a solvent, food additive, or gas leak and must succeed on a difficulty 4 Might defense task or be treated as dazed for several hours, during this time the difficulty of all tasks attempted by the character increases by one step.

10 **Micrometeorite:** A tiny meteorite holes the craft, station, or habitat, with a chance to hit one character who fails a difficulty 7 Speed defense task and inflict 10 points of damage. If in a vacuum, repairing the punctures requires two difficulty 3 Intellect tasks plus something to block the punctures.

11 **Unexpected delay:** Before the PCs can proceed, they are stopped by a habitat lockdown, a summons from station leadership, a malfunctioning AI, or some similar slowdown. The unexpected delay *could* turn out to be due to yet another, more serious threat, such as an attack of space pirates, a robotic uprising, or even the appearance of a fleet of warships.

12 **Ant infestation:** Through some monumental screw-up, crazy ants—the kind of ants that swarm inside electrical devices causing them to short-circuit and preventing them from turning on—have infested a critical component or device, such as a cryogenic sleep pod where crew hibernate in long-haul missions out to the Oort Cloud.

13 **Genetic mistake:** One PC (or an NPC ally) was the product of selective genetic tailoring, like many others. Normally a plus, the PC sometimes suffers from a "Berg syndrome" which causes palsied shaking for several hours on a failed difficulty 4 Might task.

14 **Space debris:** A falling satellite, space station, or other craft threatens to impact the moon, planet, or craft of interest. PCs might need to board the failing relic or otherwise try to change its trajectory to avoid impact.

15 **Asteroid warning:** Some observation stations have put out a warning that an asteroid of immense size is heading toward a widely inhabited planet or moon. It might be a false alarm, but PCs need to determine that or if disaster is heading their way.

16 **Fuel leak:** Reaction mass is leaking somewhere in the system, and PCs have to figure out where, and how to repair it, if they want their craft to continue to move.

17 **Solar array damaged:** Environmental subsystems that depend on solar energy are damaged through malfunction (or sabotage). PCs must venture out to the arrays and replace a power modulator by succeeding on a difficulty 6 Intellect task.

18 **Breakaway activists:** People are people, even when spread through the solar system. Violent protests (level 3) get in the way of the PCs and precipitate a riot in a habitat or station. If on a spacecraft, an NPC turns out to be a saboteur.

19	**Contract nullified:** PCs are supposed to deliver cargo or do some other kind of job for a paying client. The paying client refuses to pay the balance due or cancels the contract midway through the job.
20	**AI malfunction:** The artificial intelligence, so charming and helpful, secretly decides to kill the crew, the habitat population, or something even more dire.

RUNNING A HARD SCIENCE FICTION GAME

Just as is the case with normal science fiction games, a game in a hard science fiction setting can bog down if players don't fully understand their options. If the PCs are the crew of an interplanetary vessel, the players don't know all the things that the ship can and can't do. They may feel constrained, especially if their vessel is using precisely determined orbital mechanics to get from one planet in the solar system to another.

On the other hand, it's not like the setting is so expansive that there are hundreds or thousands of alien worlds out there to explore. Characters don't suffer from choice overload as can happen in a space opera-style game.

One way to help players out is to start them with clearly defined goals. Missions handed down from a security company one or more of the PCs work for, or from a leader of one of the planetary coalitions, or from a science agency is a good idea to give the players clarity.

Another thing to keep in mind is that even though the setting is hard science fiction, allowing players to stretch their abilities using technical prowess helps with player agency. So be generous with players who want to extrapolate the science elements of the game. If someone wants to reconfigure the ship's sensor array to do something odd but useful, let them try.

HARD SCIENCE FICTION THREATS

The Hard Science Fiction Threats table provides more dangers you can throw at your PCs playing in a setting where physics trumps fantasy. The results are not meant to be the major story arc, though you could probably spin some of them out to serve that purpose. Most of these threats should be presented as GM intrusions.

EFFECTS OF GRAVITY

Humans evolved to live and act under 1 G, Earth's gravity. Acting in other environments can be challenging.

Short-Term Microgravity Exposure: People new to low gravity might get space sickness. Newcomers must succeed on a difficulty 3 Might task or suffer mild nausea for about two to four days, during which time one step increases the difficulty of all tasks attempted. A few unlucky travelers (those who roll a 1 or who otherwise gain a GM Intrusion, usually) are almost completely incapacitated, and find the difficulty of all tasks increased by three steps during this period.

Low Gravity: Weapons that rely on weight, such as all heavy weapons, inflict 2 fewer points of damage (dealing a minimum of 1 point of damage). Weapons with short range can reach to long range, and long-range weapons can reach to about 200 feet (61 m) instead of 100 feet (30 m). Characters trained in low gravity maneuvering ignore the damage penalty.

High Gravity: It's hard to make effective attacks when the pull of gravity is very strong. The difficulty of attacks (and all physical actions) made in high gravity is increased by one step. Ranges in high gravity are reduced by one category (long-range weapons reach only to short range, and short-range weapons reach only to immediate range). Characters trained in high gravity maneuvering ignore the change in difficulty but not the range decreases.

Zero Gravity: It's hard to maneuver in an environment without gravity. The difficulty of attacks (and all physical actions) made in zero gravity is increased by one step. Short-range weapons can reach to long range, and long-range weapons can reach

EFFECTS OF VACUUM SURVIVING THE VOID

Vacuum is lethal. There's no air to breathe, and the lack of pressure causes havoc on an organic body. An unprotected character moves one step down the damage track each round. However, at the point where they should die, they instead fall unconscious and remain so for about a minute. If they are rescued during that time, they can be revived. If not, they die.

The Turing Test is a subjective test suggested by Alan Turing in which a computer is said to "pass" the test if it can convince a human, by answering a series of questions, that it is also human.

Damage track, page 202

to about 200 feet (61 m) instead of 100 feet (30 m). Characters trained in zero gravity maneuvering ignore the change in difficulty.

Long-term Microgravity Exposure: Long-term exposure to microgravity environments degrades health without medical interventions. How long one spends in such conditions is directly relevant. The GM may assign long-term penalties to PCs, if the situation warrants it, though space medicine advanced with human travel into the weightless void, and those able to exercise and take the recommended steroids and other hormones can avoid these complications.

PCS AND A SPACECRAFT

In a hard science fiction setting, PCs getting their hands on an advanced interplanetary spacecraft that presumably costs some small fraction of a nation's net worth doesn't seem especially plausible, at least immediately. During the game, of course, that could change. PCs might capture a craft, find one mysteriously abandoned, or otherwise gain access to a ship, perhaps as part of a larger mission. Either way, deciding what kind of craft PCs have means spending a little time sketching out the deck plan, even after you've assigned a general "type" to the ship.

TRAVELING THE SOLAR SYSTEM AND ORBITAL MECHANICS

In a hard science fiction setting, you might be interested in evoking the reality of travel times between colonies on planets and moons located in the solar system. Currently, the limitation of space travel with a conventional rocket is that the rocket must use nearly its entire fuel supply at once in a single, controlled explosion to reach Earth orbit. If orbits line up, it'll still take at least seven months to reach Mars, the nearest planet of interest.

Thankfully, nuclear plasma rockets have come on the scene. They can change velocity and sustain thrust for days at a time (this reduces bone loss, muscle atrophy, and other long-term effects of low gravity).

Still, plotting a course between locations in the solar system isn't simple, because everything is always moving with respect to everything else. You could exactly determine how long a trip would take with some internet research.

Or you could just evoke the effect of orbital mechanics and varying accelerations on interplanetary travel. Use the following chart to do so. For a trip between locations not directly compared, add up the destinations in between. The travel times assume a nuclear plasma engine of a kind already being tested today, but better, and a steady thrust toward the destination and an equally long and steady braking thrust over the last half of the trip before orbit insertion.

Regardless, the travel times between distant locations brings home one thing: Space is big and lonely.

OPTIONAL RULE: FINAGLE'S LAW

The extreme environment in space—hard radiation, lack of air and pressure, wild temperature variations, and lack of gravity—tends to magnify small issues into much more significant issues. While Murphy's Law, that everything that can go wrong will go wrong, is a useful reminder to keep an eye out for trouble even under regular circumstances, in space Finagle's Law reigns, which is that anything that can go wrong, will—at the worst possible moment. Not to mention O'Toole's Corollary of Finagle's Law, which is that the perversity of the Universe tends toward a maximum.

To take advantage of this aspect of activities in space, GMs can implement Void Rules. The idea is to create a feeling of increased repercussions by changing one die roll mechanic. In the game, activities on a planet's surface—or within a functioning air-filled spacecraft or habitat—remain normal. The PCs interact with each other and the NPCs, investigate, research, travel, and so on. But when they suit up and head out into the

Don't worry about the AI that passes the Turing Test. Worry about the ones intentionally failing it.

Starships, page 255

Origin	Destination	Travel Time Using Nuclear Plasma Engine
Earth/Moon	Mars	20 +1d20 days
Mars	Asteroid Belt	30 + 1d20 days
Asteroid Belt	Jupiter and its moons	30 + 1d20 days
Jupiter	Saturn and its moons	60 + 1d20 days
Saturn	Uranus	90 + 1d20 days

vacuum and weightlessness of space (or their spacecraft or station ceases to function), things change. At this time, the GM announces that the game has instituted Void Rules.

This is a key for the PCs to recognize that events can play in a far more lethal manner in space. Dropping a tool, a broken tether, or even missing a handhold could send a character spiraling out into the nothingness, lost forever. While using Void Rules, GM intrusions governed by die rolls change. Normally this happens only on a roll of 1, but when Void Rules apply, it becomes a roll of 1 or a 2. Void Rules are similar in many ways to Horror Mode, though the threat range doesn't normally continue to escalate, although it could if the PCs are clinging to the exterior of a rapidly rotating spacecraft while trying to repair a laser communication array or get thrusters working properly.

ADDITIONAL HARD SCIENCE FICTION EQUIPMENT

In a hard science fiction setting, most of the equipment described as being available in a regular science fiction setting is available. However, items like gravity regulators and potentially force field generators are not normally items one would find for sale in a hard science fiction setting. Such items are more likely to be found as cyphers, items created by black-ops research or other mysterious institutions.

Also, the items noted on the next page are also usually available.

Horror Mode, page 262

Additional Science Fiction Equipment, page 253

SUGGESTED TYPES FOR A HARD SCIENCE FICTION GAME

Role	Type
Scientist	Explorer with skills and knowledge flavor
Pilot	Explorer with technology flavor
Technician	Explorer with technology flavor
Captain	Speaker with technology flavor
Soldier	Warrior
Diplomat	Speaker
Spy	Explorer with stealth flavor
Journalist	Speaker

Character Type, page 22

Flavor, page 50

SUGGESTED FOCI FOR A HARD SCIENCE FICTION GAME

Builds Robots
Calculates the Incalculable
Conducts Weird Science
Conducts Rocket Science*
Doesn't Do Much
Entertains
Fights Dirty
Fights With Panache
Fuses Mind and Machine
Hacks Networks*
Infiltrates
Interprets the Law

Is Idolized by Millions
Loves the Void*
Looks for Trouble
Masters Defense
Masters Weaponry
Moves Like a Cat
Murders
Needs No Weapon
Negotiates Matters of Life and Death*
Never Says Die
Operates Undercover

Pilots Starcraft
Resides in Silicon*
Serves in an Elite Military Squad*
Transcends Humanity*
Solves Mysteries
Wears Power Armor
Works the Back Alleys
Works For a Living*
Works the System
Would Rather Be Reading
*Introduced in this book

Focus, page 90

Foci, page 14

SUGGESTED CREATURES AND NPCS FOR A HARD SCIENCE FICTION GAME

Assassin
Crucible*
Detective, master*
General*
Guard
Hacker*
Mad Scientist*

Mechanical soldier
Politician*
Priest*
Professor*
Replicant
Robot mimic*
Secret agent

Soldier*
Soldier, elite*
Thug/bandit
Vat reject

*Introduced in this book

Creatures, page 274

NPCs, page 334

Creatures, page 126

NPCs, page 152

OTHER CREATURES AND NPCS FOR A SCIENCE FICTION GAME

Asteroid miner: level 3, tasks related to mining in a low or zero gravity environment as level 5

Ship mechanic: level 2, tasks related to spacecraft repair as level 6

Toxic slime mold: level 1; moves an immediate distance each round; poison inflicts 2 points of Speed damage for 3 rounds

EXPENSIVE ITEMS

Weapons	Notes
Syringer	Light weapon, short range, inflicts drugs, poisons, and radio transponders in target
Grapple gun	Light weapon, long range, inflicts 1 point of damage, tip adheres to foe and connects via slender cable back to gun wielder

Armor	Notes
Paint-on impact armor	Not armor, offers +1 to Armor, applied by spraying nanosolution over clothing, lasts ten minutes. 1d20 applications

Other Items	Notes
Drone and wrist controller	Microdrone (no larger than a fly) with range of 10,000 feet (3,048 m)
EVA pack	In low or zero gravity environments, allows normal maneuverability
Fusion battery	Provides power to nearly any device short of a spacecraft for variable period depending on power requirements
Fusion torch	Cuts through substances of up to level 9 after a few rounds of application
High-rad prophylactic	One month dose protects from negative effects of prolonged high radiation exposure
Low-grav prophylactic	One month dose protects from negative effects of prolonged low gravity exposure
Molecular bonder	One dose of glue that provides a level 6 bond between two touching objects after application
Sensor bit	Wrist mounted instrument provides data on surrounding conditions, energy sources, atmospheric contaminants, and similar information
Smartacs	Augmented reality display contacts with advanced smartphone functionality
Spacesuit	Provides three days of breathable air and protection from average conditions found in the vacuum of space
Trauma kit	Pack with 1d6 doses of drugs that countermand effects of shock and injury, allowing patient to function normally even if down one or two steps on the damage track and stops bleeding

EXORBITANT ITEMS

Weapons	Notes
Rail gun	Long-barreled rifle with computer sight assistance that inflicts 8 points of damage; range is 10,000 feet (3,048 m)

Armor	Notes
Holobit	Projects offset hologram of wearer, provides asset to Speed defense tasks
Paint-on military armor	Not armor, offers +3 to Armor, applied by spraying nanosolution over clothing, lasts ten minutes. 1d20 applications

Other items	Notes
Prosthetic arm, advanced	Replaces normal arm, provides asset to one preprogrammed noncombat physical task
Prosthetic organ, cleansing	Artificial organ provides asset on all Might defense tasks to resist poison, disease, and the negative effect of stimulants, depressants, and other drugs
Prosthetic organ, military	Flushes blood with battle hormones that grant an asset to all attacks and defense for one minute, after which the target becomes helpless for three rounds
Data archive	Brain chip implant that provides asset to all knowledge-based tasks.

PART 4
GAMEMASTER SECTION

CHAPTER 10

CREATURES

Creatures, page 274

The creatures presented in this section are designated as being part of particular genres in Part 2, but of course, GMs are free to use a creature however and wherever they want. The number of genres possible in roleplaying games, including genre mashups, may be almost limitless. That means that this chapter only begins to explore the types of creatures that characters might encounter. Of course, the new creatures here are designed to expand those presented in the *Cypher System Rulebook*.

The most important element of each creature is its level. You use the level to determine the target number a PC must reach to attack or defend against the opponent. In each entry, the difficulty number for the creature is listed in parentheses after its level. The target number is three times the level.

A creature's target number is usually also its health, which is the amount of damage it can sustain before it is dead or incapacitated. For easy reference, the entries always list a creature's health, even when it's the normal amount for a creature of its level. For

Understanding the Listings, page 274

more detailed information on level, health, combat, and other elements, refer to Understanding the Listings.

CREATURES BY LEVEL

Glowing roach	2
Bogeyman	3
Faerie	3
Fusion hound	3
Nightgaunt	3
Shoe thief	3
Devolved	4
Robot mimic	4
Mad creation	4
Midnight scrabbler	4
Abomination	5
Cambion	5
Crucible	5
Cryptic moth	5
Killer clown	5
Prince(ss) of Summer	5
Satyr	5
Erlking	6
Gamma worm	6
Reanimated	6
Demon, chain	7
Hydra	7
The Minotaur	7
Cerberus	8
Typhon	10

ABOMINATION 5 (15)

In a post-apocalyptic setting, abominations were bred in the toxic aftermath of the fall of society, and are sometimes called mutants.

An abomination is a hideous bestial humanoid covered with thickened plates of scarlet flesh. Their eyes glow with the stagnant glow of toxic waste dumps. Standing at least 7 feet (2 m) tall, abominations are drawn to movement. Always famished, abominations consume living prey in great, tearing bites.

Motive: Hungers for flesh
Environment: Almost anywhere hunting alone in or in pairs
Health: 22
Damage Inflicted: 6 points
Armor: 2
Movement: Short
Modifications: Might defense as level 6; sees through deception as level 3.
Combat: Abominations use scavenged weapons to attack prey at range, but probably switch to biting against targets within immediate range. Targets damaged by a bite must also succeed on a Might defense task or descend one step on the damage track as the abomination tears off a big piece of flesh and gulps it down.

Abominations regain 2 points of health per round and have +5 Armor against damage inflicted by energy (radiation, x-rays, gamma rays, and so on).

Those who survive an abomination attack must succeed on a Might defense task a day later when they come down with flu-like symptoms. Those who fail begin to the process of transforming into a fresh abomination.

Interaction: Most abominations can speak, and have vague memories of the people they were before transforming; however, those memories, motivations, and hopes are usually submerged in a hunger that can never be sated.

Use: Abominations hunt ravaged wastelands and bombed-out spacecraft hulks, lurk in basements where mad scientists have conducted illicit experiments, and haunt the dreams of children who've gotten in over their heads.

GM Intrusion: The abomination isn't dead; it stands up on the following round at full health.

BOGEYMAN   3 (9)

When a child comes crying about a monster lurking under the bed, hiding in the closet, or scratching its claws against the window, parents usually assume the culprit is a pile of clothes or the wind. Parents are wrong. There are things in the night that hunt children and drag them from their beds.

Bogeymen feed on fear. The more frightened their prey, the more real they become until they assume whatever form their victim fears most. Thus, a bogeyman can wear a multitude of forms, looking to one person like a giant spider and to another like a werewolf. The form doesn't matter as much as the fear they create, fear strong enough to kill.

Motive: Hungers for emotion (courage)

Environment: Under beds, in closets, outside windows, or in toy boxes

Health: 9

Damage Inflicted: 3 points

Movement: Short, short when flying or moving through solid material

Modifications: All tasks related to intimidation as level 6.

Combat: A bogeyman begins an encounter as an insubstantial pair of disembodied eyes blinking from the shadows. As its action, a bogeyman reaches out to feed on fear. Any creature within immediate range that can see it must succeed on an Intellect defense task. On a failure, the creature inflicts 3 points of Intellect damage (ignores Armor) as the target's courage drains away, and blood seeps from the victim's eyes, nose, and ears. In addition, the difficulty to resist the bogeyman's future attacks increases by one step. This is a cumulative increase up to a maximum of five steps.

Each time the bogeyman inflicts Intellect damage, it becomes more solid, more real, taking the shape of whatever its beholder most fears. Its appearance is subjective to the viewer. One person might see a vampire, another a werewolf, and another a clown covered in blood all at the same time.

Bogeymen flee from bright light, and take 3 points of damage from bright light each round they are fully exposed to it or successfully attacked by it.

Interaction: Bogeymen are sneaky and wicked creatures. They love eavesdropping on people to steal secrets. If a bogeyman fails to frighten a creature, its demeanor changes and it becomes whining and cringing, offering tantalizing secrets to ingratiate itself with such a clearly powerful opponent.

Use: A bogeyman attaches itself to an item taken from a place reputed to be haunted and emerges under the cover of night to terrorize the person who took the object.

GM Intrusion: A character who sees the bogeyman and fails an Intellect defense roll reacts viscerally, screaming long and loud, and takes no other action that round.

CAMBION   5 (15)

"CAMBION—Child of Demons. Delancre and Bodin think that incubus demons could unite with succubus demons, and that born of their exchange were hideous children called cambions [...]"

—translated from the 1825 edition of the French-language *Dictionnaire Infernal*

Fine ebony scales cover a cambion's perfectly athletic figure. Two reddish horns grow from its brow, and the tips of fangs emerge from between its dusky lips. Its eyes, absent iris and pupil, are the color of driven snow. Cambions are cursed creatures, born of mortal and demonic parentage, and are also sometimes called helborn. Most cambions give in to what everyone expects of them, and embrace evil.

Motive: Revenge on a world that's rejected them

Environment: Anywhere, often hiding in plain sight

Health: 25

Damage Inflicted: 6 points

Armor: 1

Movement: Short

Modifications: Disguise as level 7.

Combat: Cambions sometimes wield heavy weapons in combat, especially if they come across an artifact that can enhance their attacks.

Some cambions develop their natural and magical abilities to become powerful sorcerers, but most cambions can call up hellish fire merely by willing it at least once per day, as follows.

Soulfire Blast: An explosion of soul-rending black and crimson fire explodes around up to three targets standing next to each other within short range, inflicting 4 points of damage and stunning targets so that they lose their next action on a failed Speed defense task.

Finger of Torture: A ruby ray lances out from the cambion's finger to strike the enemy prone with torturous pain on a failed Might defense task. The target automatically takes 6 points of damage each round until they can escape the effect with an Intellect task.

Interaction: Cambions are bleak, depressed, and misunderstood. Most have turned to evil, but a few can be redeemed.

Use: A great fire is seen burning on the horizon. The next day, travelers come across a burned region with a crater that has destroyed a farmhouse. At the center of the crater is an unconscious human with hornlike growths on its head.

Loot: Powerful cambions sometimes wield artifacts as weapons.

GM Intrusion: *The character's cypher explodes when touched by cambion demon fire on a failed Speed defense task.*

CERBERUS

8 (24)

The guardian of the land of the dead appears at every opening into the underworld. The three-headed hound is 16 feet (5 m) high and a vision of terror. The heads represent the past (youth), the present (adulthood), and the future (old age), and victims bitten by a particular head suffer an associated chronological affect. Voracious for living flesh, the beast can also eat spirits should any draw too close and attempt to escape their undead land.

Motive: Hungers for flesh

Environment: Anywhere paths lead to the land of the dead

Health: 99

Damage Inflicted: 10 points

Armor: 3

Movement: Short, immediate when burrowing

Modifications: Speed defense as level 6 due to size.

Combat: Cerberus can bite three times as a single action. Each bite inflicts 10 points of damage to corporeal and insubstantial foes alike.

A bite from the head representing the past also restores 10 points of damage to Cerberus. A bite from the head representing the present means the victim must also succeed on a Might defense roll or be held fast by the maw and automatically suffer 10 points of damage each round until they can escape. A bite from the head representing the future also requires that the victim succeeds on an Intellect defense roll or lose access to all their special abilities granted by foci and type for one round.

Interaction: Cerberus is a bound guardian, but chafes under the weight of its responsibility. It may allow creatures to slip in or out of the underworld if presented with a worthy gift. An intelligent beast, it can speak all the languages known by souls languishing in the underworld.

Use: The characters must retrieve a rare ore found only in the underworld, but must contend with Cerebus before entering or leaving.

In a game using power shifts (or divine shifts), GMs should provide the same advantage to Cerberus.

GM Intrusion: *On a failed Intellect defense task, the damaged PC's soul is also bitten (or bitten instead), and they suffer 8 points of Intellect damage.*

CRUCIBLE 6 (18)

A crucible is a supercomputer that broke the leash of its programmers and creators and now operates as an independent, secret AI with inscrutable goals.

A crucible is a machine with organic parts. Polymers and alloys seamlessly fuse with warm flesh and pumping blood. A living supercomputer, a crucible is a creature of frightening intelligence with the ability to absorb surrounding matter to repair itself or adapt to new situations.

Crucibles act on subtle, decades-long plans, usually using intermediaries to hide themselves as the true masters of the situation. What their ultimate goal is, and whether they're working together or at cross purposes, isn't something any crucible has yet revealed.

Motive: Unpredictable

Environment: Usually in secure facilities guarded by loyal followers and technicians

Health: 21

Damage Inflicted: 5

Movement: Immediate

Modifications: Speed defense as level 2; knowledge of current events and scientific topics as level 8.

Combat: As one action, a crucible can pummel up to three foes within short range with long, silvery tendrils it can extrude from its core.

A crucible can absorb matter, so physical attacks against one can go awry. A character who successfully attacks a crucible with a melee weapon or an unarmed strike must succeed on a Speed defense roll. On a failure using a weapon, the crucible absorbs the weapon, destroying it and regaining 1 point of health. On a failed roll with an unarmed strike, the attack is negated, and the character takes 3 points of Speed damage (ignores Armor).

A crucible can also spend its action absorbing matter around it (such as walls, floor, equipment, unresisting living creatures, and so on), regaining 5 points of health.

A crucible that has cyphers or artifacts uses them in combat and also relies on guardians to aid it.

Interaction: A crucible usually speaks by plugging into nearby electronic systems to generate a synthetic voice. A crucible is willing to negotiate if physically tracked down and threatened.

Use: The characters are contacted by a crucible that wants them to accomplish a task on a moon of Jupiter. The job: assassinate a security officer (who the crucible paints as corrupt).

Loot: A crucible might have 1d6 cyphers and possibly an artifact.

GM Intrusion: *The character damaged by a silvery tendril must succeed on a Might defense task or be snatched into the crucible's embrace. Until the PC escapes, they can't take any other actions. While caught, the character is forced to speak in the crucible's voice, issuing threats to the other characters.*

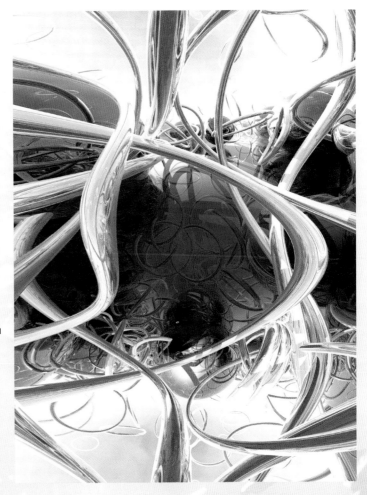

CRYPTIC MOTH   5 (15)

Normal moths are enigmatic, gauzy haunts of twilight. The feathery touch of their wings on your face can startle, even frighten. This is only to be expected, since moths are the children of cryptic moths, who are malign and intelligent entities of another realm. Sometimes referred to as a mothmen, other times as shadow faeries, cryptic moths are certainly alien. Each possesses a unique wing pattern and coloration and to some extent, body shape. These patterns and colors may signify where in the hierarchy a particular cryptic moth stands among its siblings of the night, but for those who do not speak the language of moths, the complexity of their social structure is overwhelming.

Motive: Capture humans, possibly for food, possibly for breeding purposes

Environment: Almost anywhere, usually at night

Health: 23

Damage Inflicted: 5 points

Movement: Short; long when flying

Modifications: All knowledge tasks as level 6; stealth tasks as level 7 while invisible.

Combat: Cryptic moths usually only enter combat when they wish, because until they attack and become visible, they can remain unseen and invisible to most eyes.

The touch of a cryptic moth's wing draws life and energy from targets, inflicting 5 points of Speed damage (ignores Armor).

Once every hour or so, cryptic moths can summon a swarm of normal moths (these moths act as level 2 creatures that can fly) to aid them in combat, or more often, serve as a fashion accessory or component in a piece of living art.

If a cryptic moth is prepared, it may carry cyphers useful in combat, and perhaps even a faerie artifact.

Cryptic moths regain 1 point of health per round while their health is above 0, unless they've been damaged with a silvered or cold iron weapon, or by electrical attacks.

Interaction: Although very few cryptic moths speak human languages, peaceful interaction with these creatures is not impossible. It's just very difficult, as they see most humans as a source of food or as breeding stock (to lay their eggs in).

Use: A character is followed by a cryptic moth intent on capturing and enslaving them.

Loot: A cryptic moth usually has a few cyphers, and possibly a delicate artifact.

GM Intrusion: The cryptic moth grabs the character and flies up and away, unless and until the character escapes the grab.

DEMON, CHAIN 7 (21)

The ring and clatter of metal on metal precedes the arrival of a chain demon. Lengths of rusted chains wrap this humanoid figure like funerary linens wrap a mummy. Chain, barbed and hooked, unfolds like ungainly wings from the demon's back. Additional lengths extend from both its forearms, giving the creature a greatly extended reach with claws of animate, hooked iron links.

Chain demons are denizens of Hell (or similar realms, depending on the setting). A chain demon is usually created from a human soul of such wretched evil that, upon reaching the afterlife, it is promoted to become a bleak angel of its new environment. Chain demons are great at torturing those already trapped in the demon's native hellscape, but even better at catching fresh targets and pulling them down with molten chains.

Motive: Delight in causing anguish

Environment: Any hellscape, but sometimes they escape

Health: 27

Damage Inflicted: 10 points

Armor: 3

Movement: Short; long when being lowered, raised, or pulled by animate chain wings

Combat: A chain demon can animate its chains to attack up to three targets within short range as a single action. If the demon desires, one creature damaged by its attack must succeed on a Might defense roll or be snared by a chain hook. The snagged target is drawn into the demon's embrace if it fails a second Might defense task on its next turn (on a success, the victim breaks free). A victim drawn into the embrace takes 10 points of damage each round if the chain demon wishes to inflict it (no defense roll allowed), and the difficulty of the Might defense roll to break free is increased by one step.

Interaction: A chain demon is diabolically motivated to inflict anguish, and it may engage in drawn-out negotiations only to betray its target at a time guaranteed to inflict the most spiritual pain.

Use: An influential occult researcher without a moral compass sends a chain demon to kidnap a target.

Loot: Most chain demons string trophies of victims on their chains, including expensive amulets, some of which could be cyphers or even artifacts.

Chain demons are just one variety of demon. Many more exist, including those able to possess the bodies of others.

Demon, page 284

GM Intrusion: *Instead of being drawn into the demon's embrace, the character is wrapped in animate chains where they stand, which threaten to completely cocoon them. Meanwhile, the chain demon turns its attention to other victims.*

DEVOLVED   4 (12)

Military experiments to create a super-soldier produced hundreds of dead ends, literally, plus a few dangerous failures. The devolved are one of those failures. These malformed, hideous brutes share a common heritage but display a wide array of maladies and mutations in the flesh, including limbs withered or elephantine patches of thick, scaly skin, misplaced body parts, and mental abnormalities. Simple-minded and afflicted with pain from their twisted, broken forms, the devolved vent all their hatred and wrath against all others, including other mutants, cannibals, and marauders.

Mutant, page 43

Cannibal, page 153

Marauder, page 156

Motive: Hungers for flesh

Environment: Groups of three to five that roam the ruins, raiding for fresh meat

Health: 21

Damage Inflicted: 4 to 8 points; see Combat

Movement: Short

Modifications: All tasks related to intimidation as level 6; Intellect defense and Speed defense as level 2 due to malformed nature.

Combat: Devolved attack with a claw, a bite, or some other body part. They throw themselves at their enemies with mindless ferocity and little regard for their own safety. Easily frustrated, a devolved grows stronger as its fury builds. Each time it misses with an attack, the damage it inflicts increases by 1 point (to a maximum of 8 points). Once the devolved successfully inflicts damage, the amount of damage it inflicts returns to normal. Then the cycle starts anew.

Interaction: Devolved speak when they must, punctuating their statements with growls and barks. Their understanding seems limited to what they can immediately perceive, and they have a difficult time with abstract concepts. If plied with gifts, they might be convinced to share what they know about the lands around their camps.

Use: An expedition to an old government facility uncovers a cyst of devolved that live within its sheltering bunkers.

Loot: For every three or so devolved, one is likely to carry a cypher.

GM Intrusion: *A devolved that is damaged by a character takes only half damage from that character for the next minute as its body adapts to whatever the PC used to make the attack.*

ERLKING   6 (18)

This vaguely humanoid creature is an animated accumulation of woodland debris—bark, lost teeth, matted weeds, and dirt. It wears a crown of oak leaves and a cloak of mist. Its eyes are knotholes, and its hands are sharpened twigs. An erlking is a greedy spirit of hunger deemed Unseelie by the faerie nobility of that wild and wicked realm. Erlkings love to hunt and eat children, who are particularly susceptible to the promises and glamours that erlkings spin.

Motive: Hungers for flesh and to reclaim stripped titles

Environment: Almost anywhere wooded at night

Health: 27

Damage Inflicted: 6 points

Armor: 4

Movement: Short, immediate when burrowing

Modifications: Level 7 for stealth tasks.

Combat: An erlking prefers to attack from hiding, and whisper a child or other target within short distance from its bed out into the night if the target fails an Intellect defense task. An affected target remains under the erlking's spell for up to an hour or until attacked or otherwise harmed.

When it physically attacks, an erlking can attack with three root tendrils divided any way it chooses against targets within immediate range. A target hit by a tendril must also succeed on a Speed defense roll or become grabbed until it escapes. Each round, the erlking automatically inflicts 6 points of damage on each grabbed target until the victim succeeds on a Might-based task to escape.

Silvered and cold iron weapons ignore an erlking's Armor. If an erlking's remains are not burned or otherwise destroyed, it will sprout and grow a new body from the corpse within a day.

Interaction: An erlking may negotiate if creatures have something it wants, or if targets are armed with silvered or cold iron weapons.

Use: An erlking is active only by night; by day, it hides beneath a mound of weedy earth indistinguishable from the surrounding terrain.

An erlking is a former noble stripped of title, lands, and even form, and exiled into the night for crimes unimaginable in their cruelty. An erlking's victims are found in the cold sunlight, pale and bloodless, with their vital organs nibbled out.

GM Intrusion: *Being surprised by an erlking in the darkness requires that the character succeed on an Intellect defense task or lose their next action as they faint in terror, run screaming, or stand paralyzed in terror.*

FAERIE   3 (9)

Faeries are magic creatures of music, mirth, tricks, and taunts. Seeing one is an omen. Hopefully, an omen of a silly song or the first appearance of an annoying new road companion (the very faerie sighted) flitting around, asking the questions of a curious four-year-old hyped up on sugar water and ice cream. Some faeries are crueler and delight in stealing clothing, equipment, or prized objects. And a few are malicious and, under the guise of a helpful guide or a pretty light in the distance, lure lost travelers to various dooms.

Motive: Unpredictable

Environment: A faerie can be encountered alone or in a flutter of three to twelve

Health: 12

Damage Inflicted: 4 points

Movement: Immediate; long when flying

Modifications: Tasks related to performance and deception as level 5; Speed defense as level 5 due to size and quickness.

Combat: A faerie hurls sparkling magic dust at a target within short range to inflict damage. In addition, if a faerie is touched or struck by a melee weapon, more magic dust puffs away from the faerie and clouds the attacker, who must succeed on a Speed defense task or suffer the same amount of damage they just dealt to the faerie. Sometimes faeries wield tiny weapons, such as bows, spears, or swords; treat these as light weapons.

A faerie can see in the dark, but it can also emit bright light (often colored) and appear as a glowing humanoid or an illuminated sphere.

Faeries regain 1 point of health per round while their health is above 0 unless they've been damaged with a silvered or cold iron weapon.

Some faeries can attempt to use a song or light display to charm others within short range. The target must succeed on an Intellect defense task or fall into a suggestible state for one hour. During this period, the target can be led by the faerie until attacked, damaged, or shaken from their glamour.

Interaction: Faeries are mercurial creatures, but except for the malicious ones, they can be negotiated with, especially if offered sweets, wine, or other gifts. That said, faerie attention spans are limited, so even one that means well could end up leaving the PCs in the lurch at just the wrong moment.

Use: The dancing light in the distance, leading curious PCs deeper and deeper into the dark woods, is a faerie.

Loot: The tiny pouches faeries carry are stuffed with forest bric-a-brac, but some of those pouches are ten times larger on the inside and could contain expensive items or cyphers.

GM Intrusion: Another faerie appears, and if the character fails a Speed defense roll, it flies off with their weapon or another important possession.

FUSION HOUND   3 (9)

In the radiation-scoured wastelands, creatures either adapt to the deadly energies of their environment, or they die. Fusion hounds are mutant canines able to absorb unbelievable amounts of radiation and thrive on it. They roam in packs, killing and devouring everything they come upon.

A fusion hound's entire head appears to be a blast of flame, and gouts of dangerous radiation flare from its body.

Motive: Hungers for flesh

Environment: Packs of three to eight can be found almost anywhere

Health: 10

Damage Inflicted: 5 points

Armor: 1

Movement: Long

Modifications: Speed defense as level 4; stealth and climbing as level 2.

Combat: Fusion hounds move very fast and use that speed to their advantage in combat. A hound can move a long distance and still attack as a single action. It can also use its action to run about in random patterns, increasing the difficulty to attack it by two steps.

A fusion hound's head is completely haloed in a seething mass of radioactive energy for a head, so unlike traditional canines, it has no bite attack. Instead, it pounces on prey with its clawed forelimbs, which causes a burst of radiation to flare from its body, burning whatever it touches.

Anyone within close distance of a fusion hound for more than one round suffers 1 point of damage in each round after the first.

Interaction: Fusion hounds are animals. Creatures immune to radiation sometimes train the hounds to become guardians or hunting dogs, but such creatures are rare.

Use: An NPC delivering something the characters need never made it to the rendezvous. If they backtrack to where the NPC should have come from, the PCs are attacked by a pack of fusion hounds on the road. Clearly, the courier was attacked by the pack as well, and the characters must discover if the NPC is dead or merely injured, and where the package now lies.

Many people believe that a fusion hound has no head hidden beneath their halos of seething radiation; they think the halo is their head.

GM Intrusion: *The hound flares with energy and the character must succeed on a Might defense task or go blind for ten minutes.*

GAMMA WORM   6 (18)

Gamma worms are also known as gamma spikers in some locations.

Gamma worms hide their large forms by burrowing beneath the ground, and when they emerge on the surface, behind psychic distortion fields. The only clue someone has that they're being stalked is a smell of cloves over the stale whiff of death. Unfortunately, if someone smells a gamma worm's distinctive odor, it's probably already too late.

Motive: Hungers for flesh, unpredictable

Environment: Almost anywhere

Health: 18

Damage Inflicted: 6 points

Armor: 4

Movement: Short when slithering or burrowing

Modifications: Stealth tasks as level 8 when psychic field active; Speed defense as level 5 due to size; ability to see through tricks as level 4.

Combat: A gamma worm can unfold from its wormlike length two arms, each ending in massive chitinous blade which they use to make melee attacks.

The gamma worm can unleash a hail of gamma spikes against up to three targets within short range once each hour. Foes struck by the spikes take damage and must succeed on a Might defense roll or fall unconscious. Unconscious targets wake up a few rounds later feeling dizzy and slightly sick to their stomach—they've developed radiation sickness. Each day, the victim must succeed on a Might defense task or take damage and fall unconscious again. If this happens three times before the victim succeeds on a Might defense task, they do not wake up the third time.

When a gamma worm restricts its movement to an immediate distance in a round, it can generate a psychic field that grants it invisibility.

Worms are immune to radiation but vulnerable to cold; cold attacks are not affected by their Armor.

Interaction: Irradiated and hungry gamma worms emerge from the ruins to hunt fresh meat in outlying communities. Gamma worms don't seem intelligent, but they have a secret language and purpose, which they are loathe to reveal to others.

Use: Newly discovered corpses that seem alien (corpses from gamma worms) reveal some kind of subterranean life form living beneath the city, which PCs are called on to investigate.

GM Intrusion: An irradiated character continues to experience strong vertigo and disorientation. For the next minute, they must succeed on a difficulty 3 Speed-based task each round or fall down.

STAWICKI '14

GLOWING ROACH 2 (6)

The oft-cited truism that roaches would do fine in the aftermath of a nuclear war proved true.

Radiation-born mutant roaches are terrible individually, but absolutely horrible in swarms. The size of small dogs, these firefly-lit creatures prefer the dark, subways, and basements.

Motive: Hungers for flesh

Environment: Anywhere dark, usually in nests of ten or more

Health: 6

Damage Inflicted: 2 points

Armor: 2

Movement: Short; short when flying

Combat: A glowing roach attacks with radioactive mandibles. When four glowing roaches act together they act as a swarm able to make a single attack as a level 4 creature inflicting 4 points of damage. Targets damaged by a glowing roach swarm must also succeed on a difficulty 4 Might defense task, or face additional consequences from the effects of radiation and slashing mandibles, as determined on the following table. The effects are cumulative, and last until a target can make a recovery roll.

1	**Head wound:** The difficulty of all Intellect defense tasks is increased by one step.
2	**Wounded leg:** The difficulty of all Speed defense tasks is increased by one step.
3	**Gut wound:** The difficulty of all Might defense tasks is increased by one step.
4	**Eye gouged:** The difficulty of all tasks related to perception is increased by one step.
5	**Arm numb:** One arm goes limp.
6	**Leg numb:** One leg goes limp.

Roaches dislike bright illumination; in sunlight or other bright light, the difficulty of Speed defense tasks against glowing roach attacks is decreased by one step.

Interaction: Glowing roaches almost always react like voracious insects, despite their size.

Use: Any visit to the ruins usually scares up a few glowing roaches when light is introduced to a dark place.

GM Intrusion: *The radioactive glowing roach sickens the character unless they succeed on a difficulty 4 Might task. A sickened character is overcome with nausea and loses their next action.*

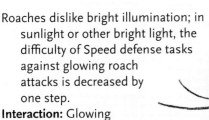

HYDRA 7 (21)

Sometimes newly encountered hydras have seven or more heads instead of "just" five.

In a game using power shifts (or divine shifts), GMs could provide the same advantage to hydras.

This mythological reptile has five writhing serpent heads, each of which constantly exhales a venomous plume. Well over 20 feet (6 m) long from the tip of its longest head to its thrashing tail, the toxic beast's most discomfiting feature is its magical ability to sprout new heads when it's wounded. Some hydras dwell on land, others in water. Most seem to have been set as guardians of important places by higher powers, which is probably why they're so difficult to kill.

Motive: Hungers for flesh, defend a location

Environment: Usually in hard-to-reach, out-of-the-way locations

Health: 24

Damage Inflicted: 7 points

Armor: 1

GM Intrusion: The character reacts poorly to the poison in the air or a bite and on a failed Might defense task, goes into helpless convulsions for one round.

Movement: Short when walking or swimming

Modifications: Perception as level 8 due to its many heads; Speed defense as level 5 due to size.

Combat: Even approaching a hydra is dangerous; the air around it is poisoned by its venomous breath. Each round a creature is within immediate range of a hydra, it must succeed on a Might defense task or take 1 point of Speed damage (ignores Armor).

All five of a hydra's heads can simultaneously bite foes in immediate range. If three or more heads coordinate their attack, the heads make one attack as a single level 9 creature dealing 9 points of damage. A target bitten by the venomous hydra must also succeed on a Might defense task or take an additional 2 points of Speed damage (ignores Armor).

Whenever the hydra takes 4 or more points of damage from a single attack, a healing pulse surges through the creature a round later. The healing pulse returns the health just subtracted from the attack and triggers the immediate growth of two additional heads that sprout from the creature. (The same thing happens if one of the creature's snakelike heads is decapitated.) The new heads are just as effective as the original ones in a fight.

Fire, electrical, and other extreme energy attacks do not trigger the healing pulse and head genesis.

Interaction: A hydra is a cunning predator, but not intelligent. It can't bargain or negotiate.

Use: The PCs investigate an ancient ruin hoping to find artifacts of the gods. A hydra saw the PCs enter and trails them through the crumbling structures at a considerable distance, waiting for them to take a rest or become otherwise distracted before attacking.

Loot: Hydras sometimes collect cyphers and artifacts in their lair, or failing that, guard something of value.

KILLER CLOWN 5 (15)

Clowns are great, but only at the circus.

A clown—whether it's a doll or what seems to be a person wearing clown make-up—could be entirely benign. But if you see one sitting alone in a dark room, lying under your bed, or gazing up at you through the sewer grate in the street, it might be a killer clown. Killer clowns might be evil spirits possessing an object or an insane person living out a homicidal fantasy. Either way, they're as dangerous as anything you'll ever likely meet. If you see a clown, run. Because it might be a killer.

Motive: Homicide

Environment: Almost anywhere

Health: 25

Damage Inflicted: 5 points

Movement: Short

Modifications: Detecting falsehoods, deception and persuasion as level 7.

Combat: A killer clown attempts to deceive its victim into believing that the clown is a friend. In fact, the clown is setting up an ambush where the victim can be strangled to death in private. When a killer clown successfully attacks, it inflicts 5 points of damage and locks its hands around the victim's neck. In each round that the victim does not escape, it suffers 5 points of damage from being strangled.

Some killer clowns know tricks which border on the supernatural. Such a clown may do one of the following as its action during combat.

> **GM Intrusion:** *The clown snatches a weapon, cypher, or other object from the character's hand as a level 6 attack, and if successful immediately uses it on the character.*

1	Reveal a secret that one character is keeping from one or more of their allies.
2	Poke target in the eyes as level 6 attack, blinding target for one minute.
3	Activate a trap door beneath victim that drops them 20 feet (6 m) into a cellar or basement.
4	Disappear into secret door or hatch and reappear somewhere hidden within short range.
5	Jab target in the throat as level 6 attack; resulting coughing fit causes target to lose next action.
6	Down some kind of elixir or energy drink that heals the killer clown of all damage sustained.

Interaction: A killer clown is all jokes, magic tricks, and juggling, until it decides it's time to strike.

Use: The creepy circus that just pulled into town is guarded by a killer clown, as late night investigators soon learn.

Loot: Amidst the joy buzzers and cards, a killer clown might also have one or two cyphers.

MAD CREATION   4 (12)

Artificial life could be created by inducing mutation, magic, selective breeding, after decades of scientific research in biology and synthetic engineering, or by wishing on a fairy locket; it depends on the genre.

In a fantasy or mythological setting, mad creations are called homunculi.

When artificial life takes a wrong turn, the results range the gamut from disappointing to dangerous. If an artificial entity starts out benign, it's difficult to know if a hidden or slowly developing flaw will tip it over the edge into dangerous dysfunction—or if it just acts oddly because it doesn't know the social cues.

Should synthetic beings be treated as people, pets, or monsters to be stamped out and destroyed? That's the eternal question and one that's usually answered wrong in fiction. It's no mystery why mad creations encountered are usually insanely dangerous.

Motive: Defense or destruction

Environment: Usually in secluded locations alone unless hiding in plain sight

Health: 27

Damage Inflicted: 5 points

Armor: 2

Movement: Short

Combat: A mad creation can release an electrical discharge against a target within long range. In melee, a mad creation's poisoned claws inflict damage and require the target to succeed on a Might defense task. On a failure, the poison induces a coma-like slumber in the target. Each round the target fails to rouse by succeeding on an Intellect task inflicts 3 points of Intellect damage (ignores Armor) to the target.

Interaction: A mad creation is intelligent and can be swayed by reason. It might be passive, but if disturbed in a place it thought was secure against intrusion, it could grow belligerent and even murderous. Once so roused, a mad creation might still be calmed, but the difficulty of all such attempts is increased by one step.

Use: Mad creations are sometimes fashioned to serve as guards or soldiers. These beings protect rather than attack unless their initial imprinting is overwritten by experience or their own flawed creation. Sometimes such a guardian goes rogue and must be tracked down and dealt with for the safety of others (or at least for the safety of its creator's reputation).

Loot: A mad creation requires many parts. Salvage from a destroyed mad creation could result in a cypher or two and another item that, with a bit of jury-rigging, works as an artifact.

GM Intrusion: *The character hit by the mad creation's melee attack doesn't take normal damage. Instead, the mad creation drops onto the character. The PC is pinned until they can succeed on a difficulty 6 Might-based task to escape. While pinned, the creation whispers mad utterances into the target's ear.*

MIDNIGHT SCRABBLER 3 (9)

Who knows what midnight scrabblers are up to when they're inactive and entombed in solid floors or walls? Maybe they don't even exist, until twilight or full darkness calls them forth. When it's dark, midnight scrabblers struggle out of solid surfaces, raising a cloud of shadow. Midnight scrabblers are many-limbed, like spiders, but have pale, hairless bodies that more resemble 3 foot (1 m) long cloth dolls sewn from dark thread and colorful—though now stained—fabric.

Motive: Hungers for flesh

Environment: Anywhere dark

Health: 9

Damage Inflicted: 3 points

Movement: Short; short when burrowing through solid material

Modifications: Speed defense as level 4 due to cloud of shadows raised by a moving or fighting scrabbler.

Combat: A midnight scrabbler attacks with needlelike claws. A victim that takes damage must succeed on a Might defense task, or become poisoned and drop one step on the damage track. The victim must keep fighting off the poison until they succeed or drop three steps on the damage track; however, those who fall to the third step on the damage track from a scrabbler's poison are not dead. They are paralyzed and can't move for about a minute. If a scrabbler isn't otherwise occupied, it can grab a paralyzed victim and drag the victim down into the ground or a nearby wall. Most victims drawn into walls are never seen again.

Midnight scrabblers can see in the dark.

Scrabblers regain 1 point of health per round while their health is above 0, unless they've been damaged with a silvered or cold iron weapon, or if they're in the presence of bright light.

Interaction: Midnight scrabblers are about as intelligent as canny predators like wolves.

Use: Hotel guests report the sounds of strange scrabbling noises under the floor and suspect rats.

Loot: If a wall or floor is physically excavated where midnight scrabblers were seen to emerge, belongings of past victims apparently "petrified" into the wall can be discovered, which sometimes includes a few cyphers.

GM Intrusion: *Characters with torches must succeed on a difficulty 5 Intellect defense task or their flashlight or another light source fails.*

MINOTAUR, THE   7 (21)

Most believe there's just one Minotaur, but there could be many.

In a game using power shifts (or divine shifts), GMs could provide the same advantage to the Minotaur.

The most famous minotaur is *the* Minotaur, the singular beast from which all lesser minotaur myths descend. The product of a god-cursed union between human and bull, the Minotaur is monstrous, and only the flesh of people can nourish it. It is usually lost in a labyrinth created to contain it. But it occasionally gets free in order to hunt the wider world before the labyrinth pulls it back. Some demigods claim to have slain the Minotaur, but the Minotaur always returns.

Motive: Hungers for flesh

Environment: Usually in mythological labyrinths, but sometimes metaphorical ones

Health: 33

Damage Inflicted: 10 points

Armor: 3

Movement: Short

GM Intrusion: The Minotaur smashes into the wall, causing a section of the tunnel or hallway to collapse on the character (or characters), inflicting 10 points of damage and trapping them until they can escape the rubble.

Modifications: Level 9 for breaking through barriers.

Combat: The Minotaur attacks by goring foes on its horns, inflicting 10 points of damage on a successful attack. If the Minotaur charges a short distance, it can attack as part of the same action, and inflict an additional 5 points of damage.

The Minotaur is simultaneously trapped by the labyrinth, but also part of it. Whenever a character attacks the Minotaur, they must succeed on an Intellect defense task or be claimed by the labyrinth themselves until they can escape with a successful difficulty 7 Intellect task. Those claimed by the labyrinth seem to disappear, though the claimed find themselves wandering a dark maze. Once a character successfully escapes a labyrinth, they are no longer subject to being claimed by the labyrinth for several days.

If killed, the Minotaur's body is claimed by the labyrinth. Thirty-three days later, the Minotaur is resuscitated.

Interaction: The Minotaur can speak, but usually chooses not to. It is belligerent and cruel, and always hungry.

Use: The Minotaur has escaped the labyrinth, and now wanders the narrow streets of a metropolis, treating the winding alleys and twisting roads as its new maze.

NIGHTGAUNT

3 (9)

"Shocking and uncouth black things with smooth, oily surfaces, unpleasant horns that curved inward toward each other, bat wings whose beating made no sound, ugly prehensile tails that lashed needlessly and disquietingly. And worst of all, they never spoke . . . because they had not faces at all . . . but only a suggestive blankness where a face ought to be."

—H. P. Lovecraft

A nightgaunt's hands and feet have no opposable digits. All its fingers and toes can grasp with firm but unpleasant boneless strength. Nightgaunts swoop out of the night, grab prey, and fly off into darkness. Nightgaunts are hungry, but they sometimes "work" for other agencies, though often enough, their goals are obscure.

Motive: Unknowable

Environment: Anywhere dark, usually in groups of four to seven

Health: 9

Damage Inflicted: 4 points

Armor: 1

Movement: Immediate; long when flying (short when flying with a victim)

Modifications: Perception and Speed defense as level 4; stealth as level 7.

Combat: A nightgaunt can attack with its barbed tail (and it also uses the tail to tickle prey caught in its boneless clutches). To catch a foe, a nightgaunt dives through the air from just outside of short range. When it does, it moves 100 feet (30 m) in a round and attempts to grab a victim near the midpoint of its movement. A target who fails a Speed defense roll (and who isn't more than twice the size of the nightgaunt) is jerked into the creature's clutches and upward, finding themselves dangling from a height of 50 feet (15 m).

The nightgaunt automatically tickles grabbed victims with its barbed tail. This subtle form of torture increases the difficulty of all tasks attempted by the victim by two steps, including attempts to escape.

Interaction: Nightgaunts never speak, and they ignore anyone who attempts to interact with them, whether the communication takes the form of commanding, beseeching, or frantically pleading. Such is the way of nightgaunts.

Use: Someone who bears one or more of the PCs a grudge discovered a tome of spells and summoned a flight of nightgaunts, which set off in search of their prey.

Loot: One in three nightgaunts has a valuable souvenir from a past victim, which might be an expensive watch, a ring, an amulet, or sometimes a cypher.

GM Intrusion: The character is startled by the nightgaunt and suffers the risk of temporary dementia. On a failed Intellect defense roll, the character shrieks and faints (or, at the GM's option, babbles, drools, laughs, and so on). The character can attempt a new Intellect defense roll each round to return to normal.

PRINCE(SS) OF SUMMER   5 (15)

A Queen or King of Summer is a level 8 version of the Prince or Princess of Summer

Fey nobility are as numberless as cottonwood seeds on the June breeze. But that doesn't mean each isn't unique, with a quirky personality and a specific role to play in the mysterious Court of Summer. Demonstrating life, vigor, predation, growth, and competition, the Princesses and Princes of Summer are beings of warmth and generosity, usually. But catch them during the change of the season, and they can be deadly adversaries just as easily. Fey nobles dress in costly diaphanous and flowing garments, and often wear some sign of their noble lineage, such as a circlet or diadem.

Motive: Unpredictable; defend fey territory and prerogatives

Environment: Almost any wilderness region alone or commanding a small group of lesser faerie creatures

Health: 22

Damage Inflicted: 5 points

Armor: 2

Movement: Short; short when gliding on the wind

Modifications: Tasks related to deception, disguise, courtly manners, and positive interactions as level 7.

Combat: Most fey princesses and princes are armed with an elegant sword and possibly a bow carved of silverwood. Also, each knows one or more faerie spells. Faerie spells include the following.

Thorns: Target suffers 5 points of Speed damage (ignores Armor) and must succeed on a Might defense task or lose their next turn entangled in rapidly grown thorny vines.

Summer Confidence: Selected targets in short range have an asset on tasks related to resisting fear and acting boldly.

Brilliant Smile: Target must succeed on an Intellect defense task or do the fey creature's will for up to one minute.

Golden Mead: Allies who drink from the fey's flask gain an asset to all Defense tasks for ten hours.

Night's Reward: Target suffers 5 points of Intellect damage (ignores Armor) and must make an Intellect defense roll or fall asleep for up to one minute.

Princes and princesses of summer regain 2 points of health per round while their health is above 0 unless they've been damaged with a silvered or cold iron weapon.

Interaction: Most fey are willing to talk, and those of the Summer Court are especially eager to make deals. However, those who bargain with fey nobles should take care to avoid being tricked.

Use: The characters find a fey noble wounded and in need of aid.

Loot: In addition to fine clothing, fine equipment, and a considerable sum of currency, a prince or princess of summer might carry a few cyphers and even a faerie artifact.

GM Intrusion: *The character is blinded for up to one minute by a shaft of brilliant sunlight unless they succeed on a Might defense task.*

REANIMATED 6 (18)

"I beheld the wretch—the miserable monster whom I had created. He held up the curtain of the bed; and his eyes, if eyes they may be called, were fixed on me."

—Mary Shelley, Frankenstein

A reanimated is a humanoid creature patched together from corpses, then returned to life through a hard-to-duplicate series of electromagnetic induction events. Though made of flesh, a reanimated's return to consciousness and mobility is marked by a substantial increase in hardiness, resistance to injury, and longevity. On the other hand, the process usually obliterates whatever mind was once encoded in the donor's brain, giving rise to a creature of monstrous rage and childlike credulity. Sometimes the reanimated is bound to its creator in service, but such ties are fragile and could be snapped by an ill-timed fit of fury.

Motive: Defense, unpredictable

Environment: Anywhere in service to a mad scientist, or driven to the edges of civilization

Health: 70

Damage Inflicted: 7 points

Movement: Short; long when jumping

Modifications: Speed defense as level 4; all tasks related to interaction as level 2; all tasks related to feats of strength and toughness as level 8.

Combat: A reanimated attacks foes with its hands. Any time a foe inflicts 7 or more points of damage on the reanimated with a single melee attack, the creature immediately lashes out in reactive rage and makes an additional attack in the same round on the foe who injured it.

If the reanimated begins combat within long range of foes but outside of short range, it can bridge the distance with an amazing leap that concludes with an attack as a single action. The attack inflicts 4 points of damage on all targets within immediate range of the spot where the reanimated lands.

Some reanimated are psychologically vulnerable to fire, and they fear it. When these reanimated attack or defend against a foe wielding fire, the difficulty is modified by two steps to its detriment.

If struck by electromagnetic energy, a reanimated regains a number of points of health equal to what a normal creature would have lost.

Interaction: Fear and food motivate a reanimated, though sometimes beautiful music or innocence can sway its fists.

Use: Depending on where a reanimated falls along its moral and psychological development, it could be a primary foe for the PCs, a secondary guardian to deal with, or a forlorn beast in need of aid.

GM Intrusion: *The character's attack bounces harmlessly off the stitched, hardened flesh of the reanimated.*

ROBOT MIMIC   4 (12)

Robot mimics have been called many things, including synths, androids, and killer robots.

The origins of robot mimics are obscure. Many believe they're the result of a state-sponsored program to develop war machines or automated assassins that looked like regular people. Once deployed, these fake people slipped free of their programing. Now they roam their environment looking like anyone else. Some robot mimics try to fit into whatever kind of society they can find. Some may not even know that they are not human. Others are bitter, homicidal, or still retain their programming to kill. These later have shed their synthetic skins with hot plasma, revealing the inner red-hot metallic form.

Motive: Varies

Environment: Nearly anywhere, either out in plain sight or disguised as a human, alone or in groups of two to four

Health: 16

Damage Inflicted: 6 points

Armor: 2

Movement: Short

Modifications: Disguise and one knowledge task as level 6.

Combat: A punch from a robot mimic can break bones. In addition, most robot mimics can generate a red-hot plasma sphere once every other round and throw it at a target within long range. The target and all other creatures within immediate range of the target must succeed on a Speed defense task or take 6 points of damage.

A robot mimic can repair itself if it spends an action and regain 10 points of health. A robot mimic at 0 health can't repair itself, but unless the creature is completely dismembered, the robot mimic may spontaneously reanimate 1d10 hours later with 4 points of health.

Interaction: Robot mimics that pretend to be (or think that they are) human interact like normal people. But an enraged robot mimic or one that's been programmed to kill is unreasoning and fights to the end.

GM Intrusion: *The character is struck blind for one or two rounds after being struck by the robot's searing plasma.*

Use: A group of refugees who need help turn out to include (or be entirely made up of) robot mimics. Whether or not any of the robot mimics harbor programs that require that they kill humans is entirely up to the GM.

Loot: One or two cyphers could be salvaged from a robot mimic's inactive form.

SATYR 5 (15)

Satyrs are inveterate mercenaries. They gladly work for strong drink and other treasures, and ally with almost any creature capable of meeting their price.

Apparently always male, these muscular humanoids sport small, short horns and furry, hooved legs. They are self-centered, greedy, and sybaritic creatures, dedicated to food, drink, and other pleasures. They rob and steal from others as it pleases them, often relying on tricks and lies, or alluring music they play on pipes.

Motive: Play tricks; gather treasure; fulfill desires

Environment: In woodlands where other faerie or mythological creatures are found

Health: 18

Damage Inflicted: 6 points

Armor: 1

Movement: Short

Modifications: Tasks related to persuasion and deception as level 7; resists mental attacks as level 7.

Combat: Satyrs usually carry spears that they can use in melee and against foes within short range.

Satyrs can also create magical effects by playing on their pipes as an action, which can either bolster allies are harm enemies.

Feral Overture: An ally within short range is infused with magic, and the difficulty of one attack it makes on its next turn is reduced one step, and if it hits, it inflicts +3 damage.

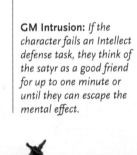

Dance of the Leaping Stag: Foes within short range who fail an Intellect defense task lose their next turn dancing and leaping. Attacks made against affected targets are one step less difficult.

Tune of the Clouded Mind: A foe within short range who fails an Intellect defense task spends its next turn attacking one if its allies.

Interaction: A satyr is always willing to start negotiations, but is prone to lying and exaggeration. Offering excessive libation, food, and other treasures is the only way to ensure a satyr remains honest, and then only for a short period.

Use: Strange piping music in the forest lures away young men and women from a nearby community. Community elders say a charismatic cult leader has set up in the woods, and clouds the minds of all who come near.

Loot: A satyr is likely to carry one or two cyphers.

GM Intrusion: *If the character fails an Intellect defense task, they think of the satyr as a good friend for up to one minute or until they can escape the mental effect.*

SHOE THIEF 3 (9)

What's the tale behind the one lone shoe? If you're lucky, the other shoe got kicked under the bed. If you're unlucky, a shoe thief has infested your home. You'll know it's the latter if other things begin to go missing, too. Small things at first, like single socks, pens, and paperclips. But single shoe thieves may become many. That's when larger stuff begins to go missing, like books, money, pets, and your little brother. Shoe thieves, only about 1 foot (30 cm) tall, appear like animate accumulations of lint, dust balls, matted hair, and teeth.

Shoe thief infestations can be traced back to dark cubbies in a home or nearby shack, littered with what they've stolen. Particularly well-established cubbies lead by crooked basement paths to a fey realm where things even more dangerous than shoe thieves stalk.

Motive: Accumulate "treasure" and food

Environment: Anywhere dark

Health: 12

Damage Inflicted: 3 points

Movement: Short; immediate when phasing through solid walls, floors or ceilings.

Modifications: Speed defense as level 4 due to small size; deception and trickery as level 2.

Combat: A shoe thief's fierce bite is, like a cat's, liable to get infected. In addition to 3 points of damage inflicted from the bite, a victim who fails a Might defense roll becomes dazed within the hour from the feeling of sickness, and finds the difficulty of all tasks increased by one step. Infected victims don't get better unless their wound is healed with magic, a faerie salve, or some similar unusual intervention.

Four or more shoe thieves can attack together as a swarm, making a single attack as a level 5 creature that inflicts 5 points of damage.

Shoe thieves regain 1 point of health per round while their health is above 0 unless they've been damaged with a silvered or cold iron weapon.

Interaction: Shoe thieves have the wit and language skills of five-year-old children. Evil and greedy five-year-olds, granted, but they can be tricked.

Use: Shoe thieves might infest an old apartment building, an abandoned well, a junkyard, a run-down keep, or the basement of the school.

Loot: Amidst the litter of trash, single shoes, keys, books, bones, and dirt, items people value can usually be discovered in a shoe thief burrow, including coins, equipment, and even a few cyphers.

GM Intrusion: The shoe thief's bite is not only infectious, but it's also venomous. If the character is bitten, they must succeed on a Might defense task or immediately move one step down the damage track.

TYPHON   10 (30)

"The hands and arms of him are mighty, and have work in them, and the feet of the powerful god were tireless, and up from his shoulders there grew a hundred snake heads, those of a dreaded drakon, and the heads licked with dark tongues, and from the eyes on the inhuman heads fire glittered from under the eyelids."

—Hesiod, The Theogony

In a game using power shifts (or divine shifts), GMs should provide the same advantage to Typhon.

GM (Group) Intrusion: *Typhon summons one or more dragons to aid it.*

Dragon, page 287

This monstrous entity called the "Father of Monsters," arose from a union of rude matter and the fires of Hell. Typhon can change his apparent size, ranging from 9 feet (3 m) tall to heights of more than 500 feet (152 m) when fully uncoiled and standing. Typhon is imprisoned deep beneath the earth. When the earth shakes, it's Typhon, trying to escape.

Motive: Destruction

Environment: Usually sealed beneath the ground, unless he gets free

Health: 140

Damage Inflicted: 20 points

Armor: 15

Movement: Long, long when flying

Modifications: Speed defense as level 6 due to size.

Combat: Typhon, when fully enlarged, can pummel with his wings or bite with his many snake heads at something within 200 feet (61 m) range. Damage is also inflicted on everything within short range of the target, and even those that succeed on a Speed defense roll take 6 points of damage. If Typhon focuses on a single target with its snake heads, the difficulty of the attack is reduced by two steps and the attack inflicts 30 points if successful.

Typhon can breathe fire from his dragon hands, twin pillars of destruction that can reach as far as the horizon, inflicting 20 points of damage on the target and everything within immediate range.

While standing on the ground, Typhon regains 5 points of health each round.

Interaction: A force of destruction, Typhon won't negotiate with anything short of a god, and usually not even then.

Use: Volcanoes and earthquakes in a wide region are on the rise. Typhon's imprisonment grows tenuous.

NPCs

The NPCs in this chapter are generic examples of character types that can be used in many genres. GMs will find that with a few tweaks, an elite soldier can be a sci-fi stormtrooper, a fantasy knight, or a post-apocalyptic survivor.

Remember that NPCs don't have stat Pools. Instead, they have a characteristic called health. When an NPC takes damage of any kind, the amount is subtracted from its health. Unless described otherwise, an NPC's health is always equal to its target number. Some NPCs might have special reactions to or defenses against attacks that would normally deal Speed damage or Intellect damage, but unless the NPC's description specifically explains this, assume that all damage is subtracted from the NPC's health.

NPCs BY LEVEL

Politician	2
Priest	2
Professor	2
Cannibal	3
Hacker	3
Soldier	3
Mad scientist	4
Marauder	4
Detective, Master	5
General	5
Soldier, elite	5

APPROPRIATE WEAPONS

NPCs use weapons appropriate to their situation, which might be swords and crossbows, knives and shotguns, malefic psychic weapons, blasters and grenades, and so on.

CANNIBAL 3 (9)

Cannibals in a modern, horror, or crime and espionage setting seem like normal and perhaps even charming people, except to their victims.

A cannibal is someone who has decided that eating other people is not only necessary but desirable. Whether this decision was forced by circumstance or out of some secret, maladaptive urge, cannibals are dangerous because they hide in plain sight, pretending friendship and aid for strangers until their prey lowers their guard. That's when a cannibal strikes. Some cannibals like it raw; others delight in elaborate preparations.

Motive: Hungers for human flesh

Health: 12

Damage Inflicted: 5 points

Movement: Short

Modifications: Deception, persuasion, intimidation, and tasks related to friendly interaction as level 6.

Combat: Cannibals use whatever weapon is at hand. Cannibals usually don't attack unless they can surprise their prey. When cannibals have surprise, they attack as level 5 creatures and inflict 2 additional points of damage.

Interaction: Cannibals seem friendly and charming until they decide you are for dinner.

Use: Characters looking for a place to sleep, hide, or stay for the night are invited in by one or more cannibals.

Loot: A cannibal has currency equivalent to a very expensive item and possibly a cypher.

Surprise, page 204

GM Intrusion: *The cannibal reveals a severed and gnawed upon body part of a previous victim, which requires the character to succeed on an Intellect defense task or be stunned and lose their next turn.*

DETECTIVE, MASTER 5 (15)

Master detectives are in a category all their own, and far outshine others in their ability to deduce facts from evidence that most people fail to recognize as relevant, even other detectives. Master detectives are singular, highly sought and even celebrated.

Motive: See what is hidden

Health: 20

Damage Inflicted: 5 points

Movement: Short

Modifications: Tasks relating to perception, intuition, initiative, and detecting falsehoods as level 9.

Combat: Master detectives can defend themselves in a fight because they are good at almost everything they do. However, they prefer to maneuver foes into situations where the fight, if any is to be had, is already lost.

Interaction: Master detectives can come across as inscrutable as they pursue their craft, or rude and denigrating if they decide that someone is of no use to them, or worse, an idiot.

Use: While following up a lead on a missing object or person, the PCs run into a master detective brought in by a third party to discover the same lead or missing item or person.

Loot: Aside from their weapons, most master detectives have currency equivalent to a very expensive item and a cypher.

GM Intrusion: *The master detective reveals the perfect piece of knowledge or item to defeat the character's ploy, having earlier deduced what the character was going to do.*

GENERAL   5 (15)

Battle-hardened and tough, generals are both physically powerful and able to multiply their power by commanding subordinates, usually according to a militarily maintained hierarchy. Rarely encountered alone, a general is usually within shouting distance of soldiers (or marauders). A general could be a modern five-star commander, a Mongol chieftain, or the leader of a mercenary band.

Motive: Defense, or conquest
Health: 25
Damage Inflicted: 5 points
Armor: 1
Movement: Short
Modifications: Tasks related to commanding others, tactics and strategy, persuasion, and intimidation as level 7.
Combat: Soldiers and other followers deal 1 additional point of damage when the general can see them (or communicate directly) and issue commands. If possible, generals avoid fighting altogether.
Interaction: Generals are strict in their interpretation of their orders if they are not the ultimate leaders in a particular situation.
Use: An opposing army is vast, but it might collapse and fade if the general leading it can be found and dispatched (or kidnapped).
Loot: A general has currency equivalent to a very expensive item in addition to weapons and miscellaneous gear.

GM Intrusion: The general draws on their reserves and regains 15 health.

HACKER   3 (9)

Anyone who pursues a passion with flair, especially if that passion is understanding the workings of computers and networks, is a hacker. They live and breathe computers, and can get these networked machines to do nearly anything. Most hackers pursue their passion as a hobby, some work to improve the security of the internet, while some seek to exploit computers and people who use them.

Motive: Understand computers
Health: 12
Damage Inflicted: 4 points
Movement: Short
Modifications: Tasks relating to knowledge of, programming, and repairing computers as level 7.
Combat: Hackers use whatever weapons are on hand, but if they have time to prepare, can set up computer-moderated cameras for surveillance, doors with auto-locks, semi-autonomous drones, and other networked devices to delay and even trap foes.
Interaction: Some hackers can't contain a disdainful attitude toward those who haven't dedicated themselves to understanding computers.
Use: While trying to solve a case, the PCs discover that someone really good with computers has been erasing logs, caches, and databases to prevent their success.
Loot: Some hackers have online accounts filled with digital currency such as bitcoin.

GM Intrusion: The hacker launches a level 2 (Speed defense as level 4 due to size) micro semi-autonomous drone at the character, which bedevils the character, increasing the difficulty of all tasks by one step until the drone is disabled.

MAD SCIENTIST 4 (12)

If you're willing to put a needle in someone else's brain and stir the grey matter, you might be a mad scientist. If you've reanimated dead flesh or created a freeze ray, you are.

Every scientist interrogates reality's underlying laws to find answers. Science is a tool of evidence accumulation, deduction, and experimentation that almost anyone can employ, no matter their means. Thus, to be a mad scientist, one must go much further, and not merely ask anything, but also act recklessly. Mad scientists wonder "can we?" but never "should we?" If they can do something, they do it, or at least try, if they can claim to be expanding the horizon of scientific understanding. If innocent people are harmed or even killed during a mad scientist's experiments, it probably doesn't bother a mad scientist.

Motive: To understand and exploit reality

Environment: Usually in secure scientific facilities

Health: 15

Damage Inflicted: 7 points

Movement: Short

Modifications: Defends as level 6 due to a scientific gadget (or cypher) of the mad scientist's creation; knowledge of advanced science and engineering techniques as level 7

Combat: Mad scientists not already accompanied by security personnel, robotic defenders, reanimated bodies, or some other perk of their position or fruit of their labor can usually call something up at a moment's notice if they are encountered in their labs. Also, a mad scientist can attempt to take command of an enemy's technological device—be it armor, a weapon, a cypher, a robot, and so on—within short range for up to one minute using a handheld device.

Mad scientists usually have access to an energy or high-velocity weapon capable of attacking within long range that inflicts 7 points of damage. Also, they carry a couple of extra cyphers that allows them to increase Armor, confuse the senses of other creatures for a few rounds, and possibly even to briefly transform themselves so that the difficulty of all tasks performed by the mad scientist is two steps easier for up to an hour.

Interaction: Mad scientists are narcissistic and love to talk about their work, especially if it is self-aggrandizing. They negotiate but usually don't care about another person's well-being; they're sociopathic. A few mad scientists are self-loathing, hating themselves for what they've created, but too far down the path to feel like they can change.

Use: Blackouts and strange noises have been traced to a location that is found to hold a secret and secure lab where a scientist labors to create something amazing, or amazingly monstrous.

Loot: Mad scientists have a few cyphers and possibly an artifact.

GM Intrusion: *The mad scientist produces a gadget or cypher that proves to be the perfect answer to a dilemma at hand.*

MARAUDER   4 (12)

Marauders in a modern, horror, or crime and espionage setting might ride right through the heart of a city in a pickup truck with gun rack in the window, or in a motorcycle gang.

Marauders are sometimes called berserkers in historical and mythological genres.

Stripped of humanity by brutal living conditions, radiation, drugs, or magic, marauders still *look* like humans. But they delight in unremitting and extreme violence. They torture their victims to death over excruciating minutes or hours and take trophies of flesh.

Motive: Raid and kill for what they want
Health: 18
Damage Inflicted: 6 points
Armor: 1
Movement: Short
Modifications: Tasks related to initiative, intimidation, and Intellect defense as level 7.
Combat: Marauders are armed with weapons taken from past victims. They never stop—the first time a marauder would normally be killed, savagery revives them with 12 health.

GM Intrusion: The marauder screams and makes an especially violent attack—treat the attack as level 6 inflicting 8 points of damage.

Interaction: It is essentially impossible to negotiate with marauders. They only laugh as they stab for the eyes.
Use: A group of marauders is squatting in a location the PCs need to explore for unrelated reasons.
Loot: Marauders carry weapons and light armor. One in three might carry a cypher.

POLITICIAN   2 (6)

Diplomats are also often politicians briefly appointed to serve as a mouthpiece by an even more senior politician.

A politician consistently holds some elected public office. A politician could be a mayor, a city councilperson, a senator or representative, a governor, prime minister, president, and so on. To enact policy change, most politicians must compromise. To some politicians, retaining their position is the most important goal.

Motive: Enact policy change and/or win the next election
Health: 9
Damage Inflicted: 2 points
Movement: Short
Modifications: Tasks relating to knowledge of current events, government, and civic operations as level 6.
Combat: Politicians are more talkers than fighters, and those of sufficient importance are either accompanied by bodyguards or can call some to their presence at a moment's notice. Politicians try to negotiate to avoid or end combats.
Interaction: Politicians welcome interaction. Some politicians will say anything, even if they don't intend to follow through. Others try to hold to promises made, especially if those promises were publicly made. Many collect favors but intend to call those favors in at a later date.

GM Intrusion: Two level 3 police (or some similar official civil peace-keeping force) arrive to protect and serve the politician.

Use: A politician to whom one or more of the PCs owes a favor asks for a meeting, then requests they undertake some action which might be construed as bordering on the illegal. But a favor is a favor.
Loot: Many politicians have at least one very expensive item, such as a designer watch, on their person.

PRIEST 2 (6)

Priests serve as intermediaries to higher powers. Whether those higher powers know, care, or even exist depends on the genre. For most priests, faith is their primary motivation. Priests minister to the sick and sorrowful, lead communities of the faithful, and sometimes serve as missionaries in rough locations.

Health: 9

Damage Inflicted: 2 points

Movement: Short

Modifications: Tasks related to persuasion; detecting lies and trickery; lore, knowledge and understanding; and pleasant social interaction as level 6

Combat: A priest rarely or never fights, but instead tries to persuade foes to negotiate and lay down arms. If fighting can't be avoided, a priest is usually defended by one or more members of their flock who attacks and defends as one level higher than normal while fighting on the priest's behalf.

Interaction: Most priests are concerned with others' welfare and health, even their foes. A few only pretend to these concerns.

Use: A priest in the countryside has gathered a flock and built a church in a rural or wilderness area. But something is wrong at the church—either among the flock, or external to it. Either way, the church has come under threat.

Loot: In addition to their clothing and religious paraphernalia, priests have currency equivalent to an expensive item and a cypher (though possibly a subtle cypher, depending on the genre).

GM Intrusion: *The priest intuitively finds a character's hidden spiritual weak spot, and verbally probes it. On a failed difficulty 5 Intellect defense task, the character is stunned and loses their next action.*

PROFESSOR 2 (6)

Professors are either currently or were once part of the faculty of a school or university. Some are PhDs; others are self-taught researchers. All seek to find the truth hiding right under our noses, using the scientific method to tease out their answers. Professors are natural teachers, and often seek to help others find the truth, too.

Motive: Find answers

Health: 9

Damage Inflicted: 3 points

Movement: Short

Modifications: Tasks relating to intuition, persuasion, detecting falsehoods, most knowledge tasks as level 6.

Combat: Professors prefer to avoid a fight. If a fight can't be avoided, a professor tries to deduce a foe's weakness (if any) and exploit them in combat.

Interaction: Most professors are helpful, informative, and with children may be maternal or avuncular. A few also manage to come off as insufferable know-it-alls.

Use: To the PCs, professors can be obstacles (a researcher who won't reveal their patron) or allies (a patron who provides answers to hard questions and other occasional aid).

Loot: Most detectives have currency equivalent to a very expensive item and a one or two cyphers.

GM Intrusion: *After watching the character fight or interact for one or more rounds, the professor gains an asset on all tasks they make to oppose or get the better of the character.*

SOLDIER   3 (9)

Armies fielded by nations (or rich city-states) are composed of soldiers. Soldiers receive training, weapons, and support to achieve their goals. They can be deployed in fire-teams of up to four, squads of up to twenty-four, companies of up to 250, or battalions of up to 1,000 strong.

Motive: Accomplish specific military missions

Health: 12

Damage Inflicted: 4 points

Armor: 1

Movement: Short

Modifications: Perception as level 4.

Combat: Soldiers are armed with melee and ranged weapons appropriate to their genre. When two or more soldiers work as a unit on the same task (such as attacking the same target), they function as if level 4 on that task.

Interaction: Soldiers take orders from commanding officers, negotiating with a soldier provides little gain.

Use: A small squad of soldiers has been commanded to take out a post defended by the PCs.

Loot: Every soldier carries weapons, light armor, and possibly useful things (binoculars, food rations, collapsible shovel, radio —whatever's appropriate to the genre in which the soldier appears).

GM Intrusion: The soldier calls in an airstrike. Characters in an immediate area must succeed on a difficulty 5 Speed defense task or take 5 points of damage and be stunned, losing their next action.

SOLDIER, ELITE   5 (15)

Elite soldiers begin as talented and motivated individuals trained to the limit of their ability to improve. These individuals are subsequently subjected to so many life-or-death missions that they'd be considered veterans in any other unit.

Motive: Accomplish specific military missions

Health: 27

Damage Inflicted: 5 points

Armor: 2

Movement: Short

Modifications: Perception as level 6; resistance to intimidation and trickery as level 7.

Combat: Elite soldiers are armed with weapons appropriate to their genre and are so skilled that they can attack with those weapons twice as a single action.

When two or more elite soldiers work as a unit on the same task (such as attacking the same target), they function as if level 6 on that task.

Interaction: Although it would be virtually impossible to convince elite soldiers to abandon their mission, they are trained to look for alternate routes to success. If a PC can make a convincing argument why helping would advance the elite soldier's mission, they might make a short-term ally.

Use: Elite soldiers are rarely encountered unless the characters regularly rub shoulders with those in society powerful enough to order such squads. To the PCs, elite soldiers can be obstacles, allies, or both, but they are rarely a way for the characters to hand off responsibility for accomplishing a hard task.

Loot: Every elite soldier carries weapons, medium armor, and possibly useful tools (for sapping, electronics work, bioinfiltration—whatever's appropriate to the genre in which the soldier appears).

Whether it's the Navy SEALs, the Space Marines, or the vanguard of Zeus's host, special forces are a breed apart thanks to their limited numbers, their extreme training, and their enviable physical capabilities.

GM Intrusion: The elite soldier produces a rocket-propelled grenade (RPG) and fires it at the PC.

Rocket-Propelled Grenade, page 80

INDEX

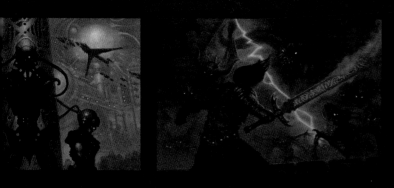